Machine Translation

Trends in Linguistics
Studies and Monographs 11

Editor

Werner Winter

Mouton Publishers
The Hague · Paris · New York

Machine Translation

Bożena Henisz-Dostert
R. Ross Macdonald
Michael Zarechnak

Mouton Publishers
The Hague · Paris · New York

ISBN 90 279 7836 0
Typesetting: Otto Gutfreund & Sohn, Darmstadt. – Printing: Karl Gerike, Berlin.
– Binding: Lüderitz & Bauer Buchgewerbe GmbH, Berlin.
Printed in Germany

This book is dedicated to the memory of
Léon Emile Dostert,
a leading light in machine translation

Preface

We hope that this book will be of interest and use to the many persons who, for a variety of reasons, have recently been showing an increased interest in machine translation, and also to those who may be developing such an interest. The main reasons for the recent significant and growing consideration given to machine translation fall into two major categories: the practical need for large volumes of translation, and the theoretical challenge posed by the linguistic problems involved in machine translation and machine-aided translation. These factors have always, of course, been the driving forces in the development of product-oriented, experimental machine translation. The main purpose of this book is to state and exemplify the principles which have guided this development. The organization of the book presents the various yet integrated phases of practical machine translation within the general historical and intellectual setting which has surrounded its development. The three parts of the book are designed to present an overview of machine translation from its earliest stages to the recent reactions of its users, while discussing the linguistic problems involved. Machine translation, in the context of these discussions, means fully automatic translation, with no post-editing, and with the barest minimum of essentially automatic pre-editing. This pre-editing is carried out in the course of the keying of the input text by operators usually unfamiliar with the language of the text. Central to the discussion are references to the Georgetown Russian-to-English Machine Translation System, in the development of which each of the authors has been involved for a number of years. The discussions are of a much broader and more general nature, however, in Part I: The history of machine translation, and in Part II: The problem of machine translation. Part III: Users' evaluation of machine translation, is based entirely on the reactions of users of translations made with the Georgetown system.

Part I is not simply a background. Rather, it is a considered description of a multifaceted phenomenon. A variety of views of the development of machine translation are presented and discussed, and this allows the reader to obtain a comprehensive view and to arrive at an individual judgment.

Part II is a matter-of-fact statement of some of the major problems of machine translation; it does not attempt to give all of the answers. The solutions employed in the Georgetown system are frequently used as illustrations typical of an experimental, product-oriented system. A number of other possible solutions and examples involving languages other than Russian and English are given. Theoretically-oriented systems are also considered.

Part III is a straightforward report on scientists' reactions to texts which had been machine-translated at their request. The reactions are to unedited machine translations made in the decade of 1963–1973. The study is supported by a detailed statistical analysis which reveals very positive attitudes on the part of the users.

Since the manuscript was completed, the evidence for renewed interest in machine translation has increased. In Part I, a United States government-sponsored seminar is discussed – the Rosslyn Seminar, organized in 1976. Another seminar, similarly sponsored, was organized in May, 1978. The proceedings were still to be published at the time of writing. It is not clear to what extent machine translation was a matter of consideration, although scholars currently involved in machine translation were consulted, notably B. Vauquois.

A substantial review of the current interests, needs and research relating to machine translation on the international scene emerged from the Seventh International Conference on Computational Linguistics, held in Bergen, Norway, in August, 1978 (COLING 78). These proceedings are available. Machine-aided translation was also a subject of considerable discussion at the Bergen conference and at other recent conferences, but that topic is outside the bounds of the present volume.

The recent developments in machine translation can be characterized as having two main foci: systems actually producing usable translations, and research on systems (especially of the Artificial Intelligence type) aimed at machine translation in some longer-range perspective.

Among the systems actually producing usable translations, we may note the following.

In the United States, the Georgetown System is routinely used to produce translations at the request of scientists at the Oak Ridge National Research Laboratory in Oak Ridge, Tennessee. The translations are produced on an IBM 360 computer. A considerable percentage of all translations made there are computer-produced. The System is also operating at Georgetown University itself where low-key research on linguistic improvements is continuing.

Recent developments in the Soviet Union are discussed in Part I, and evidence that the official recommendations for the development of practical, user-oriented systems have been followed was provided at COLING 78 in the system described by O. Kulagina (FR-II, French to Russian). This system has been put to the test by users, and the users' evaluations are very similar to those discussed in Part III. Kulagina is in the process of describing her system and presenting the users' evaluation in a book.

In bilingual and language-conscious Canada, the need for large volumes of translation, the high cost of human translation and the government's substantial sponsorship have combined to create a situation in which practical machine translation is being developed to serve as a daily means of public information. At COLING 78 it was reported that the operational system METEO, developed at the University of Montreal for national weather reporting, which automatically translates from English to French eighty percent of the sentences submitted to it, is now to be followed by a system called AVIATION, which will translate technical texts in aeronautics.

In France, where the work of Vauquois' group has always combined theoretical sophistication with practical orientation, Vauquois describes his system as serving important customers.

It is interesting that these practical systems have a marked tendency to display striking similarities in their design and operation, much stronger similarities than may appear from the superficialities of divergent terminologies and methods of discussion.

Among the more theoretically oriented systems, the Artificial Intelligence Project at Yale University was also described at COLING 78; the discussion emphasized the need for a full understanding of texts and for relying on a store of world knowledge which may not be found in the texts themselves. The research is as yet limited to microworlds, and its aim is the rendition of pertinent information in a semi-paraphrase form rather than in what is commonly understood as translation. Since the information of the texts is represented in terms of deep structures, the possibility of generating translations in a number of languages is envisioned. A similar point of view was presented at COLING 78 by the SALAT Project of the University of Heidelberg.

It would be premature to attempt to predict the direction which the development of machine translation will take. Our still inadequate knowledge of the phenomena of language is challenged particularly acutely by encounters with the computer. This book attempts to expose some of our strengths and limitations, and to serve as a source of information for ongoing and future efforts. We desire both to lessen the amount and scope of possible misguided efforts in the future, and to increase our awareness and our mental capabilities in the environment in which man's most expressive tool—language—interacts with his most ingenious tool—the computer.

Anyone who has worked on complex computational systems knows that they are the result of the efforts of many individuals. The Georgetown System, which is central to parts of this book, has been built by various members whose efforts are acknowledged in other publications, and especially in the General Report. However, the work of Dr. A. F. R. Brown, who bravely and ingeniously put together a variety of linguistic formulations to build an operational machine translation system, requires special mention whenever the Georgetown System is discussed.

We offer thanks to those who have helped us to put this book together and to publish it. And, following the time-honored tradition, we extend our thanks, jointly and severally, to our respective spouses.

Bożena Henisz-Dostert
R. Ross MacDonald
Michael Zarechnak

December 1978

Contents

Preface VII

Part I The history of machine translation
    Michael Zarechnak

Introduction 4
1 Early concepts of machine translation 7
  1.1 Pre-computer machine translation 7
  1.2 New impetus to machine translation with the birth of
     computers 9
  1.3 Booth's article on the historical background of machine
     translation 12
  1.4 Outside evaluation of the Georgetown University machine-
     translation system 14
2 Léon Dostert and the 1954 experiment 20
  2.1 Professor Léon Dostert 20
  2.2 Linguistic basis of P. Garvin 22
  2.3 Macdonald's general report on the Georgetown Unyversity
     machine translation research project 27
3 Description and analysis of machine-translation development .. 34
  3.1 Bar-Hillel's report on automatic translation of language ... 34
  3.2 Josselson's views on the historical development of machine
     translation 39
  3.3 Government support of machine translation and its
     advisory committee (ALPAC) 47
  3.4 Machine translation in Western Europe 57
  3.5 Klein's criticism of practical machine-translation research .. 60
  3.6 Machine translation in Bulgaria 62

4 Machine translation in the Soviet Union 64
   4.1 Kenneth E. Harper's article on machine translation in the
        USSR 64
   4.2 The theoretical approach toward machine translation
        in the USSR 65
   4.3 The latest developments in the USSR 72
        4.3.1 History of the development of machine translation
               in the USSR 73
        4.3.1.1 The first stage (1954–1958) 73
        4.3.1.2 The second stage (1958–1961) 73
        4.3.1.3 The third stage (1961–to date) 73
5 Directions for future development of machine-translation
   research: the Rosslyn machine-translation seminar 76
6 Conclusions 85

Part II The problem of machine translation
         R. Ross Macdonald

Introduction 91
1 Preliminary 93
   1.1 The text 93
   1.2 The computer .... · 94
   1.3 Pre-editing 94
   1.4 Transcription 95
   1.5 The dictionary 102
2 Processing 109
   2.1 Segmentation 109
   2.2 Idioms 111
   2.3 Exclusions 113
   2.4 Interpolation 114
   2.5 Gap analysis 115
   2.6 Syntactic analysis 115
   2.7 Semantic analysis 121
   2.8 Artifical intelligence 124
   2.9 Synthesis 126
3 Post-editing 128
4 Types of systems 130
   4.1 Empirical vs theoretical 130

4.2 A typical empirical approach 133
4.3 A typical theoretical approach 135
4.4 Melded systems 143

Part III Users' evaluation of machine translation
        Bożena Henisz-Dostert

Introduction 149
1 Machine-translation activity at Euratom and Oak Ridge 157
   1.1 Analysis of records 158
   1.2 Requests from outside 161
2 How the data were collected 164
   2.1 The nature of the questionnaire 164
   2.2 How the users were reached 167
3 Analysis of questionnaire results 169
   3.1 The users 169
   3.2 The analysis of the answers 170
   3.3 Summary and conclusions 206
Appendix 209
   1 Questionnaire on the use of machine translation 210
   2 Partial list of ETC clients 216
   3 A sample of users' letters of evaluation 220
Bibliography 245
Machine translation samples 250
Author index 257
Subject index 259

PART I

The history of machine translation

MICHAEL ZARECHNAK

Introduction

Upon undertaking this short history of machine translation (MT), I did not realize the many varied difficulties I would encounter in such an attempt. Just the list of questions I would hope to answer is staggering:
- What were the causes for the emergence of MT?
- Who were the people who tried to prove the feasibility of MT?
- What was the purpose of MT?
- What tools were available?
- What theoretical foundations were available or sought for MT?
- Was there any continuity with previous basic concepts of translation?
- What languages were studied for the purposes of MT?
- What methods were suggested, tried, and found to be successful in carrying out the MT system?
- What were the basic stages in the research and development of MT?
- What correlation exists between MT and information retrieval?
- What were the financial sources?
- What evaluations were applied?
- What kinds of algorithms were proposed, tested, successful?
- What perspectives are ahead for us after 25 years of research and development?
- Is the path to the correct answers to these questions a difficult one?

In trying to answer these questions, I will analyze and evaluate, in historical terms, publicly available information contained in various books, monographs, articles and special computer outputs which display final or intermediate stages in particular machine-translation systems. In addition to the public data I will, where appropriate, mention my own experience in the field, evaluate other machine-translation systems, and contrast these with Georgetown Automatic Translation (GAT).

One of the difficult problems in historical analysis is to separate fact from opinion and scale the contributions of various individual researchers within the historical perspective, trying to emphasize the fruitful efforts of each machine-translation group and individual workers within each group. I am not trying to promote heroes in the machine-translation field. The most valuable aspect of this study is not any person or persons but what I have seen as a set of procedures aiming at adequate description and explanation of the truth. Needless to say, seeking the truth may look anecdotal, as was shown by a Russian poet, Alexej K. Tolstoy. In his poem he describes how seven brothers decided to go to various parts of the world to study the attributes of truth, then return to Russia and compare notes. The result was that each brother saw the truth from a different viewpoint and could not compromise with the others. Evidently, this version of machine-translation history is just a particular viewpoint in describing and explaining the available data and opinions.

What is the point of view of this author? It is an organic fusion of various compatible views geared toward automatic processing of translation from the source to the target language. I shall mention some highlights amongst those views. I see the concepts as a logical intersection between various classification schemes applicable to a particular purpose. Thus, given any specific concept in the linguistic field to be automatically processed, one has to recognize that such a concept must be represented by a code or a series of codes. Further, since linguistic codes are simultaneously used for both paradigmatic and syntagmatic axes, one has to subcode both paradigmatic and syntagmatic codes into context-free and context-sensitive groups. We have good theoretical und practical reasons to believe that whatever the degree of sophistication of the specific classification system, both unwanted acceptances and unwanted rejections inevitably occur. To illustrate this point, no matter how "hard" one works or thinks on an algorithm for a particular function, such as the subject function in a sentence, the general application of this algorithm to many arbitrary cases will more than likely include inappropriate subjects and rejected subjects. This situation prevails in almost any subroutine developed either at GAT or by other machine-translation groups. This indubitable fact makes one wonder if in final analysis the researchers in the machine-translation field will have to settle for a machine-translation product which is far from perfect, yet useful in a particular information subfield, and which will slowly but surely improve qualitatively through feedback utilization and further investigation. One of the specific difficulties encountered during this investigation has been the determination of how and why machine translation started. The general consensus as to "how?" is expressed by Warren Weaver in his memorandum on translation in 1948. Weaver was interested in machine translation for two reasons – first, to extend the use of computers to the humanistic field; second, to discover decomposable elements in the translation process. The "why?" is answered in terms of "information explosion" and the natural desire of mankind to extend its physical and intellectual organs artificially, following the historical pattern of the telescope extension of the human eye, the car extension of the human leg, the telephone extension of the human ear, etc. Certainly, assignment of some intellectual operations to the computer might free man from mundane tasks and allow him to apply his creative power to the results produced by computers.

Determining the "how" and "why" of the origin of machine translation has proved difficult in part because of the quotation techniques used by various researchers in the machine-translation field. It is almost a prevailing pattern for a researcher to freely quote opinions in support of his own views and to neglect contrary opinions. Another aspect of quotation techniques which creates difficulties is the widespread habit of quoting out of context, thus distorting the general impression upon the reader. To illustrate the point, one could quote various researchers concerning the starting point in their machine-translation research. Quite a few of them would say that they started in 1946 or 1948 or 1952, but that real progress started after 1955. If the reader wonders why progress did not begin until after 1955, either there is no answer or the answer is not very convincing; e. g., "Although the subject of machine translation was considered at the RAND Corporation in 1950, the workable scheme developed then was not carried out. Its authors became involved in other matters, and it was not until the late fall of 1957 that a continuing research project was established" (Hays 1967: 15). I shall try to prove that progress from 1955 was possible because of the Georgetown University-IBM machine-translation experiment carried out at the initiative of Professor Léon E. Dostert with the linguistic algorithm worked out by Professor Paul Garvin. I share the views of Professor Garvin and Professor Dostert that the G.U. experiment of 1954 proved and demonstrated beyond any doubt the feasibility of machine translation. The fact that some of the rules used in that experiment were of an *ad hoc* nature (not *ad omnia*) in no way detracts from the validity of the *ad omnia* rules. In addition, the Georgetown experiment, as any experiment which blazes a path into an unexplored region, is bound to raise objections and create misconceptions on the part of those machine-translation researchers who judge that experiment in retrospect.

This history of machine translation will be based upon reviews of past attempts at writing the history of machine translation by Weaver, Booth, Bar-Hillel, Garvin, Macdonald, Harper, Lehmann, Kulagina, Mel'čuk, Klein, and others. These and similar efforts will be discussed in detail and followed by commentary of this author.

The purpose of this commentary will be to clarify previously unexpressed points, to correct erroneous statements and to reject false judgments such as Josselson's "GU MT experiment did not prove anything" (Josselson 1971: 7). The hope is that the reader will obtain a balanced and correct view of machine-translation research and development.

At the end of this study I arrive at certain descriptive and explanatory statements or conclusions. I have tried to present this study in such a way that the reader will be able to verify my train of thought and agree that necessary and sufficient evidence exists for these conclusions. In particular, these conclusions can be verified (or refuted) by following the chapters of this book chronologically, using the output of the preceding chapter as an input to the following chapter. On the other hand, the reader can first study the items in the bibliography, then check the cross-references and footnotes and finally read as much as necessary from each chapter to be able to agree or disagree with the conclusions of this study.

1 Early concepts of machine translation

1.1 Pre-computer machine translation

As early as the 1930s there were several investigators who envisioned the use of automatic machines to assist in the translation of languages.

In 1933 George Artsruni, a French engineer, Armenian by birth, was issued a certificate patent for a translation machine which was called "Mechanical Brain" by its inventor. The constituent parts of this machine were described (Corbé 1960: 87–91) and information was given on the translation process. It is noted that despite the inadequacy of Artsruni's machine in comparison to contemporary computers, its principle can be still used for some practical experiments: for a rapid teletype translation and replacement of words from one dictionary or word combinations from another dictionary.

In 1933 P. P. Trojanskij in the USSR proposed a detailed process of translation from one language into another language with the aid of machines (Mološnaja 1961: 288).

Trojanskij worked out a process of automatization of translation in the following manner:

1. The input text is analyzed with the aim of transforming it into a particular logical form: all the inflected words are represented in canonical forms (thus, a noun is represented in the nominative case, the verb in the infinitive, etc.). The forms are ascribed their syntactic functions in the sentence in terms of, to use Trojanskij's words, "marks of the logical analysis".
2. The text transformed in this manner is replaced by the text of the other language transformed in the same manner by the logical analysis marks.
3. The transformed text is substituted into a normal form of the target language; the required grammatical forms are chosen in agreement with the marks of the logical analysis.

Trojanskij envisioned that the first and the third stages would be carried out by a human being. The second stage was to be performed by machine.

Thus Trojanskij's translation machine was an automatic dictionary which required pre- und post-editing by an editor. Trojanskij understood the unity of the logical content, expressed by a pair of languages with different grammatical and lexical structures. Basing his thought on this understanding of the logical unity, he suggested that a sufficiently clear translation through a universal logical intermediary language is possible. Trojanskij asserted that the translation could take place both from one language to another language, and from one set of languages to another set of languages.

The basic content of the essentially new method suggested by Trojanskij consists of the separation of the process of translation into three individual components: analysis, transfer, and synthesis. Trojanskij proposes to use not only the final results of this process but also the intermediate results: 1) presentation of the source text in terms of the logical form, and 2) representation of the translated text in a logical form.

The knowledge of these logical forms would even be an economic advantage to people who knew only their native language in communicating with people who spoke other languages. The suggestion of representing the source text in a logical form contains in its rudimentary form the general idea of designing a standardized language for scientific literature.

The machine was assigned only the role of the transfer from the source to the target language, but Trojanskij explicitly held that the whole process could be automated.

Trojanskij's project was not worked out in linguistic detail; the specifics of the analysis and synthesis were not expressed; the treatment of idiomatic expressions and the lexical homonymy were given only in a most general form. As a result, one feels that he was not sufficiently acquainted with the level of linguistic and logical knowledge of his time.

Understanding Trojanskij's work is made more difficult by his peculiar and sometimes vague terminology, deviating from the prevailing linguistic terminology. However, on the whole, the ideas are interesting not only because they are original but also because they are useful, creative, and fruitful. As contemporary works on machine translation show, the independence of analysis from synthesis, and the use of an intermediary language, are the leading principles of scientific investigations in the field.

For the technical realization of his project, in 1933 Trojanskij proposed a model of the translation machine. This machine consisted of a tape moving across a table. On this tape equivalent words or units from various languages were written in vertical columns. The principle of the work was purely mechanical. In 1941 Trojanskij built an electromechanical model, and in 1948 he proposed to build his machine on an electronic magnetic device for communication. However, the technical support which appeared only with the emergence of the electronic computers was lacking at this time and his machine did not reach the level of practical application.

1.2 New impetus to machine translation with the birth of computers

One of the widely held impressions regarding the start of machine translation is that the idea of machine translation emerged during a personal conversation between Warren Weaver (Director of the Natural Sciences Division, Rockefeller Foundation) and A. D. Booth in 1946. This was a time when people were looking for wider applications for the newly born machine – the computer. In 1947 the scheme for detailed dictionary coding was developed by A. D. Booth and D. H. V. Britten. A year later R. M. Richens introduced and tested the concept of split vs. full dictionary entries, thus achieving more economic use of the memory of the computer.

First machine translation research was formally announced by Ervin Reifler at the University of Washington as a result of Warren Weaver's memorandum, *Translation*, which appeared in July 1949.

Weaver's Memorandum was widely discussed and was reprinted in *Machine translation of languages* by Locke and Booth (1955) as a document suggesting research in the machine-translation field.

Mortimer Taube in his book *Computers and common sense* (1961) calls attention to three basic points made in the memorandum. The first point, according to Taube, is connected with the logical proof that machine translation is possible. This proof is based on arguments by McCulloch-Pitts (1943). The second point concerns the dependence of the meaning on context, proposing to study this relationship by "the statistical semantic character of language". Taube stresses the fact that "statistical" indicates not the frequency of occurrence but the relative length of phrases required for reduction of ambiguity of meaning. In this context, the concept of the minimal context that has any meaning at all is discussed. Bertrand Russell, Willard Van Orman, Quine, and other philosophers are of the opinion that it is the sentence, not the word, that is the minimum carrier of meaning. The third point is Dr. Weaver's assumption that computers could be effective in machine translation since they were effective during World War II in cryptographic work.

Weaver did not expect the results of machine translation to have aesthetic value, but to be of "wide service in the work-a-day task of making available the essential content of documents in languages which are foreign to the reader" (Locke and Booth 1955: vii).

He starts his *Translation* with the statement that "There is no need to do more than mention the obvious fact that a multiplicity of languages impedes cultural interchange between the peoples of the earth, and is a serious deterrent to international understanding. The present memorandum, assuming the validity and importance of this fact, contains some comments and suggestions bearing on the possibility of contributing at least something to the solution of the world-wide translation problem through the use of electronic computers of great capacity, flexibility, and speed" (Weaver 1949: 15). Weaver became convinced that there are linguistic universals in all languages and that they could have some common logical structure. He mentioned in particular some remarks made to him by the German mathematician and logician Reichenbach. Reichenbach published his views in a book (1947) where he stressed several points of direct importance for the translation process (see his introductory remarks, p. 4, and Chapter VII completely devoted to analysis of conversational language, pp. 251–354).

One of the assumptions that seemed valid to Weaver but is not convincing to the linguist is his belief that "it is very tempting to say that a book written in Chinese is simply a book written in English which was coded into the 'Chinese code'. If we have useful methods for solving almost any cryptographic problem, may it not be that with proper interpretation we already have useful methods for translation?" (1949: 22).

The linguist has some doubts, since the cryptographic code is a one-to-one relation, while in the language even the phonological level has variations, and the higher levels are not reproducible (not ready made); they are creative, and any new message may have a slightly different shape from any other previous message. Of course, the sentence is nevertheless an invariant set in any language if we understand a sentence to be certain formation techniques for propositions which carry specific information. One translates propositions, not words in isolation. Thus, one can take a proposition in English such as:

I shall be able to buy

which consists of six words (if one counts spaces between each set of letters as word boundaries) and could be translated as

Ja smogu kupit'

(Russian) with three words, and as

alabilecegim

(Turkish) with a single word. Nevertheless, the cognitive value in all three is the same.

Needless to say, some procedures from cryptography are useful. The main one is the statistical study of language unit distributions on any level. I think that Weaver is convincing when he suggests "perfect" translation is almost surely unattainable. Processes which at stated confidence levels will produce a translation which contains only X per cent 'error' are almost surely attainable.

"And it is one of the chief purposes of this memorandum that statistical semantic studies should be undertaken, as a necessary preliminary step" (p. 22).

Weaver was guided in his memorandum by four assumptions:

1. There is a vital need for contributing toward the worldwide translation problem.
2. The meaning of words of polysemic nature could be uniquely identified within a sufficiently large context.
3. Computers with large capacity and speed are useful tools.
4. The presence of linguistic universals could be subjected to logical analysis for identifying the common features in all language structures.

For additional comments and a summary of Weaver's contribution to the development of machine translation the reader is referred to E. Delavenay (1960: 5, 8, 27–28).

1.3 Booth's article on the historical background of machine translation

There are several articles on machine translation in *Mechanical resolution of linguistic problems* by Booth, Brandwood and Cleave (1958). The first article is devoted to the history of concepts which lead eventually to several experiments in the field of machine translation. Booth, Brandwood and Cleave were working in the Computation Laboratory at Birkbeck College, London University, to find new applications for digital calculators and to apply these applications to calculators in linguistic problems. The authors claim that the idea of machine translation originated at Birkbeck College in 1947, but that extensive efforts were made possible due to financial assistance only since 1955. They give credit to Dr. J. F. Lockwood, a mathematician, for mathematical contributions. In introductory remarks to the historical background of machine-translation development, the authors explain that it is quite difficult to say when precisely or at what point in time people started to think formally in analyzing language problems. Even the ancient Greeks talked frequently about the ideal language which could replace existing languages after being subjected to mechanical treatment. The authors claim that in a conversation between A. D. Booth and Warren Weaver in New York in 1946, the idea of using calculators to analyze linguistic problems was discussed. At that time this was little more than an intellectual exercise since computers were just coming into existence, though it was very interesting to find new applications for testing the capabilities of those new machines. At that time there was little financial support given to practical experimentation in this field. Machine translation, as an operational system, was not considered worthy of developing special-purpose computers for specific treatment of language problems.

   In 1947, A. D. Booth and K. H. V. Britten at the Institute for Advanced Studies, Princeton, New Jersey, produced a program which enabled an automatic digital calculator to make use of a dictionary stored in its memory. This facilitated the looking up of words presented to the machine. What was interesting in that particular program was the recognition that, as in any regular dictionary lookup, one cannot use the dictionary unless one is acquainted with certain syntactical features of the language with which the dictionary is concerned.

   In 1948 Booth and Richens, in studying procedures for the improvement of the dictionary lookup, came up with the idea that, rather than entering complete word forms in the dictionary, it would be better to give only stems, and store the endings separately. But it was also thought that storage required for natural language would exceed the capacity of existing machines and limit vocabulary. In addition, it was not at all clear whether programs would be available which would encompass the scope of linguistic comprehension by using bound morphemes or some other code to accompany the word entries. But one thing came immediately to the foreground: that given a particular field from which one is going to translate, one should have macro- and micro-glossaries. The assumption at that time was that approximately 1 000 technical terms from any particular field would suffice, while the rest of the words would come from the general dictionary. It was also discovered that, in random tests for the particular machine-translation system, there would be words in the source language not found in the dictionary. In this case the machine would reproduce the word or words in a modified form at the output so the translator could give it detailed attention.

In July 1949 the Warren Weaver memorandum led to an upsurge of interest in the subject of translation in the United States. In 1950 E. Reifler produced his first studies in machine translation in which he tried to justify two concepts: pre-editing and post-editing. The pre-editor would remove all known ambiguities and difficulties from the source language text in a mechanical way. The post-editor, on the other hand, would render the output of the machine in a respectable grammatical form of the target language. At that time there was fairly widespread opinion that in the future there would be no need for either the pre-editor or the post-editor. Ten years later A. D. Booth was not as convinced. In my opinion, there are definitely some areas for which pre-editing could be justified. Of course, there are also areas in machine output that could justify post-editing rather than development of more algorithmic programs of such high quality as to eliminate post-editing. It is more than probable that certain pre-editing and post-editing will go on for some time.

In 1952 the growing general interest in machine translation led to the sponsorship by the Rockefeller Foundation of a conference devoted entirely to machine translation, held at MIT in Boston, Massachusetts. Georgetown University was represented by Professor Léon Dostert. There were no formal results of the week-long discussions, but the prevailing feeling could be summarized as: 1. linguistic problems were too difficult for any practical experiments, and 2. experiments were the only way in which the subject could make progress at all.

Two additional observations were made at the MIT conference: 1. analysis of word frequency and word meaning should be conducted on a large scale, in various fields and in as many languages as possible, and 2. operational analysis and syntax should be developed and be available when required; namely, for use with available large and high-speed computers. After the conference work proceeded on a considerable scale, both in England and in the United States. In America K. E. Harper and A. G. Oettinger published papers on mechanical translation, dealing with some aspects of the Russian language and with the construction of a Russian dictionary for machine-translation purposes (Oettinger 1954).

In 1954 an experiment in machine translation was conducted at Georgetown University with the assistance of the IBM Corporation. (We shall deal with that experiment in more detail in the next chapter.) In that experiment a machine was programmed to translate selected sentences from Russian using a restricted vocabulary of 250 words. In that same year, 1954, V. Yngve and W. N. Locke started publishing the first journal completely devoted to machine-translation problems, called *Machine Translation*. The British authors claimed in 1955 that results were achieved in solving problems connected with dictionary lookup and that their experiments showed the feasibility of translation from French to English. In the same year the first book on machine translation appeared (Locke and Booth 1955).

1.4 Outside evaluation of the Georgetown University machine-translation system

While it is rather natural for Soviet linguists to study in detail foreign machine-translation systems and report about them in objective descriptive terms, and evaluate them, it is very unusual for an American linguist to study someone else's program and report his findings objectively. One of the reasons usually given is the proverbial "I do not want to be influenced". Eugene Pendergraft of the University of Texas is a pleasant exception. He did study varieties of American machine-translation systems and wrote about them in an interesting and illuminative manner.

Pendergraft's descriptions and evaluations of Georgetown University machine translation are selected from the paper "Translating languages" (Pendergraft 1967). According to Pendergraft, the attitude of Léon Dostert, the director of the Georgetown machine-translation project, was primarily molded on the basis of his experience and general observation in connection with his teaching at Georgetown University, where he introduced the system of simultaneous interpretation and was busy with other linguistic projects at the newly established School of Languages and Linguistics (1949). Dostert became very active in machine translation after attending the MIT conference on mechanical translation in 1952. Pendergraft notes that Dostert stated on various occasions that the focus in machine translation must be on the linguistic side. Dostert enjoyed designing experiments in order to attempt to widen the scope or the procedures of machine-translation research.

We shall now briefly present the views of Pendergraft on various machine-translation systems which existed in the US after ten years of machine-translation research, in order to contrast his evaluations of other machine-translation systems with that of Georgetown University.

Pendergraft credits E. Reifler with the suggestion made in 1950 that machine-translation research should be looked upon as a cooperative effort carried out by the pre-editor, the partially automated dictionary lookup, the automated but facilitated operation of selection, and the post-editor. Pre-editing will add needed diacritics to the source text to facilitate mechanical operation. Post-editing will take care of the word rearrangement of the target language. The pre-editor need not know more than the source language; the post-editor not more than the target language.

Anthony Oettinger, in his doctoral thesis, proposed to eliminate the problem of pre-editing entirely (Oettinger 1954). This was done by listing all the available target equivalents in the target text preserving the original word order. Pendergraft notes that while the function of pre-editor was done away with, that of the post-editor was doubled. The post-editor had to select the adequate target equivalents and rearrange the word order in the target language.

Obviously, the post-editor had to know both the source language and the target language, and also the subject matter being translated. Oettinger is also credited with having made contributions to the technical problems of automatic storing and of retrieving full and split forms.

Victor Yngve did not believe in omitting the problems of word selection and rearrangement in automatic solutions. He estimated that a source word may have, on the average, three or four possible equivalents. This ratio was too high for the addressee in the target language.

Yngve did not share the opinion that partly useful results could be secured by a short-range goal in machine translation. He believed in long-range machine-translation research of a basic type. The real purpose of his interests lay in trying to learn about language as much as possible prior to attempts at mechanization of the basic operations involved in automatic translation, i.e.,

1. looking up in a bilingual dictionary the individual words occurring in the running source text;
2. selecting from the available target equivalents the single most probable one;
3. synthesizing the proper forms and word order in the target language independently of the source language on the basis of the contrastive descriptions of the specific pair of source and target languages.

Yngve was able to achieve parts of his ideal for machine translation.

The difficulties encountered in finding solutions to selection and rearrangement problems led machine-translation workers to call this kind of low-level quality machine translation "word-by-word translation".

There were some people among the early machine-translation pioneers who believed so strongly in the power of the newly-born computer that linguistic analysis was considered by them as being of only marginal importance. Gilbert King and some of his associates from IBM were inclined to test the hypothesis that the syllable is the carrier of the morpheme as the minimal semantic unit. Accordingly, they assumed that, given a large special computer with direct access, one would be able to store both the dictionary and the grammar rules, and thus carry out the whole translation process automatically (IBM 1960). The output was not as good as they expected it to be. (We may add that it was rather surprising to learn that syllables in Indo-European languages frequently do not carry the meaning of a morpheme. Thus, the Russian word *kondensatsija* which is "condensation" emerged from King's machine as "horsedensatsija", since the first part of the Russian word ["kon"] (actually *kon'*) as a syllable could mean also "horse", while the second part ["densatsija"] was not in the dictionary and was left as it was.) The positive feature of King's system was the availability of a large-capacity computer with the integral address procedure; the special-purpose circuitry was capable of performing, in addition to selection and rearrangement operations, also those for the treatment of idioms. Among the machine-translation workers the original model of the machine was known as "Mark I", and its later modification as "Mark II". The hardware research was sponsored by the U.S. Air Force. The sponsor abandoned its support for "Mark III" which was planned to incorporate in its circuitry the capabilities for performing selection and rearrangement. The word lookup was based not on the word length but on the letter-by-letter sequence. This explains how "horse" came from "kondensatsija".

Dostert's general work procedures were a cross between the long-range goal of Yngve and the short-range goal of Reifler. At first he set himself apart from the others by stating that one should work the way Descartes did – tackle one part of a problem at a time, learn from it, take another part, and eventually, through these cumulative efforts, insights will be increased and general comprehension might be closer at hand. He agreed with Reifler that diacritics (special codes) would be helpful, but tried further to insert them, as much as was feasible, into the dictionary in order to facilitate the two processes of machine translation – selection and concatenation.

Pendergraft is correct in stressing the difference between Reifler's diacritics and those of Dostert, and saying that "... the diacritic marks assigned by Reifler's pre-editor gave information about the word-event (instance, token), while those obtained from Dostert's dictionary gave information about the word-design (pattern, type)" (Pendergraft 1967: 299).

According to Pendergraft, syntactic analysis at Georgetown is performed in terms of immediate constituent analysis applied to each sentence. Each major constituent serves as a "fulcrum" and is used as a tool for getting more information about the rest of the units in the sentence.

After Garvin's departure from Georgetown the contest between the GU machine-translation groups had narrowed to a choice between GAT (General Analysis Techniques) and SLC (Simulated Linguistic Computer), a system devised by Dr. A. Brown and recoded by him for the 709–7090 IBM computer in 1959.

Pendergraft observes that "GAT became the symbol and embodiment of the empirical approach" (p. 306). Pendergraft reports that by 1963 "Dostert considered GAT completely operative and able to routinely translate texts in several scientific and technical disciplines from Russian to English. Nevertheless, GAT was not accepted for use by its sponsoring agencies, and the Georgetown project has been practically disbanded" (1967: 306). He gave no explanation.

It is my feeling that Pendergraft is historically justified in defending Dostert's linguistic base as being traceable to Leonard Bloomfield (p. 307). Pendergraft is quite correct in noting similarities between certain aspects of Yngve's views and those of Dostert. In particular, Pendergraft notes that both Dostert and Yngve assumed that the lexical meanings would be found in any language, and that their translation would be feasible. This postulate was expressed by Yngve in the following manner: "Since a strict sentence-for-sentence translation is entirely impractical, and since word-for-word translations are surprisingly good, it seems reasonable to accept a word-for-word translation as a first approximation and then see what can be done to improve it" (p. 309).

After presenting some of the theoretical and practical considerations entertained by Yngve, Pendergraft states "Surely these speculations were not markedly different from those that occurred at Georgetown University. Nor would Dostert disagree with Yngve's conclusion that a solution of the grammatical multiple meaning problem requires a solution of the syntactic problems, including the changing of word order upon translation. Dostert's analysis group made a similar decision in its first few months of deliberation" (p. 311).

Pendergraft quotes Dostert's statements covering the principles used in constructing the dictionary and rules of grammar. Thus, the dictionary entries contain diacritics of three different types: 1. program-initiating; 2. choice-determining, and 3. address-diacritics.

Program-initiating diacritics were used to determine which rules of selection or rearrangement should be used in processing specific words. Pendergraft lists all six program-initiating diacritics with the following interpretation in the translation process:

0. The order of the original text is to be followed.

1. There is to be a difference of order in the translation from the order in the original, and an inversion is necessary.
2. There is a problem of choice; the choice depends on an indication which follows the word under consideration.
3. There is a problem of choice; the choice depends on an indication which precedes the word under consideration.
4. A word appearing in the original text is to be dropped, and no equivalent will appear in the translation.
5. At a point where there is no equivalent word in the original text, a word is to be introduced into the translation (p. 300).

The second type of diacritics, choice-determining, had two functions. Either the word under consideration was coded as a resolution cue for other ambiguities, or the context words were indicated to define or clarify the word under consideration.

The third type, address-diacritics, were symbolic coding for the locations of the words under consideration.

In addition to these three types of diacritics, the words and sentences containing these words were assigned such additional codes as might be determined by the lexical and syntactic searches during further operations in the course of the translation.

Lexical searches were activated by program-initiating diacritics 2 or 3 above.

Syntactic scanning was activated by the program-initiating diacritics 0, 1, 4 or 5 above. The words belonging to a specific syntagmatic linkage such as agreement, government, or adjoining would be properly coded and linked together.

2 Léon Dostert and the 1954 experiment

The Georgetown University machine-translation project, headed by Dr. Léon E. Dostert, is described or referred to in practically all reviews and articles dealing with the history of machine translation, as it was the first experiment proving the feasibility of machine translation. The most accurate descriptions of the GU machine-translation project were given by some authors who, in one way or another, were intimately involved or acquainted with the GU machine-translation system. This chapter is based on articles written by L. Dostert, the founder of the GU machine translation, Professor Paul Garvin, the senior linguist, Professor Ross Macdonald, the editor of the GU machine-translation papers, and E. Pendergraft, the senior machine-translation researcher at Texas University. I myself was the senior researcher of the GAT (General Analysis Techniques) as one of the four sections of the GU machine-translation project and will comment on the articles written by these authors. I hope that the reader will see from the context which comments are mine and which are the opinions of the others.

2.1 Professor Léon Dostert

L. E. Dostert, founder of the machine-translation research at GU, did not write extensively about the history of machine translation; he made it. Except for his article, "Brief history of machine translation research" (1957a), where he describes the beginnings of the research, he was too busy experimenting, directing and coordinating machine-translation research activity at Georgetown to formulate historical description or evaluation of this new and exciting research field. As a true pioneer in his field he combined vision and practice. He was bold enough to break totally unknown ground and modest enough to listen to the suggestions of others in the field. He was one of those pioneers who "set out bravely to manipulate natural language in relatively small computers and more often gained the scars rather than the plaudits of their victories" (Pendergraft 1967: 291).

L. E. Dostert was a person toward whom an observer could not display a neutral attitude. One felt like becoming one of his loyal followers, or one felt antagonistic towards him as a result of his machine-translation methods. This feeling was created by Dostert's straightforward attitude in his relations with people. He had an inventive mind. He told me how he came upon the idea of simultaneous translation, which he developed during the Nurenberg Process in 1946. He watched as interpreters tried to whisper unobtrusively to one of the speakers what had been said by the other speaker. This observation led Dostert to the idea of equipping the speakers with earphones and putting the interpreter into a separate area where he could translate into a microphone. Thus, everybody could hear what was said simultaneously into two or even more than two languages.

The first interest in machine translation at GU arose in 1952. In June of that year Professor L. E. Dostert, at Georgetown, was asked to participate in a meeting on machine translation at MIT. As a result of the meeting and consultation with linguists and engineers, Dostert started an experiment in collaboration with the International Business Machine Corporation to produce an actual machine translation.

Russian was to be translated into English by use of three codes: program-initiating diacritics, choice-determining diacritics and a code indicating the locations in the computer of the first two types of codes.

The goal was to produce the quality of the machine-translation output such that the outside evaluator, specialist in the field, would find this quality acceptable as a source of information contained in the source language.

The dictionary entries containing the Russian words, their English equivalent(s), their codes, and the syntactic rules were keypunched and introduced into the memory of the computer to allow the computer to translate the Russian source text into English.

I believe, as did Dostert, that much of the computational activity in language translation which followed was due to that experiment.

For further reference the reader may wish to consult the articles written by L. Dostert listed in the bibliography at the end of this book. What is most apparent in these articles is the uniqueness of Dostert's personality, his spirit of inventiveness, and his strong desire to develop a new tool to service the community. He knew how to motivate his co-workers by letting them conduct research independently provided only that in the final analysis they would be willing to come down from the level of theoretical thinking and try to embody the theory in some practical system. Those among his co-workers who thought that they already had such a system felt no need for theoretical analysis. On the other hand, those who felt it was unnecessary to apply it in practice did not want to produce a comprehensive system with the necessary and sufficient amount of detail. Both of the latter types of co-workers eventually had to part ways with L. Dostert, whose approach was characterized by a creative balance between theoretical analysis and practical application.

2.2 Linguistic basis of P. Garvin

Professor P. Garvin created the linguistic basis for this classical GU machine-translation experiment (1967: 46–56).

In order to understand the basic principles and procedures developed by Garvin, it will be useful to become acquainted with the input data he used to prove the feasibility of machine translation. The Russian sentences that were transliterated and coded for the translation algorithm are the following:

Test sentences:

1. PRYIGOTOVLYAYUT TOL
2. TOL PRYIGOTOVLYAYUT YIZ* UGLYA
3. TOL PRYIGOTOVLYAYETSYA YIZ UGLYA
4. BOYETS PRYIGOTOVLYAYETSYA K BOYU
5. KACHYESTVO UGLYA OPRYEDYELYAYETSYA KALORYIYNOSTJYU
6. TOL PRYIGOTOVLYAYETSYA YIZ KAMYENNOGO UGLYA
7. BYENZYIN DOBIVAYUT YIZ NYEFTYI
8. BYENZYIN DOBIVAYETSYA YIZ NYEFTYI
9. AMMONYIT PRYIGOTOVLYAYUT YIZ SYELYITRI
10. AMMONYIT PRYIGOTOVLYAYETSYA YIZ SYELYITRI

11. SPYIRT VIRABATIVAYUT YIZ KARTOFYELYA
12. SPYIRT VIRABATIVAYETSYA YIZ KARTOFYELYA
13. KRAXMAL VIRABATIVAYUT YIZ KARTOFYELYA
14. KRAXMAL VIRABATIVAYETSYA YIZ KARTOFYELYA
15. TOL PRYIGOTOVLYAYETSYA XYIMYICHYESKYIM PUTYEM YIZ KAMYENNOGO UGLYA
16. AMMONYIT PRYIGOTOVLYAYETSYA XYIMYICHYES-KYIM PUTYEM YIZ SYELYITRI
17. KRAXMAL VIRABATIVAYETSYA MYEXANYICHYES-KYIM PUTYEM YIZ KARTOFYELYA
18. TSYENA KARTOFYELYA OPRYEDYELYAYETSYA RIN-KOM
19. VYELYICHYINA UGLA OPRYEDYELYAYETSYA OTNOSHYENYIYEM DLYINI DUGI K RADYIUSU
20. KALORYIYNOSTJ OPRYEDYELYAYET KACHYESTVO UGLYA
21. OBRABOTKA POVISHAYET KACHYESTVO NYEFTYI
22. ZHYELYEZO DOBIVAYETSYA YIZ RUDI
23. MYEDJ DOBIVAYETSYA YIZ RUDI
24. DYINAMYIT PRYIGOTOVLYAYETSYA YIZ NYTRO-GLYITSYERINA S PRYIMYESJYU YINYERTNOGO MATERYIALA
25. VOZVISHYENYIYE OPRYEDYELYAYETSYA NYIVYELYIROVANYIYEM
26. UGOL MYESTA TSYELYI OPRYEDYELYAYETSYA OPTYICHYESKYIM YIZMYERYENYIYEM
27. TSYENA PSHYENYITSI OPRYEDYELYAYETSYA RINKOM
28. TSYENA PSHYENYITSI OPRYEDYELYAYETSYA SPROSOM
29. TSYENA KARTOFYELYA OPRYEDYELYAYESTYA SPROSOM
30. DOROGI STROYATSYA YIZ KAMNYA
31. VOYSKA STROYATSYA KLYINOM
32. MI PYERYEDAYEM MISLYIPOSRYEDSTVOM RYECHYI
33. ZHYELYEZO DOBIVAYUT YIZ RUDI
34. MYEDJ DOBIVAYUT YIZ RUDI
35. ZHYELYEZO DOBIVAYETSYA YIZ RUDI XYIMYI-CHESKYIM PROTSYESSOM

36. MYEDJ DOBIVAYETSYA YIZ RUDI XYIMYICHYESKYIM PROTSYESSOM
37. DYINAMYIT   PRYIGOTOVLYAYETSYA   XYIMYI-CHYESKYIM PUTYEM YIZ NYITROGLYITSYERYINA S
38. DOMA STROYATSYA YIZ KYIRPYICHA / / / PRYIMYES-JYU YINYERTNOGO MATYERYIALA
39. DOMA STROYATSYA YIZ BYETONA
40. VOYENNIY SUD PRYIGOVORYIL SYERZHANTA K LYISHYENYIYU GRAZHDANSKYIX PRAV
41. UGOLOVNOYE PRAVO YAVLYAYETSYA VAZHNIM OTDYELOM ZAKONODATYELJSTVA
42. NAUKA O KYISLORODNIX SOYEDYINYENYIYAX YAV-LYAYETSYA VAZHNIM OTDYELOM XYIMYIYI
43. VLADYIMYIR YAVLYAYETSYA NA RABOTU POZDNO UTROM
44. MYEZHDUNARODNOYE PONYIMANYIYE YAVLYA-YETSYA VAZHNIM FAKTOROM V RYESHYENYIYI
45. VYDUTSYA   PYERYEGOVORI   O   PYERYEM-YIRYIYI / / / POLYITYICHYESKYIX VOPROSOV
46. FYEDYERATSYIYA SOSTOYIT YIZ MNOGYIX SHTA-TOV
47. RADYIOSTANTSYIYA PYERYEDAYET POSLYEDNYIYE SOOBSHCHYENYIYA O POGODYE
48. RADYIOSTANTSYIYA PYERYEDAYET POSLYEDNYIYE POLYITYICHYESKYIYE YIZVYESTYIYA
49. VLADYIMYIR POLUCHAYET BOLJSHOYE ZHALOVANYIYE

I would like to draw the reader's attention to the fact that these sentences are highly constrained. None of them have a negative particle. All of the sentences are declarative and no interrogative or compound sentences are included. As for the verbs, they are given in reflexive or nonreflexive form, in the third person singular or plural; there are no other person conjugational forms, singular nor plural, involved. In relation to the subject and predicate functions, there are complements in the genitive, extending the noun as well as some prepositions which govern the nominal phrases.

The GU experiment was carried out in conjunction with IBM on January 7, 1954. The purpose was to test the feasibility of machine translation by devising a maximally simple, but realistic, set of translation rules which were also programmed on a computer. The particular IBM computer which was used was the IBM 701. However, the computer was of secondary importance. The syntactic rules developed by P. Garvin and the organization of the dictionary should be of primary importance. These rules are based on the underlying concept of recognition routines which have one or two simple commands; two commands if there is a branching, and one if there is an absolute transfer. Garvin is quite right in stating that his rules are realistic, in the sense that he succeeded in solving general linguistic problems, with the qualification, of course, that those problems were only of two fundamental types connected with translation decisions. The first type is: given a pair of English equivalents for a single Russian unit, one of the English units is selected. The second translation decision is word arrangement: given the Russian units A and B, they are rearranged if necessary into English to give the order B and A.

There are, however, some specific limitations imposed upon this procedure. Given the particular problem he tried to solve, Garvin defined his search limits as only one step to the left and one to the right, or both if necessary. Given the problem of arrangement of units, he would rearrange items only if they were continuous. No discontinuous rearrangements were made. The program applied to Russian sentences, one at a time, and the word lookup of the sentence in the dictionary was carried out on a sentence-by-sentence basis. After the words from the sentence were looked up in the dictionary, the code attached to each word was coupled with matching words from the sentence. The information thus collected was brought to the internal memory of the computer, and the algorithm was activated to operate on those words to generate the expected translation.

Despite the heavy restrictions imposed on the rules, these rules used by Garvin seemed adequate at that time for the purpose of proving the feasibility of machine translation. Garvin provided logical analysis for a few translation problems and expressed the rules for their solution in programmable terms. Given the state of knowledge of computational linguistics at that time, Garvin noticed and analyzed several variables of the problems to be solved. Then he produced a specific one-to-one rule for each isolated variable. If a particular problem were of no interest to him, or he did not know how to solve it, he usually set the problem aside, since he could add further rules later. He could test the rules which he had developed, without the additional rules applicable to this particular experiment. To give some specific examples, we can mention the translation of cases from Russian into English. Each case form had to be analyzed in two ways: first, whether or not it was to be translated by a preposition and, second, what preposition was to be chosen. The experiment did not advance to the second step, namely what preposition to choose, but rather the preposition was arbitrarily assigned, based on the text. In that sense the English equivalent was pre-edited. Similar examples were represented by the first person plural verb form, where the ending was not translated if the verb was preceded by the plural personal pronoun *my* 'we'. The Russian language does not have articles and yet in that first experiment articles were inserted into the English translation at the suggestion of Professor Archibald Hill.

Now a few words about the organization of the dictionary. The dictionary entries were split if the entry was inflected (e.g., if it was a verb, noun, adjective, etc.). These inflected and uninflected entries were stored in the computer memory in alphabetical order. The specific technical procedures used by Garvin to solve a given problem were based on two criteria: the recognition points and the decision cues. The entries in the dictionary were accompanied by two-positional digits or three-positional digits, and each digit had a particular function to play. In the whole experiment there were only five rules; these five rules of translation are those controlled by a set of two-digit and three-digit numerical code symbols, or diacritics. The first of the digits was used to indicate whether the diacritics were assigned to a decision-point entry or a decision-cue entry. The second digit indicated the number of the rule to be applied, and the third digit, used only for some decision-cue diacritics, marked which of two choices was to be made.

Garvin (1967: 48) characterizes the 1954 experiment in the following way:

1. The scope of the translation program was clearly specified.
2. The lookup routine was designed for maximum efficiency of the translation algorithm.
3. The translation algorithm was based on the collocation of decision points and decision cues, rather than directly on the linguistic factors involved.
4. The word length of a sentence turned out to be operationally insignificant.

5. Selection and arrangement were confirmed as the basic algorithmic operations.

The importance of the 1954 experiment, according to Garvin, "... lies in the fact that it formed a significant first step in a continuing research process which is just now nearing completion. This first step consisted in providing an essentially correct formulation of the problem of machine translation which can be succinctly stated as follows:

1. The machine translation problem is basically a decision problem.
2. The two fundamental types of decisions are selection decisions and arrangement decisions.
3. For the automatic implementation of a translation decision, the algorithm has to have the capability for recognizing the decision points and the appropriate decision cues."

In conclusion, Garvin says: "The research derived from this formulation has therefore been focused on the detection of the recognition criteria needed for the identification of the decision points and the decision cues. The approach to the decision problem is based on an understanding of syntactic structure which increases as our empirical treatment of it develops." (1967: 48–49).

In my considered opinion, nobody can detract from Professor Garvin's pioneering contribution in providing the first beginnings in solving, on a computer, the two basic problems involved in the translation problem: 1. the decision steps connected with the lexical unit selection, and 2. the arrangement units of the target language. Those two problems reflect the two axes in the natural language structure referred to by de Saussure as the associative and syntagmatic axes.

Any further elaboration and improvement of machine-translation systems may add more levels, including the semantic level, to the translation process, but it must follow the general principles successfully tested by Garvin in the 1954 GU machine-translation experiment.

2.3 Macdonald's general report on the Georgetown University machine translation research project

The general report (Macdonald 1963), covering the achievements of the Georgetown machine translation project from June 1952 to March 1963, draws from three sources:

1. It is a revision of the *Occasional Papers* published in order to present these papers in a consistent style, to improve their readability and to provide summaries and explanations. However, the *Occasional Papers* covering Comparative Slavic are not individually described in the general report because some of them were published elsewhere, and due to their scope they would require separate attention. Brief descriptions of the Direct Conversion and the Simulated Linguistic Computer (SLC) programming systems are given at the end of this report.
2. It is a description of the research at Georgetown from 1956 to 1963.
3. It covers the terminal reports which were submitted to the Central Intelligence Agency at the termination of support.

A brief description of the form of the presentation of some linguistic statements, following the papers on morphology, is given to provide some insight into the problems involved. Greater emphasis is given to the principles involved rather than to specific details of coding and classification.

It is reported that Russian was to be translated into English using three codes: program-initiating diacritics, choice-determining diacritics and a code indicating the locations in the computer of the first two types of codes.

The quality of the Russian-to-English machine-translation output was considered acceptable to outside readers who were requested to evaluate the translation. The dictionary, its codes, and the syntactic rules were keypunched and introduced into the machine to allow the machine to translate the source text into English.

The result of GU machine translation was given wide publicity in 1954 when it was announced in New York. The announcement was greeted by astonishment and skepticism among some people.

L. E. Dostert summarized the result of the experiment as being an authentic machine translation which does not require pre-editing of the input nor post-editing of the output. He suggested that certain problems of meaning could be solved by compiling technical dictionaries for various fields and by developing a core (intermediary) language to facilitate the translation.

In 1956 the USSR Academy of Sciences announced a successful translation of English into Russian on their computer, at the same time acknowledging that their interest had been initiated by the GU experiment.

In 1956 Georgetown University received a grant from the National Science Foundation for the translation of Russian scientific materials into English, focusing on the field of organic chemistry.

Training of research workers was the first requirement. Two groups were organized: the first was to carry out translation analysis and linguistic analysis, to provide the preparation of a consistent translation; the second group was to provide analysis of the Russian language for machine translation, and was later named the experimental group. This original procedure was subsequently refined and generalized. Because of a flood of differing opinions, unanimous agreement with respect to procedure was rarely possible.

As the work of the experimental group proceeded, a divergency of points of view arose. By January 1957 there were a number of groups identified by the names of the methods they used, e. g., code-matching, syntactic analysis, general analysis, and the sentence-by-sentence method. In brief, the following are the characteristics of these methods.

Code matching is word-by-word analysis of the coding of each Russian dictionary entry for each English meaning. One function of the form applicable in each context is derived by comparing the codes of contiguous words. Those which are the same are selected and grouped; the others are disregarded in that context. Modifications are necessary when none of the codes of contiguous words match.

Syntactic analysis considers one sentence at a time. It is the analysis of immediate constituents (IC) of each sentence, and ICs of those ICs and so on until the analysis is complete. The item conveying the largest amount of grammatical information which serves as the fulcrum in the process of prying out more information from the remaining item is the focus. This method is sometimes referred to as the fulcrum method.

General analysis also works with a sentence at a time where every possible level of the analysis is important. Morphology, including idiom, is the first level. Syntagmatic processes, including agreement, government, and modification, is the second level, and syntax is the third.

The sentence-by-sentence method was purported to be the most novel method to machine translation. It is the method where the linguist can control, add, revise, subtract or alter the processes until the system no longer requires modifications or additions.

The theory as well as the operational procedures were different among various groups. For example, in the work of the experimental group the dictionary entries were first unsplit and then split. Other groups tried other methods. It became a policy that diversity of methods was accepted; that each method was tested and the method which produced the best result was adopted over the others.

In April 1957 a feasibility test on machine translation was successfully performed using a particular Soviet publication in the field of organic chemistry. The translation was to be performed on both 'prepared' and 'random' texts. The 'random' text was considered the conclusive method for proving the system. A dictionary was prepared to translate the texts. The dictionary emphasized the need for up-to-date text-based dictionaries in each technical field.

Later in the year there were several meetings and seminars on machine translation at several places in the US and abroad. In September 1957 decisions were made by the GU machine translation research project to investigate numerous methods, to research other additional languages, to investigate additional fields of scientific literature for machine translation, etc.

An additional test was then completed by the General Analysis Group (GAT) in 1958, and an acceptable translation was obtained through additional *ad hoc* procedures.

In August 1959 the code-matching group produced an excellent translation of ten sentences in length, although information on the procedures used was not revealed.

In the spring of 1959 the regular seminar papers were replaced by a new series called *Occasional Papers* which described the analysis and programs being carried out.

In June 1959 an 'examined' text was tested by the General Analysis Technique. When asked to check the translation, a chemist indicated that the texts conveyed the essential information although the style was clumsy and the reading of the texts time-consuming. At this time, the name 'General Analysis Techniques' was changed to 'Georgetown Automatic Translation' (GAT).

Simultaneously the sentence-by-sentence method, developed by Dr. A. F. R. Brown and later called the Simulated Linguistic Computer (SLC), was tested. The results of this test were not as satisfactory as the GAT results. However, when used to translate French into English, this method proved to be as significant as GAT.

From the results of these tests, research workers of these two methods identified particular deficiencies and started correcting and completing their procedures. At the end of 1959 the code-matching method was reviewed by the GU special committee and was consequently abandoned as a practical solution to the problems of machine translation.

In July 1959, at the UNESCO Conference in Paris, the first public demonstration of the translation of a random text was given by M. Zarechnak and A. Brown from Georgetown University. Later, in January 1960, trial runs of machine translation of organic chemistry were given at the Pentagon in Washington, D.C.

In February 1960 Zarechnak and Brown attended the symposium on machine translation in Los Angeles, with Dr. Dostert as a 'discussant'. Brown and Zarechnak described the research done at Georgetown.

In July 1960, at the Princeton Conference on machine translation, various aspects of the work were discussed in an effort to find research similarities between various machine-translation groups, to agree on a common format for the dictionary information and to investigate the possibility of establishing an exchange procedure.

Subsequent to the discussions with Professor Dostert, the government of Yugoslavia decided to initiate a project for machine translation from English into Serbo-Croatian.

Prior to 1961 an IBM 705 computer had been used. Early in 1961 the IBM 705 computer was converted to an IBM 709 and all computer programs were rewritten.

The linguistic formulations designed and coordinated by M. Zarechnak were the same for both programming efforts. The first programming team headed by Peter Toma was characterized as 'Direct Conversion Programming' because it did not use any subroutines, and kept programming all the linguistic operations as many times as were called in by the main control linguistic system. This system had a nickname, *SERNA*, given to it by this author, which was an acronym for *S (e) Russkogo Na Anglijskij* [from Russian into English], with 'E' added for euphony. The word *serna* is also a regular Russian word for the English 'chamois' from the deer family. The idea was to have a picture of a deer swiftly and gracefully moving over the mountainous regions. A good machine-translation system should by analogy move in a similar manner over the linguistic landscape of the source text and synthesize its target equivalent.

I stress this small detail missing from Macdonald's paper since Peter

Toma later left the GU machine-translation group, formed his own private company, and has claimed that the machine-translation system called SERNA was created by him. In reality, he merely coordinated the programming efforts and functioned as a liaison officer between M. Zarechnak, the senior researcher for the GAT, and the programming team.

The second programming team acquired the name Simulated Linguistic Computer (SLC). Its sole author and programmer was Dr. A. F. R. Brown, who analyzed the linguistic base of the GAT and wrote as many subroutines as he found useful. In addition, Dr. Brown wrote his programming language. It is with his language that the GAT-SLC is running now at the Oak Ridge, Tennessee National Laboratory (ORNL), and at Georgetown University, where the GAT-SLC as rewritten for IBM-360 has been running since 1977.

In April 1961 at the conference on Russian-English grammar codes at Georgetown, types of dictionary codes, as well as other coding systems, were discussed.

In September 1961 the first international conference on machine translation was held in Teddington, England. Georgetown University was represented by Professor Dostert, Dr. Brown and Mr. Zarechnak (Zarechnak 1963).

Research work was also initiated on the problem of machine translation from Chinese into English, even though the problems differ from Russian or French into English due to the nature of the languages.

Investigations of certain points of view through the research of other languages were also carried out, e.g., comparisons between French and English, and Turkish and English. Each comparison was beneficial to both the SLC and machine translation begun in Turkey.

In October 1961, through a comparative study of the Slavic languages by the Comparative Slavic Research Group at Georgetown, a system of transcription compatible with the orthographies of these languages evolved and the work on the morphology of the individual languages began. It was expected that establishing core languages through this comparative research would be possible.

In the latter part of 1961 the SLC system was generalized so that it could be adapted to any machine translation situation.

In April 1962 another test on Russian-into-English translation was made which showed a noticeable improvement over the former translation.

In May 1962 Dr. Macdonald visited Ankara, Turkey, to orient and coordinate the staff of a project for English-to-Turkish translation. In the same month the Reverend Roberto Busa, S. J., of Rome, Italy, held two seminars at Georgetown University to discuss machine translation and other closely related topics.

In June 1962 the Chinese group of the GU machine translation research project published a telegraphic-code Chinese-English Dictionary for machine translation. The completion of the dictionary made a pilot project in the translation of Chinese to English possible. A text in mathematics was selected for the project.

At the NATO Conference on Automatic Translation in Venice in the summer of 1962, Professor Dostert and Dr. Brown presented a paper reviewing the results of the GU project.

In October 1962 a demonstration translation was performed at ORNL where the text selected was in the field of cybernetics. The problems encountered were greater than in the texts in chemistry or related fields due to the difference in content and level of style. Research necessary to obtain improvements in the system was planned.

In 1962 the Euratom Center in Italy proposed developing a machine-translation system for translating from Russian to French. A contractual agreement between Euratom and GU was negotiated and GU was asked to provide a consultant to Brussels to aid in the adapting of the GAT which would be used in the analysis of Russian.

I would like to add that in 1962 the GU machine translation project stopped its work, since it was not further supported by its sponsor. The official version of the reason for phasing out the support was the sponsor's opinion that the quality of the text from Russian into English was not satisfactory, and as a result of this situation the sponsor felt that he should investigate what other machine-translation systems might produce. This author has the feeling that there were, or might have been, other reasons for stopping the financial support of the GU machine-translation project. Unless the archives of the sponsor are opened for studies, one can only guess as to what these additional reasons were.

3 Description and analysis of machine-translation development

3.1 Bar-Hillel's report on automatic translation of language

Yehoshua Bar-Hillel's 1960 report is composed of four sections: 1. *Aims and methods, survey and critique;* 2. *Critical survey and the achievements of the particular machine-translation research group;* 3. *Conclusions;* 4. *Remarks on the bibliography.* In addition, there are references and three appendices: Appendix I, *Machine translation statistics as of April 1, 1959;* Appendix II, *Some linguistic obstacles to machine translation;* and Appendix III, *A demonstration of the non-feasibility for fully automatic high-quality translation.* Bar-Hillel believes that this report, and especially Appendix III, has proven that fully automatic high-quality translation (FAHQT) is not feasible.

Bar-Hillel, an Israeli scholar, bases his report on observations made during a visit to the USA in November 1958. According to Bar-Hillel, machine translation started in 1952 and therefore the time had "come to critically evaluate the progress made during the seven years that have since passed in order to arrive at a better view of these problems and possibilities" (1960: 93). The reader should be fair to Bar-Hillel, and not be influenced by his typically harsh style and harsh judgments. Instead, greater attention should be given to his objective statements and to his descriptive characteristics and evaluation.

In the first section Bar-Hillel starts with a statement concerning machine translation funding: machine-translation has become a multi-million-dollar business.

> "It has been estimated that in the U.S. alone approximately one and a half million dollars were spent in 1958 on research more or less closely connected with MT, with approximately 150 people, among them 80 % with a MA, MS or other higher degrees, working in this field either full or part time. No comparable figures are available for

Russia, but it is generally assumed that the number of people engaged there in research on MT is higher than in the States. At a conference on MT in Moscow in May 1958, 347 people from 79 institutions were reported to have participated" (p. 92).

Bar-Hillel criticizes two short reviews on the state of machine translation which were prepared prior to his report. The first was by H. P. Edmundson, K. E. Harper, and D. G. Hays (Edmundson 1958), and the second by G. W. Reitweisner and M. H. Weik (Reitweisner 1958).

Bar-Hillel considers the first review "well prepared and excellent as far as it goes" but "too short to go into detailed discussion of all existing problems, in addition to this not always critical to a sufficient degree" (p. 93). The second review, according to Bar-Hillel, "seems to have been prepared in a hurry, relies far too heavily on information given by the research workers themselves who, by the nature of things, will often be favorably biased toward their own approaches and tend to overestimate their own actual achievements, and do not even attempt to be critical" (p. 93). Such statements are very characteristic of his style. The reader is justified in assuming that, after taking such critical attitudes toward any reports published by the participants in machine-translation research, Bar-Hillel may also have certain criteria and certain goals of his own which he considers valid for machine translation, and therefore would consider any reports which do not fit into his preconceived logical concepts "somewhat unbalanced".

The other reviews noted by Bar-Hillel, a short report by L. E. Dostert to the 8th Annual Round Table Conference of Linguistics and Language Study of Georgetown University (Dostert 1957), and the historical introduction in the book by A. D. Booth and his associates (Booth 1958) are dealt with separately.

The sources which Bar-Hillel used for describing the situation in the USSR were based either on English translations of Soviet reports produced in the US or on a personal report of A. G. Oettinger which was made readily available to Bar-Hillel after Oettinger returned from a visit to the USSR.

In the second section of the introduction to his article, Bar-Hillel criticizes the attempts at fully automatic high-quality translation (FAHQT) as an unreasonable goal. But he did not sufficiently define 'high quality' for translation in any operational sense. He used several descriptive statements; for example, the quality of the translation produced should be better than that of experienced human translators. However, the 'experienced human translator' is not an operationally defined concept, and is certainly subject to debate. In one part of his article Bar-Hillel makes reference to high-quality translation as a 'standard average translation'. In others he admits that he does not have a perfectly good translation in mind. The concept of 'fully automatic' is not operationally defined either, since the problems he considers, such as pre-editing, post-editing or interfering with the machine-translation operation by using *ad hoc* solutions (which consequently would be hypothetical solutions), are not defined in any operational way. Bar-Hillel's arguments to the effect that some contrived Russian sentences, or even those taken from the real texts, will not lend themselves to a proper translation by machine-translation systems, are basically correct. However, one has to bear in mind that none of the systems in existence and, I imagine, none of the systems in the future, will have algorithms ready to deal with whatever man is capable of creating. On the one hand, Bar-Hillel tries to prove that fully automatic high-quality translation is not feasible, and on the other he admits that a partially mechanized high-quality translation might be attainable in the near future as a machine-aided tool for the translator. This would be a compromise between various extreme goals. He states: "Those who are interested in machine translation as a primarily practical device must realize that full automation of the translation process is incompatible with high quality. There are two possible directions in which a compromise could be struck: one could sacrifice quality or one could reduce the self-sufficiency of the machine output" (p. 95). He also goes so far as to say that "There are very many situations where less than high quality machine output is satisfactory" (p. 95). Unfortunately, he does not explain what these situations are.

Some years later, in 1971, at a special conference organized by W. P. Lehmann at the Linguistics Research Center in Austin, Texas, Bar-Hillel did not defend his formula of FAHQT as strongly as he had previously done. He was willing to recognize the importance of users' evaluations of the output of machine translation. It is my belief that this conference was actually the turning point in returning to a pragmatic approach to machine translation. It was clear by 1971 that the FAHQT researchers had not come up with any operational possibilities for machine translation, and something had to be done for further development.

Let us now consider the third section of that article, referred to as 'Commercial partly mechanized, high quality translation attainable in the near future'. In that section Bar-Hillel makes some very useful prognostic statements about the future of machine translation, and I believe that they are as valid now as they were when he made them almost twenty years ago. "As soon as the aim of machine translation is lowered to that of high quality translation by a machine-post-editor partnership, the decisive problem becomes to determine the region of optimality in the continuum of possible divisions of labor" (p. 95).

Bar-Hillel names four factors essential to further development of machine translation. First, "a reliable and versatile mechanical print reader will have to become available" (p. 96). Second, "a concerted effort will have to be made by a pretty large group in order to prepare the necessary dictionary or dictionaries in the most suitable form" (p. 96). Third, "a good amount of thinking accompanied by an equally large amount of experimenting will have to go into the determination of the location of the interval in the above mentioned continuum within which the optimal point of the division of labor between machine and post-editor will have a good chance of being situated, as a function of the specific translation program and the specific qualities of the envisaged post-editor" (p. 96). Fourth, "an old question which has not been treated so far with sufficient incisiveness, mostly because the ideal of FAHQT diverted the interests of the research workers into other less practical directions, namely the question whether machine-translation dictionaries should contain as their source-language entries all letter sequences that may occur between spaces, sometimes called *inflected forms*, or rather so-called *canonical forms*, or perhaps something in between like *canonical stems*, has to be decided one way or another before mass production of translations is taken up" (p. 97).

In comparison to the present-day situation we can see that the first factor, the 'print reader', or mechanical scanner, has made some progress in the last twenty years but is still not available for machine-translation purposes. The second factor, the need for an adequate dictionary, has already become a reality. We have both the large dictionaries and some automatic algorithmic procedures with which the large dictionaries can be increased to any size. However, it should be acknowledged that semantic coding and programming is still absent from the machine-translation systems, and without semantic coding the quality of the translation cannot be significantly improved. Therefore, pre-editing and post-editing should be taken into consideration, and I agree with Bar-Hillel that it is "profitable to introduce as much elementary pre-editing as the keypunch operator can take into stride without considerable slowing down" (p. 97).

Detailed criticism of Bar-Hillel's specific arguments to prove that FAHQT is not feasible is given in essays published by Cambridge Language Research Unit, Cambridge, England (*Essays on and in machine translation* 1959). The Cambridge group, headed by Margaret Masterman, criticizes Bar-Hillel's tone, characterized by intense negative criticism directed personally at those with whom he disagrees, and also for writing a polemic under the format of an official document. In the second part of the Cambridge contribution, Bar-Hillel is reminded of vagueness in his writing. The well-known phrase "The box was in the pen" is also analyzed and rejected as an argument against the concept of FAHQT.

From an historical perspective we should probably agree with Bar-Hillel's reversal of his original rejection of FAHQT as a viable goal. This reversal was expressed at the Texas machine-translation conference (1971) and is quoted by Fred Hutton in one of the draft papers on machine translation at ORNL in 1975 in connection with making the GAT SLC system operational on the IBM/360 (Jordan 1975: 13).

> "When I started using the term 'high quality' a number of years ago, I was using it in a much too absolute sense which cannot be seriously justified. 'High quality' has to be relativized with regard to users and with regard to situations. A translation which is of good quality for a certain user in a certain situation might be of lesser quality for the same user in a different situation or for a different user, whether in the same or in a different situation. What is satisfactory for one need not be satisfactory for another... Every program for machine translation should be immediately tested as to its effect on the human user. He is the first and final judge, and it is he who will have to tell whether he is ready to trade quality for speed, and to what degree."

Errare humanum est. Yet if an error is propagated with the force and prestige that accompanied Bar-Hillel's pronouncements, and there is no-one to correct the error with equal force and prestige, progress in the given field will be seriously hindered and may even be temporarily halted.

Bar-Hillel's views against FAHQT were used by several researchers to justify and obtain financial support for more basic studies thought necessary for eventual successful machine translation, but which were in fact not relevant to the solution of real machine-translation problems. The end result of this attitude was the ALPAC report analyzed later in this chapter.

3.2 Josselson's views on the historical development of machine translation

Harry Josselson wrote his article on the historical development of machine translation in 1971, eleven years after Bar-Hillel's article was published.

Josselson's training is in the field of Slavic linguistics. Bar-Hillel's was in philosophy and especially in the theory of sets and logic. One significant difference between them should be noted. Josselson is a trained linguist, and a native speaker of the Russian language. Bar-Hillel was acquainted with the basic linguistic principles and linguistic schools of thought, but his knowledge of Russian was rather restricted. This explains some of the stylistic differences between the two authors. Josselson is likely to delve into linguistic details while Bar-Hillel prefers to argue his case on logical grounds, without ever approaching substantial samples from the text, in either the source or the target language.

I shall review Josselson's article in the order in which he arranges his material. His article consists of six parts: 1. introductory remarks, 2. machine translation since 1960: aims and growth, 3. linguistic problems in machine-translation research, 4. survey of machine-translation groups since 1960, 5. the ALPAC report, and 6. conclusion.

Josselson begins with an analysis of a number of Bar-Hillel's pronouncements, including the assertion that fully automatic high-quality translation (FAHQT) is exceedingly difficult, if not impossible to achieve (Josselson 1971: 2). Josselson does not critically analyze the components of Bar-Hillel's statement.

It is typical of Josselson's style to ascribe certain negative characteristics to certain machine-translation workers without identifying them by name. In addition, Josselson makes the reader feel that these negative characteristics are so obvious that there is no need to prove they are among the reasons for machine-translation failure. To cite an example for purposes of illustration: "This fact (the nature of language) escaped many early researchers in machine translation, particularly those who were hardware-oriented and who proceeded from the very naive position that since everybody speaks a language, everybody should, theoretically at least, be able to deal with any processes which involve language" (Josselson 1971: 2).

Josselson reviews the groups in the machine-translation field both prior to and after 1960. The review of work done prior to 1960 is heavily influenced by the view of Bar-Hillel. The author includes the following in the list of naive concepts: "Language was considered just a 'bunch of words' and the primary task for early machine translation (MT) was to build machines large enough to hold all the words necessary in the translation process... Overlooked was also the fact that two given languages may have two completely different structures", and "all the translation problems that were not solved by applying rules derived from grammar were lumped together under the heading of 'semantics'" (p. 3).

Although section 1.2 has the title "The nature of language and problems of language descriptions", the reader cannot find a description of the nature of language. Either the author makes statements which are obvious, or he uses terms without defining them. For example, he says that if the researcher is serious, he must know the rules under which the language operates and how the mechanism of this operation can be simulated by automatic means. Since the language changes constantly, cooperation between man and machine is necessary. Among the practical problems in machine translation, the following three are considered in Bar-Hillel's terms: 1. use of automatic print reader, 2. problems of automatic dictionary storage and retrieval, 3. micro-grammars and micro-glossaries. Josselson supports the use of micro-dictionaries and grammars.

Section 2 is devoted to the aims and growth of machine translation since 1960. The author reviews the machine-translation groups in terms of the shift of emphasis in the philosophical approach and practical application by individual workers and groups. The reader could assume that the groups would be examined on an equal basis. For example, if the GU machine-translation project was recognized as the largest of its kind, one would expect the reviewer to deal with it at a length at least equal to that devoted to other projects. This is not the case. In fact, the GU machine-translation group received half a page while the Josselson group (Wayne State machine-translation group) received several pages which were used constantly as a diagnostic guide for comparison to other machine-translation groups (p. 19). Josselson comments on the first GU machine-translation experiment and its success:

> "This was due to the fact that the first machine translation experiments were carried out on very limited small texts, with bilingual glossaries and grammars specially tailored for these texts, thus in effect creating an ideal, closed linguistic system in contrast to the openness and dynamics of natural language. The computer programs specifically designed for these small texts of course guaranteed the success of these experiments. As a consequence early machine translation researchers arrived at the conclusion that all that was necessary to achieve practical results in machine translation was to increase the size of the dictionary and to expand the grammar" (p. 7).

According to Josselson, the primary tasks for machine-translation groups in the US and elsewhere consisted of: designing bilingual dictionaries with proper morphological, syntactic and semantic coding, syntactic analytic routines, automatic sentence parsing routines, and multiple choice routines.

There were 12 machine-translation groups in the US in 1962. Josselson reports that since these machine-translation groups were supported by several US government agencies (The US Office of Naval Research, CIA, NSF, the US Air Force), there was a need for exchange of information among the research groups to minimize duplication of certain tasks and to attempt to develop machine translation along more efficient and productive lines (p. 8).

In retrospect, it seems to this author that the US Federal Government should have had people monitoring the expenditure of funds, and should have had researchers to cooperate or organize an independent, government-sponsored laboratory for testing the various theories and pragmatic aspects of the experimental systems.

Josselson reports on four conferences held for the exchange of information on machine translation. The first such conference was held in Princeton, N. J., in 1960. The second machine-translation conference convened at GU in 1961 and was devoted primarily to grammar coding.

The third conference was held in Princeton and syntactic problems were its main topic. The fourth conference was held in 1965 and dealt with the computer-related semantic analysis. Josselson writes that "various independent scholars and key representatives of research groups were able to examine together the problems either of linguistic or computational nature that have confronted several researchers" (p. 10). No specific data are given.

In addition to the national American conferences, international conferences on machine translation were organized, apparently to encourage participants to exchange information.

It is interesting to note that perhaps Josselson really believed in an atmosphere of cooperation. My own recollections are different. In both the local and international conferences a small group supervised those sessions, perhaps encouraging an atmosphere of cooperation. However, these conferences did not yield any specific results from which everyone could benefit.

The First International Conference on Machine Translation of Language and Applied Language Analysis was held in September 1961 at the National Physical Laboratory in Teddington, Middlesex, England. Proceedings of the conference were published in two volumes in 1961.

The third and fourth sections describe linguistic problems in machine translation with which many machine-translation groups dealt.

In Josselson's opinion, the descriptive linguistic materials accumulated during the last two centuries were not adequate for machine-translation purposes. He says that "serious-minded linguists", in trying to find out more about how the language operates, started studying modern linguistic theories and models. The author compares this stage to a mathematical model of the dynamics of the path of the rocket trajectory prior to the launching of a satellite. He indicates that the content area of these theories need identification and the scientific areas of linguistic units also need to be studied. The linguistic units include morphemes, words, phrases, and sentences. Josselson gives an example from Russian of the disambiguation of the personal pronouns, "he", "she", "it", etc., which need information for their disambiguation from the preceding sentence. The majority of the working systems were based on the length of a single sentence. While this statement is essentially correct, he does not mention the fact that machine-translation workers were aware of these problems and there was an attempt to find a solution to them

(Zarechnak 1957). The real reason for not including this kind of information in the working system was partly connected with the logical presentation, and partly with the memory size of IBM computers in 1957.
Josselson thinks that contrastive analysis is best suited for good translation results in machine translation. This view should be compared with
the views of other workers who believe that the source and the target
language should be analyzed independently. A set of transfer routines
between the source and target languages or an intermediary language
should be developed only after adequate independent description. In the
intermediary language transfer routines would extend from the source to
the intermediary language (IL) and from the IL to the target language.
The relative advantages and disadvantages of the IL are treated elsewhere in this chapter.

Josselson specifically mentions the lack of one-to-one correspondence
on all levels in languages. This observation is tied together with a more
fundamental statement by Roman Jakobson whom Josselson quotes:
"Most frequently, translation from one language into another substitutes
messages in one language not for separate code units, but for entire messages in some other language" (Jakobson 1959: 15).

Josselson also mentions that nested structures are important in improving the quality of the translation. He defines a nested structure as "any
language that grammatically allows sentence structures containing discontinuous constituents. Nesting has been defined as the interruption of
a main clause by an embedded phrase or clause, followed by the resump-
tion of the main clause" (Josselson 1971: 15). In discussing various levels
of nesting, Josselson quotes Murray Sherry (Sherry 1962: 143–145). For
comparison, refer to my paper on nested PN structures (Zarechnak
1961). Josselson believes that the point of view creates the system, therefore a particular syntactic recognition routine is dependent on a specific
approach to grammars such as "dependency grammar". Josselson
writes: "Dependency theory, which has primarily been employed in the
machine-translation activities of the RAND Corporation and GU, was
elaborated by David Hays, and is in principle based on the assumption
that words in a sentence are mutually dependent in a hierarchical way"
(Josselson 1971: 17). Josselson fails to mention that Hays' dependency
theory is based on the work of the French linguist L. Tesnière.

As far as the use of dependency grammar at GU is concerned, this is a
misrepresentation on Josselson's part. I do not know who among the GU

machine-translation groups used Hays' dependency grammar. Hierarchical interdependence is a traditional concept, and as far as the GAT-SLC is concerned, Harris' concepts of sentence kernels, based on Bloomfieldian concepts, were explicitly recognized as a machine translation operational influence (Harris 1962). Nor do I think that Garvin's machine-translation procedures should be explained in Hays' terms. Josselson mentions that the stratificational grammar theory was used by the Berkeley research group, while transformational theory of the Chomskyan type was used by the Center for Automatic Translation at Grenoble, France, and the University of Montreal, Canada. According to the author, the 'formational' theory applied at the Linguistic Research Center, University of Texas appears to be closely related to the transformational theory. The formational theory is based on the assumption that a mathematical theory of the formation of symbol strings is possible. Therefore, the creation of a metalanguage for processing the object language is mandatory. Among the additional grammatical approaches to syntactic analysis Josselson lists those he considers better known, namely, predictive analysis, immediate constituent analysis, the fulcrum approach, clump theory (the machine-translation group at the Cambridge Language Research Unit in England), and the correlational grammar (Ceccato, Italy).

Josselson describes components of a machine-translation system using his own system as a guide, stating that these "procedures with a few variations, were in general use by other machine translation groups as well" (1971: 19). Among the components of a machine-translation system, he mentions the following: dictionary compilations, syntactic analysis, target-language synthesis, treatment of idioms and lexical entries (both full and split entries), grammar codes, and parts of speech. As the author goes into more technical details of coding, it is clear that the special approach to syntax has less and less importance, and the data known to exist in the language take precedence over the approach. Apparently, the author himself realized this fact since he states: "Here one must distinguish carefully between the linguistic theories which are used by various machine translation groups, either in expressed form or implied in their statements, and the approaches and procedures used by them in the course of analysis and subsequent computer processing" (Josselson 1971: 21). Why? The answer is rather obvious. Given, say, a Russian expression *Srednjaja Azija* 'Middle/Central Asia', whatever one's theory, one has to produce in the target English language 'Central Asia'. In operational terms it means that the context criteria are to be used, and concatenation has to be made independently of any specific theoretical frame. The same is true in searching for the kernel type occurring in the Russian language. The algorithms have to be geared to the Russian structure signals, whatever the theoretical approach.

It is necessary to introduce modifications of the traditional descriptions, since they were written for humans and not for machine-translation purposes, which makes some of the definitions inadequate. Nevertheless, the basic categories known from the traditional description of the particular language have to be used in any machine-translation system, with the necessary modifications for automatic treatment.

Josselson informs the reader that the predictive analysis developed by the National Bureau of Standards (Ida Rhodes) was later developed further and modified by the Harvard machine-translation group (A. Oettinger and Murray Sherry). I believe that any degree of sophistication in predictive analysis for sentence parsing of natural language is bound to fail for the simple reason that the underlying concept in predictive analysis, that of pushdown store, carries the seeds of its own destruction. The reader may verify the background necessary to understand the deficiencies of the pushdown store by reading pertinent literature (Hall 1972: 282). According to Josselson, Ida Rhodes developed a set of predictions describing the Russian syntax. Each prediction has an urgency number. Predictive analysis takes the previous profiling of the sentence in which the clause and phrase boundaries are already determined as its input. At Harvard University, Murray Sherry was working with the single-path system only. Later W. Plath introduced the multipath system, thus increasing the power of predictive analysis for solving some ambiguities.

Josselson expresses the hope that "contributions in the area of semantics, which has barely begun to be investigated, including Bunker-Ramo, RAND Corporation group and others, are sure to come in the future" (p. 26).

The increase in machine-translation group activity can be seen from the figures given by Josselson: in 1956–1960 there were three groups in the US, one in Great Britain and three in the USSR, and some activity in Milan, Italy, and at Hebrew University in Jerusalem (Bar-Hillel, after leaving MIT). In 1966 there were 70 groups working in fifteen countries:

the US, USSR, Great Britain, France, Germany, Japan, Belgium, Canada, Mexico, Czechoslovakia, Yugoslavia, Rumania, Hungary, Poland, and Italy.

The fifth section of Josselson's article deals with the ALPAC (Automatic Language Processing Advisory Committee) report, published in 1966 by the National Academy of Sciences. Josselson's analysis of the ALPAC report is essentially correct. The ALPAC report recommends (ALPAC: 34) that the NSF should give financial support to research in 1. computational linguistics, and 2. improvement of translation. The committee sees, however, little justification at present for massive support of machine translation *per se*, since it finds the machine-translation results slower, less accurate, and more costly than those provided by the human translator. Josselson specifically quotes the following part from the ALPAC report, "... without recourse to human translation or editing... there has been no machine translation of general scientific text, and none is in immediate prospect" (1971: 46).

The reaction to the ALPAC report from various countries was very negative. Josselson reports on the reaction from West Germany (F. Krollmann) and the USSR. The Soviet linguists published the whole document in Russian and the conclusions of the committee. According to the Soviet analysis, the "committee displayed... a certain narrowness and pragmatic single-mindedness which is characteristic of the report", and these conclusions were not applicable in their own country (p. 47).

In the US the most detailed critical analysis was prepared by Zbigniew L. Pankowicz of the Griffiss Air Force Base, Rome, New York (Pankowicz 1967). Unfortunately, it took ten years for those responsible for language data processing within the US to realize that the ALPAC tactics were detrimental to both theoretical development and operational experiments.

In his conclusions, Josselson stresses the opinion that the continuation of machine translation is justified as an application of symbiosis between man and machine. He suggests that the user of the machine-translation product should get used to reading "MTese". Machine translation might be most effective in a small sub-area of language (scientific and technical). Josselson is aware that his bibliography is not complete. In particular, he thinks that despite the FAHQT objections, machine translation should continue along the lines of the work being done by EURATOM (European Atomic Energy Community), in Ispra, Italy, where it is being carried out under the direction of S. Perschke. The system adopted in Ispra is modeled ofter GAT/SLC used in Oak Ridge National Laboratory, Oak Ridge, Tennessee. MT systems are also used at the Foreign Technology Division, US Air Force, Dayton, Ohio, the National Physical Laboratory, Teddington, England, the Central Research Institute for Patent Information, Moscow, USSR, and some other centers.

The present author finds himself in agreement with Josselson concerning the wide range of symbiosis between man and machine, including the area of pre-editing and post-editing, some problems connected with the scanning reader, at the level of its applicability to machine translation, and also in the area of coding of words not found in the dictionary.

I agree whole heartedly with Josselson's concluding statement: "Since computers will not go away and are, quite obviously, here to stay, it makes no sense to renounce their application in such an important area of human behavior as language output. You don't throw away an important tool; you use it" (Josselson 1971: 51).

3.3 Government support of machine translation and its advisory committee (ALPAC)

In the United States it is customary that the government agencies form advisory committees around the activities they support, which can provide technical assistance and independent observations.

In April 1964 an Automatic Language Processing Advisory Committee (ALPAC) was formed at the request of the Director of the National Science Foundation (NSF) in order to advise the Department of Defence (DOD), the Central Intelligence Agency (CIA) and NSF on research and development in the field of machine translation. The Committee itself was formed by Dr. Frederick Seitz, President of the National Academy of Sciences (NAS), to evaluate the promise of machine translation and the fruitful steps that could be taken in machine-translation development. The members of the Committee included John R. Pierce, Bell Telephone Laboratories, Chairman; John B. Carroll, Harvard University; Eric P. Hamp, University of Chicago; David G. Hays, The Rand Corporation; Charles F. Hockett, Cornell University; Anthony Oettinger, Harvard University, and Alan Perlis, Carnegie Institute of Technology. Charles F. Hockett resigned from the ALPAC before the report of the Committee was written.

Among the members of the ALPAC there were only two people, Oettinger and Hays, who could not possibly be independent observers since they were actively involved in machine-translation research, although neither of them produced a working machine-translation system. The other members were unbiased in this respect, and could be considered as independent observers of machine-translation research and development.

The ALPAC, under the general guidance of J. Pierce and funded by the three agencies – DOD, CIA, and NSF – started its independent observations in April 1964.

What procedures were accepted for gathering the data and evaluating the findings? In his August 20, 1965, report to the President of NAS, J. Pierce states that the members have acquainted themselves "concerning the needs for translation, considered the evaluation of translations, and compared the capabilities of machines and human beings in translation and in other language processing functions".

The ALPAC invited 17 experts from various fields connected in most cases with human translation activities or machine-translation research. Among the latter group one sees the following names: Paul L. Garvin, Bunker-Ramo Corporation; Gilbert King, the ITEK Corporation; J. C. Licklider and David Lieberman, the IBM Corporation, and Winfred P. Lehmann, the University of Texas. (See the details in Appendix 20 of the ALPAC Report.)

The ALPAC report was published under Publication number 1416 by NAS, National Research Council (NRC) in Washington, D.C., 1966. It has a black cover, but this is not the real reason why this report is better known as the 'Black Book' on machine translation; it put practical machine translation in disfavor. It contains 124 pages and eight pages of transmittal letters.

Now, in 1977, we can read this report with a certain detachment, and compare and verify some facts and statements within the report or made later by its members. But we can only verify some facts and statements. The point is that there is no comprehensive information on the project itself, such as its cost, while the GU Machine Translation General Report contains all such information. We will have to wait for some time to obtain that information.

Kljuchevsky, a famous Russian historian, assumes that the historical activity and the participants engaged in it should be judged by the results in relation to the goals stated prior to the activity itself, and by what, if any, good or harm was done by these activities and their participants for the other members of the same professional field or the population in general whose money was spent on this activity of independent observation. It is also assumed by historians that the facts have to be verified prior to their evaluation. This was not done by ALPAC.

Let us list the chapters of the ALPAC report to see just what questions were discussed and what conclusions were reached. CONTENTS lists them as follows: Human translation 1; Types of translator employment 2; English as the language of science 4; Time required for scientists to learn Russian 5; Translation in the USA government 6; Number of government translators 7; Amount spent for translation 9; Is there a shortage of translators or translation? 11; Regarding a possible excess of translation 13; The crucial problems of translation 16; The present state of machine translation 19; Machine-aided translation at Mannheim and Luxembourg 25; Automatic language processing and computational linguistics 29; Avenues to improvement of translation 32; Recommendations 34. These topical questions are followed by 20 appendices (pp. 35–124). J. Pierce states in his report to Dr. Seitz, "We found that what we heard led us all to the same conclusions, and the report which we are submitting herewith states our common views and recommendations." The ALPAC in its recommendations suggested changes in the support of purely theoretical linguistic research so that the research has value in itself, and support for improved human translation, with an appropriate use of computers.

The reader should note that all of the Committee members came to the same conclusions. However, ten years later at a seminar on machine translation at Rosslyn, Virginia, D. Hays indicated that he was the dissenting voice in that ALPAC group.

While studying the report, the reader finds many qestions unanswered, such as: Who prepared the text of the report? We know only that A. Hood Roberts was the Executive Secretary and Mrs. S. Ferony the Secretary. Were they responsible for the preparation of the report? Did the three sponsoring agencies (DOD, NSF and CIA, later organized in the Joint Automatic Processing Group – JALPG) solicit opinions of the experts within their agencies? We shall touch on these questions as we progress in our analysis of this little black-cover book which has stopped machine-translation research and development for more than a decade.

What does JALPG stand for? The three agencies, after supporting projects in the automatic processing of foreign languages for about a decade, have decided to coordinate the federal efforts in this field and organized the Joint Automatic Language Processing Group – hence, JALPG.

The reader would expect such a committee to consider the circumstances under which machine translation started, and from there, to further analyze the specific conditions under which the three agencies started supporting machine-translation research and development. We have enough data to answer the above two questions. First, the computers arrived at the scene, and their processing of natural language could be tested. Second, the US Government supports research activity in new fields usually in the hope that, after pumping enough seed money into it, the research activity will become development research, and then a privately directed and profit-oriented activity. With regard to machine-translation history, all of these things almost happened but didn't, due to the following obstacle.

ALPAC did not consider the historical background of machine translation at all. It states in the Preface:

> "The Committee determined that support for research in automatic language processing could be justified on one of two bases: (1) research in an intellectually challenging field that is broadly relevant to the mission of the supporting agency, and (2) research and development with a clear promise of effecting early cost reductions, or substantially improving performance, or meeting an operational need."

The Committee decided that machine-translation research was justified only on the basis of the second premise above, and "in the light of that objective, the Committee studied the whole translation problem". We shall see some of their thinking and procedures on that whole problem later. Suffice it to note that while it is unnecessary for theoretical research to have application (it may be arbitrary in that respect as long as it contains internal logical integrity), practical research, even if unsuccessful, carries in it theoretical implications of a positive or negative nature, and cannot be thought of as relevant to premise (2) only. There is no mention in the whole report of the theoretical foundations supporting the GU machine-translation research project or any other project. There is no explanation given for devoting a single page to 'human translation' in the report. Experts in translation told one member of the committee only that "These experts seem to agree that the three requisites in a translator, in order of importance, are (1) good knowledge of the target language, (2) comprehension of the subject matter, and (3) adequate knowledge of the source language." (p. 1).

If the ALPAC members had invited E. Nida, a leading expert on translation in the USA, they would have learned significantly more from him than from the experts who enumerated the above three requisites. Among other things, they would have learned that the term 'target language' is not theoretically justified, since one does not 'hit' the target language with the message. The message is translated and received by people. Therefore, while there is a source language, its opposite number is a 'receptor' language. Nida's views on the theory and practice of translation are known all over the world, and he has followers in many countries, including the USSR. Why? His theories make sense. Yet he or people like him were not heard at the conference discussion organized by the ALPAC members on June 2–3, 1964, September 30–October 1, 1964, December 9–10, 1964, and March 17–18, 1965.

The words 'adequate' and 'restricted' referring to competence in the foreign language are considered synonyms. Why? Because restricted competence is adequate when the translator is an expert in the subject matter. If this were so, then one would like to assume that the expert in the field, reading the MT-ese, would find it adequate too, since he knows the subject matter and could skip over rough syntactic structures.

"The final copy… is usually produced by the central office" (p. 1). Why? Because the translators "do not always produce a final copy suitable for reproduction". The reader should note that the word "post-editing" is not used. This word will be used only if the machine-translation copy has been edited for final copy.

Some inconsistencies should be noted in the Committee's findings: on the one hand, the English language is considered on statistical grounds to be the predominant language of science, and on the other hand, American scientists and engineers try to acquire an adequate reading knowledge of Russian for material in their fields. It is reported that as of October 1962 there were 262 translators and clerk-translators employed in the USA, and 453 worldwide. Their median annual salary was $ 6,850. The supply of translators exceeded the demand of Government agencies, which paid between $ 9 and $ 66 per 1,000 words. The amount spent by several agencies during the years 1963–1965 was $ 13.07 million. If commercial translation is added, the total amount will equal approximately $ 22 million.

It is a small wonder that the Committee is not concerned with any lack of translation but "it does have some concern about a possible excess of translation" (p. 13).

According to the Committee "the total technical literature does not merit translation, and it is futile to try to guess what someone may at some time want translated. The emphasis should be on speed, quality, and economy in supplying such translations as are requested" (p. 15).

The report stresses the fact that the "quality of translation must be adequate to the needs of the requester" (p. 16) and its findings attest to the fact that the government has no reliable way of measuring the quality of translation. As a result, the correlation between cost and quality is far from precise.

Under the heading 'The present state of machine translation' it is stated that "'Machine Translation' presumably means going by algorithm from machine-readable source text to useful target text, without recourse to human translation or editing. In this context, there has been no machine translation of general scientific text, and none is in immediate prospect" (p. 19).

The reader might ask: why 'presumably'? What is 'useful'? One would expect members of the ALPAC to cite the definitions of various machine-translation systems directly. This was not done. 'Useful' is apparently synonymous with 'adequate to the needs of the users'. In Part III of the present book we report findings of the users. They are not in agreement with the ALPAC report. 'In this context' is an attempt to ascribe negative features to the opponent, and then deride him for their presence. One could say that 'none is in immediate prospect' only under the following conditions: (1) either one knows that without further support this is impossible, and the goal of the report is to recommend no further machine-translation support, or (2) an attempt at rationalization, an excuse for covering up one's own inability to foresee possible machine-translation improvement as an 'independent' finding. In principle, further machine-translation improvement is not possible until linguistic research detaches itself from the short-term machine-translation goals, and directs its attention to the basic language studies which have value in themselves, whether or not they may be applicable for testing.

It is this author's opinion that both (1) and (2) reasons were at work, judging by the text of the ALPAC recommendations stated on p. 34. The committee recommended expenditures in two distinct areas. "The first is computational linguistics as part of linguistics – studies of parsing, sentence generation, structure, semantics, statistics, and quantitative linguistic matters, including *experiments* in translation, with machine aids or without. Linguistics should be supported as science, and should not be judged by any immediate or foreseeable contribution to practical translation. It is important that proposals be evaluated by people who are competent to judge modern linguistic work, and who evaluate proposals on the basis of their scientific worth" (p. 34).

This kind of recommendation leads to support of fragmentary studies with little respect for the massiveness of the language data. This kind of study leads to publication of 400-page papers discussing a negligible number of examples. If no translation is required, and the money for translation is limited, then why not call non-translation research "translation research" in the event that the sponsoring agency would like to see items in the proposals which broadly relate to the service of the particular agency?

Who are the people competent to judge modern linguistic work? Obviously, only those who support pure linguistic research. It should not come as any surprise that the people in a position to distribute money might also be the same committee members favorably disposed toward the views of the ALPAC report.

The second area of support is aimed at improvement of human translation in nine areas:
1. practical methods for evaluation of translations;
2. means for speeding up the human translation process;
3. evaluation of quality and cost of various sources of translations;
4. investigation of the utilization of translations, to guard against production of translations that are never read;
5. study of delays in the overall translation process, and means for eliminating them, both in journals and in individual items;

6. evaluation of the relative speed and cost of various sorts of machine-aided translation;
7. adaptation of existing mechanized editing and production processes in translation;
8. the overall translation process, and
9. production of adequate reference works for the translator, including the adaptation of glossaries that now exist primarily for automatic dictionary lookup in machine translation.

The reader may note that none of the above areas mention direct machine-translation support, and all of them to varying degrees are just statistical observations of someone's work. In that sense the proposed research in the second area mentioned is essentially parasitic in its nature. Certainly, no aid is expected from this second area for machine-translation support.

When the report was ready for publication, the higher echelon in the NAS became concerned that these recommendations might stop any support for pure linguistics as well. In order to prevent this from happening, Harvey Brooks, Chairman of the Committee on Science and Public Policy, found it useful to insert his letter to the President of the NAS at the recommendation of John Pierce into the report "of the support needs for computational linguistics, as distinct from automatic language translation. This request was prompted by the fear that the committee report, read in isolation, might result in termination of research support for computational linguistics as well as in the recommended reduction of support aimed at relatively short-term goals in translation" (July 27, 1966).

The committee suggested spending approximately $ 3 million a year at four or five research centers. "The figure is not intended to include support of work aimed at immediate practical applications of one sort or another" (from Brooks' letter to Dr. Seitz on July 27, 1966).

As if the above statements were not clear enough, Brooks stresses support for the basic developmental research in computer methods for handling languages "as tools to help the linguistic scientist discover and state his generalizations, and as tools to help check proposed generalizations against data..."

This statement is not convincing for the simple reason that while computers may be useful in controlling the volume of data, they are less efficient in controlling "the data complexity". The latter should be discovered by the linguist first, and only then tested against random data.

If one wants to check theories, one has to formulate them in logical terms, and then again check them for various purposes, such as their exhaustiveness, non-contradictory nature, and simplicity. The computer itself will not provide that effort. Here, as in any other science, the engineering, experimental studies will go ahead of the theory, the theory will be adjusted and may suggest new experiments, depending upon the stated goal of the research. In this fashion an active two-way traffic may develop between theory and experiment. There is no logical reason to support theory only, without experiments, if we want the science to be taken seriously, as we certainly do in the case of machine translation.

All things being equal, one could only hope that after ten years of ALPAC's repressive influence in regard to practical machine-translation research, the government agencies will find enough practical reasons to venture into a new phase of exploring just how the existing computers can help in translating the ever-increasing amount of foreign literature relevant to the overall cultural development in the USA.

The members of ALPAC apparently decided that the reader would not see for himself what the committee tried to conceal in its report. To give an example, the GU machine-translation system is mentioned several times but only in negative terms. The first mention is on p. 19 where the evidence is sought for the statement that "The contention that there has been no machine translation of general scientific text is supported by the fact that when, after 8 years of work, the Georgetown University machine-translation project tried to produce useful output in 1962, they had to resort to post-editing. The post-edited translation took slightly longer to do and was more expensive than conventional human translation". No evidence is brought to support this statement. It is indeed true that a translator who is opposed to the machine-translation output will try to prove that translation from the original text is easier than from a machine-translation output. However, if the translator were trained in the machine-translation system which generated a particular text in English, he might have noticed the patterns of errors, and the reasons behind them. Then his translation would become only post-editing, and fast at that.

The ALPAC report tried to convey the impression that the reader is given an opportunity to read the machine-translation output of four typical but different machine-translation systems: 1. Bunker/Ramo, 2. Computer Concepts, 3. FTD, USAF, and 4. Euratom, Ispra, Italy, with the statement in parentheses "(Essentially the Georgetown machine-translation system)". This parenthetical statement should also have been inserted for Computer Concepts.

Having displayed a sample from Euratom, the authors of ALPAC found it informative to comment as follows:

> "The reader will find it instructive to compare the samples above with the results obtained on simple, or selected, text 10 years earlier (the Georgetown-IBM Experiment, January 7, 1954) in that the earlier samples are more readable than the later ones" (p. 23).

As I have explained in the chapter devoted to the first experiment on machine translation, the 1954 sample was a carefully prepared set of sentences. When ten years later a text of one hundred thousand words was translated on a computer without being previously examined, one would expect a certain number of errors on all levels of operations, and the need for post-editing. The small text in 1954 had no such random data to translate. In his letter of July 27, 1966, Brooks states "... small scale experiments and work with minature models of language have proved seriously deceptive in the past, and one can come to grips with real problems only above a certain scale of grammar size, dictionary size, and available corpus". Evidently the memory of the compiler of the ALPAC report was not very long. Contradictory statements are not infrequent in the report.

Do the authors of the ALPAC report at least once, perhaps by omission, say something positive about machine translation? Yes, they do. "However, work toward machine translation has produced much valuable linguistic knowledge and insight that we would not have otherwise attained" (p. 24).

What is this insight? There is no answer. Of course one could venture to suggest that the development of the artificial intelligence started from machine-translation roots in two varieties: 'hard workers' and 'hard thinkers'. During the last decade they were expected to produce some insights which could be helpful to machine translation. The hopes were not justified. Government support for some of these groups is fading out. In 1966 the report emphatically states "The Committee indeed believes that it is wise to press forward undaunted, in the name of science, but that the motive for doing so cannot sensibly be any foreseeable improvement in practical translation. Perhaps our attitude might be different if there were some pressing need for machine translation, but we find none" (p. 24).

In our review of Josselson's article, we have mentioned the fact that the reaction in Europe was negative toward the ALPAC report. Despite this fact, their report had negative influence upon the views of other linguists and their sponsors, including the USSR. It took ten years for the USSR to reconsider its attitude toward practical machine-translation research. In 1966 an All-Union Center for Translation was formed, within which a machine translation section was organized. I report on this development in the chapter describing the situation in the USSR under the title "Latest developments in the USSR".

The US Government saw a new need to reconsider its attitude towards practical machine-translation research also. Under the sponsorship of FBIS (Foreign Broadcast Information Service) it called a closed conference in February 1976. We analyze that conference in the chapter entitled "The Rosslyn Machine Translation Seminar".

At this time one cannot do justice to the ALPAC for a variety of reasons. No information was released on its cost. No information was provided as to what the three agencies thought of their machine-translation policies. One should await further disclosure of government papers on the background against which the ALPAC report was written, return to its evaluation, and try to provide a more balanced description and evaluation of the small group of people. This small group of people, much to its own surprise, was able to cut off the financial and moral support for many who wanted to continue collecting the real data from natural language and who wanted to improve the step-by-step existing procedures for higher quality machine-translation output.

3.4 Machine translation in Western Europe

A good overview of machine translation in western Europe was published by W. P. Lehmann and R. A. Stachowitz (1972). According to the authors, machine-translation activity in western Europe started after the first experiments in the US, the USSR and Great Britain. There was close cooperation between some of the projects and the work conducted in the

US. The greatest part of the European groups were, however, independent in their research, both in linguistic theory and research procedures. The machine-translation groups at Cambridge, Bonn and Milan included the semantic component in their research plan. The majority of the machine-translation groups were developing algorithms suitable only for a pair of languages. However, the Grenoble group in France, under the guidance of B. Vauquois, was an exception in that they attempted to design a general analyzer that could be used for any language.

HQFA (high-quality fully automatic) translation is thought to be unattainable in the near future unless the quality is sacrificed. Some groups would like to produce a usable machine translation in the near future. Others, including F. Krollmann, Director of the Mannheim Machine-Aided Translation Effort, are satisfied with aiming at compilation of multilingual dictionaries for use in computer-aided translation.

When the ALPAC report reached western Europe, it had adverse effects. According to the authors' findings, work in machine translation was sharply reduced. Some groups discontinued their work because of lack of financial support. The report recommended support of computational linguistics as a part of linguistics; for example, studies of parsing, sentence generation, structure, semantics, statistics and quantitative linguistic matters, including experiments in translation, with or without machine aids. The report stressed that "linguistics should be supported as a science, and should not be judged by any immediate or foreseeable contribution to practical translation. It is important that proposals be evaluated by people who are competent to judge modern linguistic work and who evaluate proposals on the basis of their scientific worth" (ALPAC 1966: 34).

It is not too difficult to see that if some linguists in western Europe took the recommendations seriously, they would drop any practical activity in translation, and turn their attention to the nonpractical goals. Quite a few of them thought that they had to show an interest in modern linguistics. This meant Chomsky. Yet Chomsky was not interested in machine translation. The fear of being connected with practical machine translation went so far that the organizers of papers for the International Congress on Computational Linguistics, in Sweden in 1969, warned their prospective participants not to show concern for problems of mechanical translation, unless treated by linguistic methods (Lehmann 1972: 689).

While in the US one could easily classify the machine-translation groups into purely theoretical ('blue-skies') and practical ('grey-skies'), the machine-translation groups in western Europe were very difficult to classify in those black and white terms. Therefore, the authors stress the fact that both the theoretically-oriented groups such as the LIMAS goup in Bonn, and the practically-oriented ones such as the Grenoble group *(Centre d'Etudes de la Traduction Automatique:* CETA) in France remained active.

Lehmann and Stachowitz divided the western Europe groups as follows: machine-translation groups using semantic or syntactic information, machine-aided translation, and pilot studies. We would like to focus on some of the points of view characteristic of the authors of this survey.

In describing the details of the Grenoble group, the authors credit L. Tesnière with providing the source for the dependency trees in their own machine-translation work. According to the authors, L. Tesnière "has written the most comprehensive dependency grammar, in which an excellent introduction to the theory can be found". In the US, dependency grammar is often mentioned in connection with D. Hays. Among the language-dependent algorithms, Lehmann and Stachowitz give "a short description of the most sophisticated of them, SLC (Simulated Linguistic Computer), developed by A. Brown, who began his work with the Georgetown Automatic Translation Group and then transferred his activities to Ispra" (Lehmann 1972: 694).

It is in Ispra that the Joint Nuclear Research Center Scientific Data Processing Center (CETIS) "has been using the most sophisticated of language-dependent algorithms" (p. 693).

The authors state that "for some time SLC has been used in Ispra. Recently it was acquired by the Atomic Energy Commission at Oak Ridge, Tennessee, and is used for in-house translations" (p. 695). In a report prepared by the same authors covering the Machine Translation Conference in Texas in 1971, widely divergent views and estimates on the completeness of machine translation and the need for user's evaluations were expressed by Bar-Hillel and Zarechnak. It is stated: "By contrast, the system used for machine translation of Russian at Oak Ridge is essentially the GAT system developed at Georgetown University some years

ago. The lexicon and syntactic rules are updated by Zarechnak constantly. But the basic system, based on a surface structure analysis, has been
maintained" (Lehmann 1971: 40).

The groups in western Europe engaged in machine-aided translation
and the pilot studies are described in the next chapter. Lehmann and
Stachowitz arrived at the following conclusion (Lehmann 1972: 696):

> "The groups which have maintained themselves in Western Europe
> will probably continue their work. Their existence is not influenced
> by overly optimistic expectations nor by overly pessimistic conclu-
> sions with respect to their results. These groups are gradually in-
> creasing the scope of data to be processed so as to include more and
> more semantic and even factual information in their analysis proce-
> dures. These groups are gradually improving their control of MT
> and the quality of their output."

3.5 Klein's criticism of practical machine-translation research

W. Klein's book *Parsing* (1971) represents a slightly revised version of
his dissertation.

In the Preface to the book, the author explains that in the time period
between the writing of his dissertation and the publication of his book, he
has read more publications in the field and concluded: "Computational
linguistics has made no significant progress". However, he admits that
the criticism expressed in the book had undergone modification. It is evi-
dent that were he to write the book now he would write it differently.

In the introduction to the book the author states: "The history of
machine translation is a history of negative conclusions. The various
stages of its development were determined not by profound disclosures
about the subject but rather by the recognition that the methods used so
far have not brought us closer to the goal. It is a history of a surrender before the complexities of the task, the degree of which became apparent
only through the failures of practice" (p. 7). In his desire to criticize the
efforts of the people engaged in machine translation, he indicates that
"the goal of these people was not to produce an adequate linguistic
method, but rather to code the content in whatever way, as long as it was

a mechanized way" (p. 7). Experience has shown that linguistic adequacy and practical usefulness cannot be separated.

Klein states two requirements that are essential for machine translation: 1. The linguistic theory should be adequate in terms of clarity of explanation. 2. It must lend itself to a mechanized process, i. e., transform action into a computer program. As in human translation, the author recognizes three tasks in machine translation: 1. to recognize the content of the source language, 2. to transfer the information, and 3. to synthesize it into the target language.

The book deals with the first two tasks – the "automatic syntactic analysis", i. e., the automatic recognition of the structure of a given sentence. The author intends to show how a given method, the so-called "Parser", should be applied in order to fulfill both conditions, i. e., adequacy and computability.

On the basis of a primitive language model he tries to prove that translation is impossible: it can be computerized, but is not adequate. His discussion of this sample leads him to consider three types of models: 1. the word-form model which is the prerequisite for the computerization of all the others, 2. Tesnière's dependency model, 3. Chomsky's tranformation model.

Klein agrees that a sentence cannot be considered a completely independent unit to be translated without taking into consideration the content of the preceding or following sentence. An algorithm translating a sentence as an independent unit would be completely unrealistic.

The aim of the book is to prove that mechanical translation is impossible, no matter where, how, and by whom it is done. In his chapter on the word-form model, the author tries to show the inadequacy of the word-for-word translation of the early days of machine translation and considers three researchers to be protagonists of this method: E. Reifler, A. Oettinger and L. Dostert. He admits that Oettinger and Dostert soon switched to other methods, but he uses the ALPAC Report for denouncing the quality of the Georgetown-IBM translation not only in early 1954, but also in 1965.

According to Klein, the reason for the failure of the word-for-word translation is "morphological, syntactic, semantic ambiguity". Without resolving these ambiguities, it is impossible to even formulate the problems of machine translation.

In the second chapter, on the syntactic theory of Tesnière, and the third chapter, on transformation grammars (see p. 110 footnote), the author concludes "a machine syntactic analysis in this form is not possible". As a reason for this he mentions the multiple meaning of the lexical rules and grammar. It seems that Klein did not take time to study the GU machine-translation system in detail, and his negative conclusions about the GU machine-translation system are based essentially on hearsay or the principal belief that practical machine translation is impossible because he, Klein, does not know how it could be made operational. One would expect that in a doctoral thesis the reader would find some contribution to the field under investigation. Unfortunately, this is not the case with Klein's dissertation. It is very characteristic of his argumentation to ascribe some faulty assumptions to the opponent, and then without too much trouble to demonstrate that these assumptions were illogical. He makes several such assumptions in characterizing Tesnière's parsing system. The details can be found in his chapter on Tesnière.

I have mentioned Klein's contribution for the sole reason that I wished to include a voice from the theoretical camp which is *a priori* antagonistic toward theoretical justification of practical work in the machine-translation field.

3.6 Machine translation in Bulgaria

A. Ljudskanov (1963), in his survey *Njakoj beležki otnosno obščite principi za sŭstavjane na rečnik za rusko-bŭlgarski mašinen prevod* [Certain considerations on general principles relating to construction of a Russian-Bulgarian dictionary for machine translation], reviews the goals and scope of machine translation, binary and multiple machine translation, types of analysis and synthesis of machine translation, the problem of translation equivalents, and the intermediate language (IL).

Problems of compiling a machine-translation dictionary are specially emphasized such as its importance, the list of glossary items, the structure of the dictionary, the information attached to the dictionary entry, polysemy, homonymy, etc.

Statistical information is based on preliminary research done on a Russian mathematical text: in the text consisting altogether of a length of 20,000 running words, there were 1,278 unique word forms; 87 instances of homonyms; a total of 14 cases of polysemy (one Russian word has more than one Bulgarian equivalent); and, in 200 sentences, the subject precedes the predicate in 79 % of the examples, the object follows the predicate in 90 % of them, and the adjective precedes the noun within 89 %.

In connection with the significant similarities between Bulgarian and Russian, it is suggested that those types of words which have only 1 : 1 correspondences and which do not influence the parsing of the Russian sentence be set aside (i.e. the uninflected parts of speech or inserted structures). Prior to the parsing, the sentence is "freed" from words whose equivalents can be introduced into the Bulgarian output later on. The use of the 'index of the correspondence type' is suggested; simpler algorithms should be used, given absolute and direct correspondences, instead of the relative and indirect correspondences. The terms are not defined.

In "The first machine translation experiment in Bulgaria", Ljudskanov (1966) describes the goals, the theoretical foundation and the results of machine translation from Russian to Bulgarian. The experiment was carried out in 1965 by the group called "Machine translation and mathematical linguistics" in the Mathematical Institute of the Academy of Sciences of Bulgaria.

The assumption of the isomorphism of separate linguistic levels serves as the basic concept in constructing the algorithms for the lexical, morphological, syntactic and semantic analysis. This permits the use of a standard form of analysis for all the levels. Some parts of the algorithms, such as segmentation of the input text into sentences and proper names, are worked out as universal algorithms. The other parts, sufficiently described in the literature, are of an ad-hoc type; for example, 'polysemy'.

For illustration purposes, a sample of the produced translation and the schemes of the algorithm are displayed at the end of the book.

4 Machine translation in the Soviet Union

4.1 Kenneth E. Harper's article on machine translation in the USSR

Kenneth E. Harper introduces his article on machine translation (Harper 1963: 133) with a remark that machine translation has been an active area of research in the Soviet Union during the past decade. He divides this research into two periods. During the first period, the Soviet linguists worked to develop a binary machine-translation algorithm for approximately 20 language pairs, with the main emphasis on English-Russian, French-Russian, and Hungarian-Russian translation algorithms. The information programmed was derived essentially from existing traditional grammars. Ambiguities encountered in studying small samples of texts were solved by *ad hoc* rules. The drawbacks of these studies were caused by an overestimation of computer power and of the state of linguistic knowledge.

Harper considers the year 1959 as the dividing line between the first and the second period. The second period was characterized by increased attention to the linguistic research prior to programming efforts. V. V. Ivanov (1961) used the saying "one cannot see the forest for the trees" to emphasize the need for relating the particular to the more general linguistic principles. Ivanov also emphasized the need for machine-aided linguistic study as a prior input to a general linguistic system.

In the Soviet Union scientists are always trying to fuse theory and practice. For this purpose, in 1960, a Section of Structural and Applied Linguistics was established in the Institute of Linguistics of the Academy of Sciences of the USSR.

The aim of this Institute is described by A. A. Reformackij (1961). Harper quotes the central statement of Reformackij's work: "The structural aspect presupposes the examination of a language as a whole and each level of its structure as an interconnected system of levels of significance given in a hierarchical gradation of symbols and their combination, organized in contrast with each other, paradigmatically connected, and linearly distributed in speech" (Harper 1963: 134).

Harper suggests that the Soviet linguists did not have sufficient access to computers in order to test their binary algorithms, and perhaps for this reason some Soviet linguists switched their attention to more theoretical aspects of linguistic studies. According to Harper's observation, the Soviet linguists became interested in concepts from mathematical and symbolic logic and in intermediary language. As of 1963, "although the computer has not yet been a partner in linguistic research, it has been the stimulus for critical re-examination of linguistic theory" (p. 134).

In the summary, Harper finds that the Soviet linguists are more responsive to the cross-fertilization of mathematical and computational ideas coming from other countries than are their co-workers in the West.

Most of the references listed are found in the National Bureau of Standards bibliography (Walkowicz 1963). The titles of sources used by Harper are given as translated by JPRS (Joint Publications Research Service).

4.2 The theoretical approach toward machine translation in the USSR

Historical perspectives of machine-translation research and development were extensively reported on by O. S. Kulagina and I. A. Mel'čuk in their collection of machine-translation articles under the title *Avtomatičeskij perevod* [Automatic translation] (Kulagina – Mel'čuk 1971). This was a second volume on the history of machine translation published in the USSR. The first was a translation of Booth's *Machine translation of languages* (Locke 1957). The Locke and Booth collection dealt with the initial phase of machine translation. Since that time, machine-translation development was further characterized by the emergence of trends developed by new machine-translation groups. Though not without contradictions, the new views were well aired in a rapidly growing number of machine-translation papers. The number of papers which appeared prior to 1963 was about 1,500, as indicated by the Mel'čuk – Ravič bibliography (1967).

I shall describe the views of Kulagina and Mel'čuk on the history of machine translation as presented in the introduction to their 1971 book. I will try to distinguish my own point of view, whether positive or negative, from the point of view of the authors.

Kulagina and Mel'čuk feel that the majority of machine-translation papers are published in various technical journals, and more frequently than not are of a highly technical nature, which presents difficulties for the general reader who would like to form his own opinion on the present state of affairs in the machine-translation field. The lack of historical reviews prompted the authors to translate and publish a collection composed of papers which had been published abroad depicting the machine-translation situation during 1955–1966 just as it has been depicted for the previous decade. Thus, the Soviet reader could get an idea of the state of affairs of machine translation in the USA, England, France and Italy. According to the authors, the selected papers should not be looked upon as an attempt to cover the whole machine-translation field outside of the USSR, but rather to present a general view of machine translation in the foreign countries indicated.

The GU machine-translation experiment in 1954 is prominently named "when for the first time in history a computer-assisted translation of a simple text was produced from one language to another, concentrating on finding the right approach to making machine translation feasible" (Kulagina – Mel'čuk 1971: 4). The authors stress the fact that immediately after the GU machine-translation experiment, a number of scientific machine-translation research groups emerged both in the US and the USSR with the goal of developing working machine-translation systems. In the USSR efforts were made to develop a working machine-translation system for English to Russian and French to Russian, while in the US the development of a Russian-to-English system was of primary interest.

There were quite a few external differences among the systems developing at the time. The description of these differences from the Soviet point of view is contained in another article, published by D. Ju. Panov, A. A. Ljapunov and I. S. Muxin entitled *Avtomatizatsija perevoda s odnogo jazyka na drugoj* [Automatization of translation from one language to another] (Panov 1956). The authors of this article state that the following differences between the Soviet machine-translation experiment and that of GU should be noted: "… (first) the underlying principles do not correspond to ours, and second, the Americans translated from Russian into English, while we are naturally interested in the reverse" (p. 2).

The article states that the correspondences between the target and source languages must be represented as a formal system acceptable to the computer. This difference in morphology and syntax between a source and a target language constitutes an additional difference between the initial data for the machine-translation workers. Furthermore, the word order in English differs from that of Russian; so does the number of formal classes established for English and Russian.

The authors state that, on the whole, the formal analysis for machine-translation purposes is based on a number of codes accompanying all the words in the dictionary such that the information contained in these codes should be sufficient, in the ideal situation, to secure the transfer from the source to the target language.

Kulagina and Mel'čuk think that despite all the differences noted among the various machine-translation procedures, all these developing systems could be labeled as the first-generation machine-translation systems, as opposed to second- and third-generation machine-translation systems, which will be discussed below.

According to the authors the first-generation machine-translation systems could be characterized by binarity, inseparability, and univariantness.

Binarity means a pair of languages in a specific direction, say, from Russian to English only.

Inseparability means information used in the machine translation, formulated within the analysis and the synthesis of the text actually studied, not outside of the text. The linguistic information and the algorithmic and mathematical information was not separated. Levels in the translation process serving as input to the consecutive levels were not strictly formulated. Kulagina and Mel'čuk think that it is quite difficult to analyze the sequence of instructions and evaluate the anticipated results.

Univariantness is defined as a single solution for a single problem. However, the single solution might be incorrect.

I feel that such labeling suffers from oversimplification, though at the same time one has to admit that the attributes listed by the authors are not without justification. If one examined GAT-SLC in the light of three attributes mentioned above, one would notice that GAT-SLC is binary and univariant but not inseparable, i. e., the information developed for the Russian-to-English machine translation was partly developed outside of the text to be analyzed with the aim of being useful for any Russian text. Essential information on the structure of Russian was taken from Russian traditional grammars and properly adjusted for the automatization purpose.

Let us move to the second-generation machine-translation systems. Here we discover certain features of the dialectical thought of the authors; i. e., if the first generation sets forth the thesis, then the second generation sets forth the antithesis. Accordingly, the second generation of machine translation would be characterized by the opposite features of the first-generation systems, namely:

1. Maximum independence of the analysis from the synthesis; i. e., the source text analyzed independently of the target text.
2. Maximum separability of the algorithm, and
3. Poly-variantness as opposed to univariantness.

The authors state that a level of transfer, possibly in the form of a special intermediary language (IL), was introduced in the machine-translation process; i. e., the source text is analyzed first into the categories of the IL and the target synthesis is generated from the IL input according to the rules of the target language.

In my opinion, this antithesis is also an oversimplification. Thus, GAT-SLC might be characterized as having: 1. maximum independence, and not having 2. maximum separability of the algorithms from the linguistic information. Finally, in the GAT-SLC system the question of univariantness vs. poly-variantness should also be qualified so that each problem has only one solution. This solution should be the most appropriate for the context on the assumption that functions in the context are always single-valued. Either the Saussurian "all or nothing" or the Boolean 1 or 0 apply here. However, in the GAT-SLC this single solution is arrived at only after various attempts at some other solution for the same problem fail. In other words, we might pose a particular question, e. g., how to obtain a unique English equivalent for a Russian preposition. A set of context-sensitive rules must be tested within the context of the preposition, and only one of the possible English equivalents can be selected as best suited to the given context. Of course, we also expect errors. Yet if the ratio of the errors is below 10 %, we feel quite satisfied, as we consider it the first approximation toward further improvement of the quality of the translation.

Kulagina and Mel'čuk use the word 'transfer' in two senses: first, for the representation of the source message directly in the target message without any intermediate language, and second, for representation of the source message in the target equivalent via the IL. The first type of transfer is referred to as a bipartite machine-translation system, the second as a tripartite machine-translation system.

I would like to point out that the bi- and tripartite machine-translation systems have one essential characteristic in common; i.e., in both, levels introduced during the translation process are content-justified by the data of the source and the target languages. By introducing the following linguistic levels: morphological, syntagmatic, syntactic, semantic, and possibly pragmatic, translation rules can be formulated in terms of correspondences between the translation units of the source language from the above levels and their equivalences in target languages. Thus, both the content and the formal description are present. Yet the reader must be aware that this static formal description deals with the transfer of the dynamic equivalence of information between the two languages.

My point is that the presence of the bi- or tripartite organization will in no way affect the quality of the translation. Historically, from the point of view of time and space, tripartite systems are less flexible and less economical.

Kulagina and Mel'čuk are, however, quite correct in asserting that the development of the tripartite systems was typical of some machine-translation groups in the beginning of the sixties, e. g., the system developed by V. Yngve. In a tripartite system the division of labor takes the following form: the linguist produces the adequate formalized linguistic description of the data; the mathematician works out the optimal procedures, while at the same time the linguist and mathematician together design the unified format.

Kulagina and Mel'čuk think that the poly-variantness principle has in turn caused the emergence of the filtering process; that is, only those instances of texts are accepted which are not listed as unacceptable. Each filter has a list of such unacceptable instances. The method of filters which was first proposed for machine translation by Y. Lecerf (1963) contrasts with the consecutive local method of analysis. Kulagina and Mel'čuk think that the consecutive method is characteristic of Garvin's fulcrum.

Many teams working on machine-translation problems switched from efforts to create a comprehensive (total) system of translation to the problems of syntactic analysis (fragmental approach). During the first half of the sixties various algorithms for syntactic analysis were designed. These algorithms were characterized by varying degrees of completeness and power, applicable to various languages, within the framework of machine-translation systems of that period. The level of syntactic analysis was considered to be central and decisive.

According to the authors, the essential interest in syntactic analysis is also apparent from the publications of that period. It is not without reason that half of the papers in their collection are devoted specifically to syntactic analysis.

The authors add that along with the design of syntactic systems in the sixties, concerted efforts were directed towards the completion and improvement of translations, retaining the basic, necessary features of the first-generation systems. Nevertheless, these efforts did not escape the influence of syntactic analysis, which started to play an important role in improving machine-translation systems. Also, some efforts were made to design a corresponding part of the algorithm by taking into consideration more contemporary principles. As a result, hybrid systems were developed which could be metaphorically called the "one-and-a-half-generation (polutornye) machine-translation systems".

For example, the following systems of Russian-to-English machine translation fall into this category: "fulcrum" (p. 26), a system worked out at the National Physical Laboratory, England (p. 234), and the Georgetown University system.

Such systems characterized essentially by their applied practical orientation were, perhaps, too empirical. Nevertheless, according to Kulagina and Mel'čuk, one cannot but ascribe great scientific importance to them.

These systems retained a comprehensive approach and maintained the goal of considering the translation process as a whole, from the input to the output text. This comprehensiveness was lost in the syntactic analysis carried out, as a rule, on a higher theoretical level. The danger of the dissolution of the very concrete (and therefore also challenging) task of treating machine translation in a purely academic abstract manner, which was far removed both from the language reality and the machine experiment, began to emerge.

Kulagina and Mel'čuk point explicitly to the possibility of merging research in theoretical syntax into a wider scientific frame of reference; i. e., discrete analysis, mathematical logic, the theory of programming languages, etc.

In summing up the results of the second-generation machine-translation systems, the authors stress the achievements in the syntactic field, the procedures applicable to automatic text handling, and the completion of the computer tests of efforts for further improvement of the systems of the one-and-a-half generation. It is due to the experiments of the one-and-a-half generation that the basic inadequacies of these systems were identified. The methods and means were designed for their principal improvement, thus preparing the path for the third generation of machine-translation systems.

Kulagina and Mel'čuk are apparently correct in stating that as of their writing there existed no complete and pure third-generation machine-translation system. In their opinion the closest approximation to such a system was the Grenoble Russian-to-French machine-translation system (p. 319; also Mel'čuk 1967).

The authors consider that the following features are characteristic of the emerging third-generation machine-translation system:
– Independence, separability and the poly-variantness remain as typical features.
– Syntax will be the only seriously studied component of the system.
– Much more attention will be given to synthesis, dictionary structure, monitoring programs, etc.
– A special level connected with the use of semantic information – semantic analysis and synthesis – will emerge.

The third-generation machine-translation systems are always characterized by a structure of multilevel operators for gradual transition from the source input to the target output. The division exists between the end of the semantic analysis and the semantic synthesis. According to the authors, an approximation of such a system is present in the work of Lamb, Sgall, and Kulagina – Mel'čuk in 1967.

The authors list 29 machine-translation teams outside the USSR and nine teams within it.

Kulagina's and Mel'čuk's list should not be considered exhaustive. The authors intentionally did not include in their list approximately 50 groups which work in the field of automatic textual analysis and synthesis but are not oriented toward designing working machine-translation systems.

4.3 The latest developments in the USSR

Today in the United States, contrary to the USSR, machine translation is in daily use for rough quality translations of scientific and technical texts. However, widespread disillusionment with the early ambitious goals of machine translation which sought to replace human translation altogether with high-quality machine translation has led to a lack of funding for experimental work to improve machine-translation systems. Recognition and support is now needed in the United States for experiments in designing and solving scientific and technical problems for commercially suitable machine-translation systems. Working with limited goals and on specific texts, it should be possible within the next few years to improve greatly the efficiency and quality of existing machine-translation systems. This improvement would allow greatly expanded utilization of machine translation as a tool for rapid dissemination of scientific and technical information.

After a long period of emphasizing the theoretical basis of machine translation at the expense of developing a commercially practical working machine-translation system, the Soviets are now recognizing that there is a good basis for creating a practical system in the very near future and are supporting experimental work on computers. R. G. Kotov reviews the history of machine translation in his paper, "Linguistics and the contemporary state of machine translation in the USSR" (Kotov 1976). A summary of his report is given below:

Machine translation is currently viewed in the USSR as a practical tool for obtaining rough translations in large quantities of scientific technical texts. Previously, although machine translation was being used successfully in foreign countries, in the USSR it was believed that a practical machine-translation system would not be developed in the near future.

In 1973, a special Committee on Science and Technology was organized with the goal of developing a practical machine-translation system. Their conclusion was that machine translation, which has had successful commercial application in other countries, should be developed in the USSR and that it is possible to create a practical machine-translation system that is five times cheaper and ten times faster than human translation.

4.3.1   History of the development of machine translation in the U.S.S.R.

4.3.1.1 The first stage (1954–1958)

D. Ju. Panov, I. S. Muxin, and others, did the first experimental machine translation from English into Russian on the EVM BESM computer in December 1955. A. A. Ljapunov and O. S. Kulagina did experimental translations from French into Russian in 1956 using the EVM "STRELA". These two groups concluded from their work that machine-translation problems could be solved with an analytical or empirical approach and each had its own validity, but that the individual features of the input text could not be ignored. The group also formulated the basic principles of designing a machine-translation algorithm.

4.3.1.2 The second stage (1958–1961)

Working out the theoretical basis of translation became the dominant goal in machine-translation work at the expense of the empirical approach which was suppressed at both the first machine translation conference in 1958 and a subsequent conference on machine translation in 1961.

4.3.1.3 The third stage (1961–to date)

During this period, theoretical studies of language were developed without any relation to the specific task of designing practical, working machine-translation systems. This stimulated the development of structural and mathematical linguistics and it was recognized that theoretical constructs in linguistics, as well as algorithms, should be tested on the computer. While the linguistic investigations in connection with machine translation kept enlarging toward a fundamental description of language, there was no corresponding support for research to design a working machine-translation system and as a result there are no working systems.

Following this trend, the language model of the type "sense-text" was considered the basic tool for the investigation and description of language. Its goal is the formal description, stored in the computer, of all levels of a natural language. Such a programmed mechanism will carry out the universal transformations between meaning and texts modelling human speech behavior. However, due primarily to a very loose concept of formalization the researchers were led to create very cumbersome designs difficult to inspect. After 15 years of research using the "sense-text" model, the results are fragmentary and disconnected descriptions of language data, particular incomplete 'models', and a list of problems that it is recognized will not be solved in the foreseeable future. This research has not considered at all the algorithmic aspects of models and it seems no longer creditable to support this method as the only serious task of linguistics.

In considering the shortcomings of this trend, the value of creating a formal language description is not being denied. It seems probable that by narrowing the goals, strictly delimiting the tasks, and restricting the subject of study, results can be achieved that will have applied significance. In this context, the observations of Kulagina and Mel'čuk are of noteworthy interest. In their review (1971) they presented the concept of 'three generations' in machine translation: 1. the system of word-for-word translation, 2. the system of grammar, and 3. the system of semantic translation of machine translation. This concept was considered analogous to the development of three generations of computers: 1. lamps, 2. transistors, 3. integrated solid systems. However, the concept of the three generations does not represent the real differences in the existing machine-translation systems. The other differences of the three-generation classification also turned out to be nonexistent, such as the complete independence of the analysis from the synthesis, delimiting the levels of algorithms, etc.

The principle of differentiating the linguistic description (grammar) from the algorithms (mechanisms) promoted the thesis that the linguist should be used in practice. Representatives of this trend continue to advocate finishing the theoretical goals before doing any more work on developing working machine-translation systems and refuse to recognize the value of practical experiments. Their investigations have retained the title 'automatic translation' although they have no direct relevance to the scientific technical machine-translation problem.

There is now a good basis for the creation of practical machine-translation systems, although there has been a lack of support for this in the USSR. There has been extensive experience in building a large machine-translation dictionary, algorithms for synthesis and analysis, and programming and experiments on computers. Organizational difficulties have been alleviated by the creation of the All-Union Translation Center that has as its aim the creation of a working machine-translation system in the next few years. The International Machine Translation Seminar in Moscow in 1975 showed that linguists are again doing more practical machine-translation work. A renewed emphasis on developing a practical machine-translation system as well as theoretical research should continue both in applied and general linguistics.

Notes on the International Seminar on Machine Translation, sponsored by the All-Union Translation Center, Moscow, 1975

The need for experiments on computers using large linguistic data sets was recognized along with the need for theoretical research. The basic topics of the conference were the following:

1. Machine dictionaries: Specialists in computational lexicography study and design machine dictionaries. Many papers presented the results of already existing machine dictionaries. These dictionaries play a great role in machine analysis of specific aspects in word formation and inflection.
2. Problems of automatic analysis and synthesis of texts: Interest in syntactic analysis prevails. The papers were characterized by an absence of new all-embracing theories with reliance on concepts already known. Many papers were devoted to specific syntactic problems; for example, analysis of prepositions, rules for designing predicate relations, and others.
3. Semantic analysis of texts: The experimental method was established in the semantic analysis of texts; concepts of the semantic connectedness of the text are verified by algorithms for segmentation of texts into paragraphs and connected fragments. Some papers dealt with dictionaries containing semantic information and also the semantics of specific words and word combinations in natural languages.
4. Mathematical and programming services: Several papers dealt with the programming techniques for inter- and post-editing involving the interaction of machine and man, the complex approach to mathematical and programming services for machine translation, and the design of general and specific programs.

A large participation at the conference showed the interest in machine translation and the trend toward organizational unity in designing scientific and technical problems for commercially suitable machine-translation systems.

5 Directions for the future development of machine-translation research: The Rosslyn Machine Translation Seminar

One of the components in the future development of machine-translation research will be determined by the financial support needed for carrying out research on outstanding machine-translation problems. Among them the most important is the need for introducing systematic semantic coding for the dictionary and accompanying rules for testing semantic resonance rules.

To receive financial support one must perform an act of persuasion by demonstrating the expected quality of the translation output, and showing that the underlying procedures in the system are capable of being changed without high cost.

As an illustration of the above statement, one could mention the machine-translation seminar organized in March of 1976 at Rosslyn, Virginia, for the U.S. Government Foreign Broadcast Information Service (FBIS). Summary proceedings were published in the *American Journal of Computational Linguistics*, Microfiche 46, edited by David G. Hays. The information below is based on various articles contained on the microfiche.

The topics discussed at the machine-translation seminar included the following major groups:

> Developmental machine-aided translation systems
> Available machine-aided translation systems
> Operating experience
> Optical character recognition

What was the sponsor's objective? The answer is contained in the keynote address delivered by John Yeo, FBIS. The speaker indicated that the U.S. Government was represented by most of the institutions who "are facing translation problems, and particularly those with an interest in discovering what has happened in recent years to move us forward in machine aids to translation" (p. 6). FBIS annually translates approximately one million words. It is expected that the demand for translation services will grow. "We hope to reassess the state of the art during this conference and to find out what there is in it that we ought to be thinking about. We wish to turn out the very best translation at the very least cost" (p. 6).

The evening sessions included demonstrations by commercial representatives.

Wallace L. Chafe, in his talk "Linguistics", which in his opinion should be the foundation of machine translation, noted that "linguistics has suffered a real lag in manipulation of large amounts of data". There was quite a bit of skepticism in Chafe's remark that "real machine translation takes such deep knowledge, it is utopian". Instead, one has to try to aim at the intermediate goals: stepwise simulation. This kind of attitude is not unfamiliar. The views expressed by Bar-Hillel in 1959 were very similar. In my opinion, one should not expect a different kind of perspective from a linguist who spent two years (1972–1974) dealing with the semantic prerequisites for machine translation, after which he became interested in the investigation of "various processes involved in the verbalization of recalled experience" (p. 9). An interesting stepwise simulation system is represented by the work of E. O. Lippmann, currently at IBM's Thomas J. Watson Research Center, Yorktown Heights, N. Y. Lippmann's efforts are concentrated on the development of terminal-oriented programs specifically for "nonnumerical information processing". In my opinion, Lippmann's work could easily be combined with other machine-translation research trends, and a unified program for the whole country should be planned.

The Xonics Machine Translation System was developed in the last six years, with private sources of support, by Dr. Giuliano Gnugnoli, Dr. Allen Tucker, and Mr. Bedrich Chaloupka. It is coded entirely in the PL/1 programming language. It runs in a 100K memory region and may be executed on any IBM/370 computer. The program may be executed in three different modes: 1. the batch mode, for translation of large volumes of text; 2. the sentence-by-sentence mode, for translation of articles, abstracts and titles; 3. the interactive mode, which allows translations and dictionary maintenance to be performed at a terminal. The system consists of two programs: the dictionary maintenance program, and the translation program. The dictionaries reside on direct access storage devices. The grammatical information in the dictionary is very rudimentary. There is no special skill or linguistic training required to work with the dictionaries. The dictionary contains approximately 25,000 items in physics and chemistry. The translation program consists of approximately 650 PL/1 statements. The authors claim that the "algorithm simulates the mental processes of a human translator, and is not styled on any specific linguistic theories" (p. 38). The system is capable of proper recognition of grammatical properties, properly translated prepositions and semantic units, and rearranges participial and nested structures. The system was designed for translation from Russian into English, and was demonstrated on a terminal.

Mr. B. Chaloupka has worked on machine-translation projects since 1956. He was responsible for dictionary compilation at Georgetown University with the GAT-SLC group, and also the Code Matching Techniques Group (A. Lukjanov). Dr. G. Gnugnoli is currently Professor of Computer Science at Georgetown University and systems consultant to Xonics, Inc.

There are a few researchers in artificial intelligence and related areas, such as discourse analysis and question-answering systems, who think that progress in machine translation is not possible until additional and substantial progress is made in the above areas. As an illustration, one could cite some of the arguments in favor of such views from a talk presented at the Rosslyn machine-translation seminar by Iorick Wilks (pp. 67–68). The main reason given is the fact that the notion of inference, knowledge, and preference rules are required even for the 'most congenial real texts'. Wilks recognizes that some real improvements were made in the machine-translation field and would like to avoid "the same agonizing cycle of optimism and disillusion that began twenty years ago". In his opinion, the problems not solved by machine translation are: ambiguity of word sense, case structure and pronoun reference. Wilks presented a small fragment from an English-French machine-translation system with the capability of taking a paragraph and translating it through an interlingua of deep meaning structures and inference rules. The details of the system are contained in *AJCL* Microfiche 40, 1976. Wilks thinks that his proposal could be thought of as occupying a position between the following machine-translation directions for the future of machine-translation research and development: 1. the brute-force system, 2. theoretical AI systems, and 3. techniques of on-line editors.

Robert F. Simmons, professor of Computer Science and Psychology, University of Texas, Austin, made a significant contribution in various areas related to automatic treatment of data from natural languages. Here we mention only those of his research activities that have a direct influence on the further development of machine translation: 1. Research on quantified case-predicate forms of conceptual memory structure; 2. generation of natural language outputs for summaries, abstracts, expansions, translations, etc.; 3. development of a textword management system for linguistic analysis, retrieval and lexicon development (p. 70).

S. R. Petrick, of the IBM T. J. Watson Research Center, Yorktown Heights, New York, Chairman of the American Association of Computational Linguistics, made several observations concerning the future development of machine translation. Here only the most striking of his opinions will be mentioned. Petrick starts his summary by presenting the highlights of Chafe's introductory speech to the seminar. In that speech Chafe stressed the fact that any sentence should be parsed to produce the surface structure. "The surface structure is converted by some process of comprehension into a conceptual structure, whether or not it is universal. If it is not universal, then it must be converted into a similar conceptual structure of the target language." Petrick thinks that Chafe's model provides a good basis for discussing translation efforts. Specifically, Petrick makes the following statement: "One way in which different systems roughly based on Chafe's model can vary is in the relative depth of their conceptual structures. Actual systems that were discussed vary in this respect all the way from rather abstract structures that directly represent meaning to shallow structures whose relationship to corresponding sentence meanings was, at best, tenuous" (p. 72).

In this evaluation, Petrick shows his own bias in several respects. He is certainly not against abstract research. His statement about a "tenuous" relationship is a straightforward rejection of non-abstract machine-translation work. He makes the reader feel that the ungrammatical source sentence should apparently be corrected by the system prior to its target synthesis.

On the positive side in Petrick's remarks, one should note his awareness that both the artificial intelligence and the computational linguistic systems, whether based on formal grammars or procedurally defined, cover the source language very sparsely (p. 73), as opposed to the working systems which do cover the source language extensively, since they provide the target output for every source sentence. Petrick asserts that the systems discussed at the Rosslyn conference are "rather primitive" in their treatment of verbalization (as defined by Chafe). One has a feeling that Petrick apparently has his own ideas regarding Chafe's verbalization. This inference is drawn from Petrick's following observations: "Many normally difficult facets of verbalization do not present a problem in machine translation, the current output of language processing systems is very unnatural and rough. This is true of AI systems as well as operational MT systems" (p. 74). Compare Chafe's uses of the term 'verbalizer' (Chafe 1971: 141) and verbalization symbolization in the second chapter of the same book. These two concepts have to do with expressing thoughts in terms of the surface structure. I would like to emphasize that machine translation does not pursue such goals at all. It does not verbalize in that sense, while artificial intelligence does, and Petrick should not put both of them on the same level in terms of their relationship to verbalization. In a machine-translation system, one provides the target equivalences for the translation units (words, phrases, sentences, possibly intersentential relationships) with the hope that the output will be acceptable to the user. I agree with the "roughness" of the machine-translation output but it has nothing to do with verbalization as Chafe defines it, since Chafe takes into consideration the participation of human beings. He says that "Language enables a speaker to transform configurations of ideas into configurations of sounds, and it enables a listener within his own mind to transform these sounds back into a reasonable facsimile of the ideas with which the speaker began" (Chafe 1971: 15). It is also possible that Petrick had in mind the report published by Chafe in *AJCL* 10 under the title, "An approach to verbalization and translation by machine" (this research report was financed by the U.S. Air Force during the years 1972–1974), in which Chafe does, indeed, speak about the translation model consisting of verbalization processes subdivided into the creative and algorithmic subtypes. He says that the first is employed by the speaker when he makes certain free choices in generating the message in the source language, and the speaker also employs the algorithmic process, since he has to obey the rules of the source language on various levels. On the other hand, the work of the translator, specifically the machine-translation system in its present stage, does not involve any creative process. It involves only an algorithmic process, i. e., it has to render the source message and its structures in some equivalent form and as close to the natural rule-determined structures as possible. Creativity is minimal, if at all present. While artificial intelligence can and should use both verbalization processes, machine-translation systems presently and for the foreseeable future will use only algorithmic processes.

It is a peculiar feature of some of Petrick's statements that they are difficult either to confirm or to contradict because he does not give specific information. Thus he states: "If, in fact, we examine the specific realizations of the components in Chafe's model which were reported to be included in the machine-translation systems described at this conference, we find very few changes over the situation that prevailed ten years ago... Difficulties and shortcomings related to conceptual structures have already been noted. These have changed very little over the past few years. In summary then, currently operational or projected machine-translation systems are only marginally different in their underlying organization and design than their predecessors."

The reader should note that Petrick does not say a word about the delaying effect of the ALPAC report. The marginal differences he speaks of are also not specifically illustrated. They sound more like dogmatic pronouncements than analysis of real data.

Petrick does feel that significant improvements were made in the procedural programming languages. His criticism is based on his opinion, not an analysis of specific performance. In particular, he states that many language-processing tasks are still very difficult to program, and convenient programming is no substitute for the absence of satisfactory models and algorithms (p. 74). He admits, however, that "Recent advances in editors and time sharing systems might, however, be significant factors in making the development of machine-aided human translation more attractive" (p. 74).

Talking about the cost of machine translation, Petrick states "The key issue is how much of the total effort can be handled by a computer and how much must still be done by human labor. Text input, pre-editing, and post-editing can take as much human time and effort as complete human translation" (p. 75). In my opinion, this cost evaluation is *ad libitum*. One could say that it might cost more than complete human translation, if one wanted to pile up 'arguments' against full-fledged machine-translation research. One wonders how long it will take before those who influence support for machine translation will realize that if the machine-translation output should be edited, the editor should be trained for this kind of job, and then his efforts will be judged differently, his own attitude will be different, and the cost will also differ. The basic task of a machine-translation editor should be to check the naturalness and fidelity of the translated text, and this could be accomplished without too much difficulty if the editor learned the generating machine-translation system, and the patterns of the generative behavior of the algorithm. The errors in the machine-translation output come in patterns, and editors should look for patterns, and correct them. An example: the GAT system produces the English output phrase – "By us was noted" which is a 'loan' from its Russian input 'Nami bylo zamečeno', and corrects it into 'We noted'.

Petrick considers of critical importance the evaluation of current machine-translation systems in terms of their unedited output quality, the acceptability of output for special uses, the amount of post-editing "that is required to meet well defined higher standards. No clear results of this type were provided at the conference and careful study is necessary to resolve certain seemingly contradictory claims" (p. 75).

Did Petrick himself examine the source text, its translation, and come to his own conclusion? – "Although I did not systematically examine large quantities of source language input and corresponding unedited target language output, the examples which I did examine suggested a rather low level of performance with respect to both fidelity of meaning output and to smoothness and naturalness of the output" (p. 76).

It should be noted that Petrick does not concern himself with the user's reaction to the transfer, the information, which from the user's point of view is the issue of first importance. Petrick relies also on the opinion of a colleague of his "with more experience" in machine translation than he has. The colleague assessed the output Petrick showed him "as more ambitious in its attempt to achieve natural output than past systems but probably not any more successful" (p. 76). This is a typical statement of anti-machine-translation thinking. Note the use of the word "probably", and no example of the output from which the knowledgeable reader could form his own opinion. Media feed information to the audience in the way they find it useful.

David Hays was the last speaker at the Rosslyn seminar. No time was allowed the audience to ask questions. Hays's extemporaneous remarks may be summarized as follows (pp. 84–88):

"No adequate reason for selecting a single system and excluding the rest has come to light thus far."

"The operational suitability of language-processing systems depends crucially on the smallest details of their designs. And yet, only those of clearly superior knowledge, taste, and judgment can be entrusted with the work."

The reader might wonder who will decide on the operational suitability of taste and other "supers"?

It seems to this writer that Hays's last remark may prove to be correct; he states:

"Several classes of systems are fundamentally different and cannot usefully be intermingled. Current commercial machine-translation systems, which make no provision for editorial intervention between the earliest and later stages of processing, are not suitable bases for machine-aided (editorial) systems; and the latter are not necessarily suitable bases for full-scale language-processing systems that may reach installability in as little as ten years if research and development are well supported" (p. 88). This certainly sounds like a "dissenting" voice from a participant in the ALPAC report.

Jim Mathias, the organizer of the Rosslyn seminar, included his remarks in the *AJCL* report (pp. 89–90).

In his summary he restates some common threads running throughout the seminar. Mathias states that "the moderators and commentators participated in the conference in order to assist the sponsor in arriving at reasonable decisions on planning and budgeting for possible application of computer technology... The sponsor should look beyond the function of translation and consider the purpose for which the work is done... The obvious preference is to assign to the computer functions it can perform well without imposing added undesirable tasks on the human translator in order to compensate for computer shortcomings." Mathias believes that the computer should be introduced into the FBIS translation process wherever it is possible to maximize current capabilities for current needs. In my opinion, Mathias is right in suggesting that "the verification of existing *technology* might be best achieved to establishing an in-house awareness through maximum exposure to research and development in the commercial and academic community" (p. 90). This writer also agrees with the following concluding statement of Mathias. "It was generally concluded that during the process of selecting systems or hardware, for application to sponsor tasks, that maximum flexibility be one of the principal criteria applied in order to assure long term usefulness and avoid costly replacement. The approach taken should not be set in concrete but should reflect the ability to cut off one method of approach if it appears unfruitful and shift to another effort or another direction. Avoid the forced choice of any single system by avoiding reliance on any one approach" (p. 90).

The only difficulty with this essentially negative advice is the absence of positive criteria of flexibility and of whether or not one could build a best system out of existing systems. Therefore, while the sponsor might be interested in one purpose only, the developer might have his own designs of what purpose(s) to accommodate. Some restraints on both sides are evidently in order.

6 Conclusions

In retrospect, looking back at 25 years of machine translation, three phases of its development can be clearly recognized. The first phase started with the inception of the existing idea of translating from one language to another by mechanical means. It was born in the minds of men of vision like W. Weaver in the USA, Trojanskij in the USSR, A. D. Booth in Great Britain, and others. The idea started taking concrete form with the first timid experimentation with computers and ended with the Georgetown University-IBM experiment in 1954, which is generally regarded as the "turning point" in the development of machine translation. It proved the feasibility of mechanical translation and was the starting point for the second phase and the rapid and almost feverish activity of many groups working on the same problem. A set of favorable circumstances also facilitated both the theoretical and the practical aspects of machine-translation systems. On the theoretical side, the development of structural linguistics reached a stage where it was ready for formalization of linguistic operations needed for machine translation. On the practical side, the tool for carrying out formalized linguistic statements became available, i. e., the computer was here to be tested in this area. As in human translation, the dictionary and grammar have become important components of machine translation. First, the idea of an automatic dictionary seemed bold enough to consider it the cornerstone for machine translation. But of course it was only a matter of time before the notion of the automatic dictionary gave way to the automatic grammar, and finally, the sentence was recognized as a minimum structure for expressing the message and subject to recursive analysis.

The years from 1956 to 1966 represent a very active period, due to financial support from various government agencies in several countries. It was a time when a close cooperation between various groups could have produced excellent results. Unfortunately, competition rather than coordination of separate efforts led to duplication, to the expenditure of vast amounts of time and, of course, enormous funds. In addition, the fact that some machine-translation researchers did not succeed in building their own operational systems for machine-translation purposes was used in creating a psychological point which resulted, finally, in the "black book", i.e., the ALPAC report. This report essentially killed any further machine-translation development on a large scale in the US and had similar repercussions abroad. It was the beginning of the third phase – the decline of machine-translation development.

A project as sophisticated as machine translation needed more time and better coordination of talents than was expected by the sponsoring institutions. Thus, the second phase, characterized by rapid strides, ended abruptly with the ALPAC report which prematurely cut the life line from the yet unborn child.

However, the last chapter of machine-translation development has yet to be written. Whether or not the efforts to improve the quality of machine translation will be supported on a large scale, the activity will go on, and it is only a matter of time and a question of where and by which group it will be achieved. Ideally, the need for creative balance should be accepted as a condition *sine qua non*.

In the past there was very little personal relation among machine-translation researchers that could encourage mutual trust and cooperation. Nevertheless, for those of us who were fortunate enough to participate in the first stage of machine translation, the words of Wordsworth come to mind:

> Bliss was it in that dawn to be alive,
> But to be young was very heaven.

In our future considerations we should try to evaluate different trends in automatic language research on the basis of their own procedure and purpose. Thus, if one is interested in artificial intelligence, let the proposal be evaluated as such without labeling it as to whether or not the results might be useful for practical machine translation. And vice versa, if the practical machine-translation project is considered, this should be done in terms of its own procedures and goals without trying to figure out to what degree, if any, this machine-translation project might be useful for theoretical evaluation. To mix purposes and procedures in automatic language processing is as bad as to mix levels in analyzing and generating structures in natural language.

In connection with the above suggestion, the whole problem of outside testing of the results of a particular machine-translation system should be designed similar to such tests in other areas of research. The point is made that the outside examiners should be knowledgeable in the machine-translation processes as thoroughly as the machine-translation researchers themselves. This is a necessary condition, even for their successful communication. Medical or atomic research is examined by experts from those fields. Machine-translation examination should not be in any way different.

At the Rosslyn Seminar it was very interesting and useful to hear from machine-translation users. It seems mandatory that the users' reactions be solicited, not only to the use of machine translation but also to the planning stage of machine-translation research on a permanent basis.

While certain overlapping is unavoidable both nationally and internationally (in order not to subdue some emerging new ideas or procedures), it is highly desirable that each country where machine translation is being conducted does monitor machine-translation research abroad, and make its own achievements and/or ideas known to everyone concerned.

PART II

The problem of machine translation

R. ROSS MACDONALD

Introduction

Machine translation undeniably involves many complexities.

One of the foremost of these complexities is the task of determining exactly how complex a problem machine translation is. There have been various responses to this question.

It is said that an early proposal for machine translation assumed that the direct replacement of Russian words with English words by computer would produce a usable output. Such naiveté is simply not credible. But much of the early research was carried out by those whose sense of the realities of language was only slightly better developed. Though well qualified to deal with the computational aspects of the problem, these researchers assumed gratuitously that the fact that they themselves used a language qualified them to deal with the linguistic aspects also. The possession of a compendious book on grammar seemed to guarantee success.

It is true that much important work in the area of morphology resulted from this approach.

But the level of syntactic analysis which is found in books intended for human beings is much shallower than the level needed for computational work. An adequate syntactic analysis for machine translation requires an intensive study of the language structure, and the establishment of refined subcategorizations. It is necessary to make explicit many mechanisms of the grammar which the speakers of the language, and particularly the native speakers, know only subliminally; native speakers of the language have learned to use these mechanisms at so early an age, and have so reduced that use to the level of habit that, as adults, they are not conscious of what these mechanisms are. Experienced linguists have learned to probe the syntax of languages and to explicate these mechanisms. Unfortunately, not all of the research was carried out by experienced linguists.

The depth of semantic analysis in the early days of the research was negligible. A 'word' in a language rarely has a single meaning. The choice among the various meanings is determined by an elaborate network of semantic interconnections of which even the linguists had little or no experience then, though valuable basic research has been carried out since.

The question of the need for artificial intelligence also arose. Cases seem to exist where both an effective syntactic analysis and an effective semantic organization alike are incapable of resolving ambiguity. It appears that only a knowledge of the manner in which the natural world is organized, or of the manner in which the society regards the natural world, can lead to a satisfactory interpretation. Does this mean that a translation system must provide a store of general information on which the computer can draw in resolving such problems? If such a store were indeed needed, how comprehensive must it be? Must it be a digest of all human knowledge?

As realization of the magnitude of the problem dawned, the blissful hopes for immediate and perfect machine translation began to fade; those who lost hope conceded failure; those who had failed let it be known that only failure was possible, that machine translation was not feasible, and that it would not be desirable if it were feasible. Such a point of view is too extreme.

Since any language exhibits many variations at any one time, and is further subject to change as time passes, there is undoubtedly truth in the idea that a machine-translation system can never be one hundred per cent effective. There is a considerable basis for hope, however, that a system which closely approaches one hundred per cent in effectiveness can indeed be achieved. But such a system will not be built by sudden surges of enthusiasm, nor is it likely to arise from the brilliant intuitions of one or two men. Machine translation will come into active use as the result of painstaking attention to detail and careful planning on the part of a number of research workers over a period of many years. As long as the 'confusion of tongues' continues, there will be reason to try to solve the problem of machine translation.

Let me review the various aspects of the problem.

1 Preliminary

1.1 Text

What sort of text should be chosen for machine translation?

The immediate reason for most research in machine translation has been the desire to be able to obtain quick translations of technical material. For this reason texts in scientific disciplines such as organic chemistry, aeronautics, astrophysics and meteorology, to name but a few, have been chosen. Texts of this sort reduce a number of the potential problems in machine translation since the terminology of international technology is much less likely to be ambiguous than that of literature or history, and there is likely to be much less cultural bias in technical texts to be transferred into a parallel cultural bias in the target language.

Few researchers feel that machine translation is ready to provide renderings of great literary works, since it is necessary not merely to translate the sense, but also to convey the feeling of a work of literature. In addition, literature tends to be innovative, and to present a constantly varying task to the computer. Poetry is particularly intractable to machine translation in its present state.

On occasion, it has been argued that children's stories provide suitable texts for experimental work because of their shortness and because of the simplicity of the language. Actually, the simplicity of the language is largely suppositious; perhaps there are fewer involved sentences, but all of the other difficulties remain. In addition, children's stories may introduce semantic and situational combinations which would be quite unsuitable for other types of translation. If children fly and spiders talk and wizards convert frogs into princes and vice versa, the morphology and syntax are probably not significantly altered, but the semantic apparatus, depending on how it is conceived, may have to be considerably different from the semantic apparatus necessary for a suitable translation of a newspaper editorial or a text in biology.

For these reasons, it seems best at present to concentrate on the machine translation of scientific writing.

1.2 The computer

Since the first experiments in machine translation began, there has been little question but that the computer technology has been sufficiently advanced to allow of translation.

Usually, machine-translation systems have been designed to operate on general-purpose digital computers. This system has a number of advantages. Anyone who has extensive translation needs and his own computer can operate the system on his own premises and so obtain speedy results and preserve as much secrecy as he desires as to the nature of his translation interests.

On those occasions when a special computer has been built specifically to perform translations, the work has gained in efficiency and, after the initial outlay, in cost of operation. However, since a limited number of such machines are produced, many people who need machine translation are constrained to send the texts to the point at which the computer is located, and to wait for the translations to be sent back again, losing in the process a considerable amount of time and almost all confidentiality.

The most suitable machine-translation system will be one which can be operated most conveniently by the user, presumably on his own general-purpose computer.

1.3 Pre-editing

Should the text be pre-edited in any way before being presented to the computer?

There are those who favor extensive pre-editing, including segmentation of the sentences into easily handled grammatical groups, disambiguation of potentially ambiguous words, and other similar procedures.

Editing of this sort must be looked upon as a temporary expedient, however. If machine translation is to be viable, the computer must be able to accept any reasonable keypunched text in the source language and to produce a translation without the need for a human being at the interface between the text and the computer. It is to be expected that, in the course of time, the computer will be capable of reading written texts by means of an optical scanner, and, under these conditions, there would be a very considerable diminution of effectiveness if the text had to be interpreted by a human being.

It may be argued that, under the present circumstances, where it is necessary for someone to keypunch a text, a certain amount of editing is carried out even in the keypunching, and that more editing would not make a great deal of difference. But there need be very little editing involved in keypunching, and, indeed, any translation system which is to be generally useful should not have to depend on the availability of keypunch operators who understand the source language well enough to pre-edit it even in a rudimentary way, since these may be very hard to come by. The keypunch operator should be given a set of rules (the keypunch format) by which the symbols printed on the page can be converted in a purely mechanical way into computer-operable material. It has been adequately demonstrated by practice that people who know no Russian whatsoever can quickly learn to transcribe the Cyrillic alphabet into specified characters involving the Latin alphabet, and to do so with great accuracy. There is no significant problem which arises from a direct transcription of what is on the printed page which the computer cannot be programmed to solve in a largely satisfactory manner.

It may be, in the course of time, that authors who expect their texts to be machine-processed, and who have learned that certain possibilities are less likely to be well handled than others by the machine, will choose to modify their writing so as to forestall the effects of any such limitations. But that is in the far future, if indeed it ever becomes advisable.

The ideal machine-translation system will use a minimum of pre-editing.

1.4 Transcription

A well-planned transcription, or keypunch format, is a necessity for all natural-language processing, and particularly for machine translation.

In the extreme case, where the natural language in question does not use the same alphabet as the computer, it is necessary to develop a system of correspondences between the orthographic symbols of the natural language and the character-set available on the particular computer. The character-set ordinarily provides twenty-six upper case forms of the Latin alphabet, the ten digits, and a number of marks of punctuation and mathematical signs.

In the case of Chinese the transcription has been a very complex problem, since there is no one recognized way of transcribing the Chinese characters. The government of the People's Republic of China did adopt an official Romanization in the late fifties, but it is deficient in that it does not ordinarily indicate tonal differences, and this deficiency vastly increases the number of homonyms; and homonyms constitute a formidable enough problem, even when the tones are indicated. Attempts have been made to utilize the Chinese telegraphic code, in which a four-digit numeral can be used to represent some eight thousand or more of the most frequently used characters. Such a transcription has considerable advantages for the computer, since each character is represented by a string of numbers of uniform length, but it is extremely difficult for the human being to operate with this code, since no person can remember the particular significance of every string of numbers; except in the case of a few of the more common characters, constant reference must be made to lists of characters. It is possible, of course, to develop a double transcription system, one part entirely numerical and tailored to the requirements of the computer and its program, and another alphabetical, and providing the human being with the degree of mnemonic advantage necessary for efficient reading and understanding. The computer would accept the alphabetic form and put out the alphabetic form, but would transfer to the numeric form in all of its operations in which uniformity of length would be of advantage. Other systems of rendering the ideographs computer operable have also been tried; an explanation of these must presume a knowledge of the ideographs on the part of the reader, and so is beyond the scope of this survey. Input and output in Chinese characters is now also possible.

Arabic presents particular problems. The fact that Arabic is written from right to left is not one of these, since a simple change of direction is trivial. But Arabic writing for adults characteristically records the consonants and omits the vowels. The result is that many forms are ambiguous in writing which would not be ambiguous when spoken, and a considerable reliance on the context in which such forms are found is necessary to resolve these ambiguities.

Another difficult transcription is that for Russian, if the thirty-two letter Cyrillic alphabet must be transcribed in terms of the twenty-six letter English form of the Latin alphabet. There are two possible approaches.

The transcription can be a one-for-one transcription in which each letter of the Cyrillic alphabet is represented by one character available on the computer. See Table 1. In this case, some of the digits may be used as well as the alphabetics, so that the so-called soft sign can be represented by 6, and the so-called hard sign by 7. (This will make it necessary in turn to mark strings of digits which occur in the text in some special way so that none of them is interpreted as a letter of the alphabet; otherwise there would be ambiguity, since the character 4 could be either the digit 4 or the Russian word corresponding to the English word *I*.)

Table 1

	Cyrillic Letter	Keypunch Format			Cyrillic Letter	Keypunch Format
1	А	A		17	Р	R
2	Б	B		18	С	S
3	В	V		19	Т	T
4	Г	G		20	У	U
5	Д	D		21	Ф	F
6	Е	E		22	Х	X
7	Ж	J		23	Ц	Q
8	З	Z		24	Ч	C
9	И	I		25	Ш	W
10	Й	1		26	Щ	5
11	К	K		27	'	7
12	Л	L		28	Ы	Y
13	М	M		29	Ь	6
14	Н	N		30	Э	3
15	О	O		31	Ю	H
16	П	P		32	Я	4

The keypunch transcription used in this book has been adopted by a number of machine-translation systems. It is a one-to-one transcription.

The alternative is to use a variable transcription in which one letter of the Cyrillic alphabet may be transcribed by one character, while another letter is transcribed by two. This kind of transcription has its advantages, particularly if it is so designed that the second member of each digraph is a character which is not used for any other purpose. However such a transcription is organized, it should have a considerable mnemonic advantage for the research worker, and should preferably be such that it will not be any more offensive to the native speaker of the language who may chance to see it than is absolutely necessary.

There is of course less difficulty in making such languages as French, Spanish or Czech conform with a computer which has an English character set; each of these languages uses its own form of the Latin alphabet, but amplifies it by various diacritic marks. A transcription of French, then, really only requires special signs for the three accents, for the cedilla, and perhaps for the trema or diaeresis. Thus, *é* may be represented by E1, *è* by E2, *ê* by E3. (It will not be necessary in this case to mark digit strings in the text in any special way, because presumably a digit string will always be prefaced by a space whereas these signs for diacritics will never have a space before them.) Similar adaptations can be made for other languages.

The problems of German are easily solved. The umlaut over a vowel can be replaced by the letter *e* after the vowel, since this is a convention already familiar to German.

Aspects of transcription which are sometimes slighted or even overlooked are the adequate representation of punctuation and of typographic variations in the text. The extent to which these will be handled in keypunching any one text will vary depending on the purpose for which the text is being prepared, but if it is possible that the text will be used for a number of research projects, it is desirable that all of the features of the text be preserved in the transcription; it is easy to ignore them if they are present, but impossible to create them if they are absent.

Many marks of punctuation are available on the contemporary computer. For those which are not, special combinations of signs can be devised. Two ways of handling punctuation have proven especially useful.

One is to add to the end of every sentence after its regular punctuation, a special end-of-sentence mark which can then be used in scanning the text to determine quickly and efficiently where each sentence ends. The ordinary end-of-sentence punctuation should be retained, because it is frequently useful in determining the nature of the sentence structure, while the additional standardized end-of-sentence mark eliminates the necessity for searching for a number of possible forms (.?!) during rapid scanning. Special end-of-paragraph marks, which may be only the end-of-sentence mark doubled, are also helpful.

The other especially useful procedure is to have the keypunch operator punch all marks of punctuation with a space before them and after them so that they stand in the text as separate text words. For the most part, marks of punctuation give significant indications of the manner in which a sentence is structured, and they must not be treated cavalierly. In addition, it is eminently desirable to treat marks of punctuation as text words, to enter them in the dictionary, and to generate for them, as for other words in the text, codes which resolve their potential ambiguity, and which show their particular function in the sentence under investigation.

Commas, for instance, have three functions which it might be necessary to differentiate: they mark off certain types of clauses; they may mark off the items of a list and so, in effect, function as coordinate conjunctions; they mark the beginning and the end of certain types of parenthetical insertion where it may be necessary for the analysis to ignore what is between a pair of commas, and to unify what is outside of them in order to achieve a satisfactory analysis.

Periods or full stops also have three potential functions: they may indicate the end of a sentence, in which case, if it is feasible, it may prove desirable to keypunch them with a space before and a space afterwards in order to indicate this particular function; periods may indicate abbreviations, and here it may prove desirable to keypunch them with no space before them but a space after them so that the period remains an essential part of the abbreviation; periods may also occur in digit strings to indicate the decimal point (English style) or to mark off the non-fractional part of the number in groups of three (Continental style), and in such cases the period might well be punched with no space before it or after it. It may be objected that these various ways of handling the period constitute a type of pre-editing. Perhaps so; but while it is desirable that these distinctions be made in keypunching, it is not essential. Moreover, it is not out of the question to program the computer to make these distinctions in cases where the keypunch operator is so unfamiliar with the materials as to be unable to recognize, say, whether a period marks an abbreviation or the end of a sentence or both; it will eventually be necessary to do so in cases where it is expected that the original text will be optically scanned directly into the computer.

Special attention must also be given to the hyphen. Hyphens may be essential in the orthography, in which case they must be keypunched, or facultative (introduced only to show the division of a word between two lines of text), in which case it would be easier not to keypunch them. Unfortunately, every so often an essential hyphen appears at the end of a line of text. If the keypunch operator cannot determine which hyphens are essential, they can be marked by someone familiar with the language; this again constitutes a type of pre-editing. In the long run it would be better to program the computer to deal with such problems.

It is difficult to believe that some systems have deliberately chosen to ignore blanks. The blank is, of course, just as essential a character as any of the overt alphabetic forms, and one ought really to say that the English form of the Latin alphabet contains twenty-seven characters, of which twenty-six are overt, and one is a blank. The judicious use of blanks in the transcription system may considerably expand the possibilities of the system. If, as suggested here, marks of punctuation are regularly preceded and followed by blanks when they are intended as marks of punctuation, then they can also be used to signify various diacritic marks, where this seems advisable, and their function as a diacritic will be recognizable from the fact that they have no blank on one or both sides. The same is true for special characters such as the dollar sign or the per-cent sign, which can always have their usual meaning if surrounded by blanks, and a specialized value when incorporated with other material.

It is also advisable in the transcription system to distinguish between upper case and lower case letters, between italic and roman type, and perhaps also between boldface and standard type.

Mishaps have occurred in the past as a result of ignoring the distinction between upper case letters and lower case. In particular, where someone's name is homonymous with some common word of the language, as, for example, the name *Brown* and the color *brown* in English or the name *Starik* and the noun *starik* 'old man' in Russian, it is desirable to have every possible indication as to which forms are proper nouns and which are not. In addition, capitalization may frequently give a valuable indication as to which words form a cohesive group, and indications of this sort should not be lightly dispensed with.

A common way of indicating capitalization has been to prefix a special indicator to the word beginning with a capital, as, for instance, the keypunching of Brown as $BROWN, where the $ with no space after it is not used in any other meaning. There is a possible disadvantage here in looking up words in the dictionary, because of the need for testing at some point in the processing whether the word begins with a $, and of stripping the $ off, at least in certain cases, for lookup purposes. Another method which has been suggested is that of setting up an empty word (e.g., $C) which would appear as if it were a separate text word before all words of the text beginning with a capital letter ($C BROWN). At least in certain types of system, this use of empty proclitic words may have an advantage in that codes can be generated for such words which will help in the further analysis of the text.

A special sign to indicate italics (e.g., $I) may be particularly useful in certain types of text, especially in texts in linguistics in which the presence of italics generally indicates a foreign word which is not subject to translation or to analysis in the ordinary way.

Texts in chemistry and physics might benefit from having a special indicator to mark the beginning of a formula, or, in the case of complex formulae, to mark both beginning and end. This is again a type of pre-editing, but pre-editing of this sort may prove more reasonable than an attempt to enter all possible chemical formulae, for example, in the dictionary; there is an alternative, of course: if anything which is not found in the dictionary is simply printed out without change, the chemical formulae will be simply transferred as they stand without any attempt at translation. But problems such as the following have arisen. A Russian chemical text contains the Latin letter C as the symbol for carbon; the Latin letter C is of the same shape as the Cyrillic letter which corresponds to S; if the keypunch operator assumes that the letter is Cyrillic, the translation will have the symbol for sulphur rather than that for carbon. In such cases pre-editing of chemical texts, at least to mark formulae, may be a necessity.

But naturally chemical and physical formulae also present other difficulties. Input to a computer is strictly linear, and therefore subscript and superscript items which are likely to occur in chemical formulae, or vertical arrangements on the page which may occur in mathematical formulae, must be provided for in the keypunch format so that all of these formulae can be reduced to a single line without any loss of comprehensibility.

The need for a differentiation between boldface type and standard type is less obvious. The chief advantage is that boldface type frequently represents titles and headings, which require a somewhat different analytic approach from that used for text sentences. If the boldface material occurs in a text sentence, then the fact that it is in boldface indicates that it constitutes a syntactic unit of some sort, and this is again a valuable piece of information which may be highly significant or helpful in the analysis of the text.

These are some of the considerations which must underlie the development of an adequate keypunch format. The keypunch format is the foundation of all other work, and it must be carefully prepared if the work is to be successful. Naturally it is not always possible to foresee every contingency that will arise as more and more texts are handled by the system, and so the keypunch format must be flexible enough to allow for needed expansion.

A well-organized research project will have a protocol officer who will be the only member of the project authorized to alter the keypunch conventions. Once a decision has been made in developing a keypunch format, it cannot lightly be changed. All changes in this respect, and indeed anywhere through the system, should be implemented only after considered discussion. Any change that is decided upon should be introduced at the same time in all of the material which is being worked on, and this is best done by programming the computer to change all the established work uniformly during a hiatus in other processing, since inconsistency in the keypunch format is unthinkable.

1.5 Dictionary

The buildup of the dictionary allows for considerable latitude in method and design.

There are two chief methods of building a dictionary, one of which is strictly empirical, and the other a matter of copying book dictionaries.

By the empirical method, a dictionary is constructed which is sufficient to cover the first text which is to be translated. As further texts are run against the system, the dictionary is updated so that it covers each. Each new text is run against the dictionary, and those items which are not found in the dictionary are then added, so that the dictionary becomes adequate for the latest text. Experience has shown that when some two hundred thousand words of running text have been treated in this way, provided that the texts are reasonably consistent in their subject matter, there will be very few items found in any additional text which are not already in the dictionary; in diverse texts the scanning of up to half a million running words may be necessary. Those items which will need to be added to the dictionary after this point are usually names of people and of places.

The advantage to an empirical approach to dictionary buildup is that the dictionary will contain entries of the type needed for the kind of material being translated, and will contain very little material which is not of use for this purpose. The difficulty with this kind of buildup is that an item may occur in a particular text with one meaning, and in a subsequent text with another meaning. The discrepancy will not be caught simply by running the subsequent text against the dictionary as it stands, because the entry is to be found in the dictionary; the discrepancy will only appear when the translation of that entry proves to be unsatisfactory in the final output. Since this kind of updating requires a great deal of vigilance, a fairly considerable staff of dictionary analysts must be maintained.

The second chief method of building a dictionary is simply to have the entire contents of some available book dictionary keypunched. The advantage is, if the dictionary is adequate, that all of the various morphological, syntactic and semantic idiosyncracies of each entry will be in the dictionary, and constant comparison between the dictionary and the translation output will be considerably reduced, although it will not be eliminated. The disadvantage of this method is that there may be a great many entries in the dictionary which are of no practical use in machine translation because the words are obsolete, because they are so literary that they do not occur in technical texts, or because they are so extremely informal that they do not occur in written texts. Moreover, a book dictionary is unlikely to contain a selection of personal and geographical names; the human reader easily recognizes these either on the basis of previous knowledge or from the context, but for computational work it is necessary to have all of these items individually listed. In the case of personal or place names it will probably be advisable to provide in the dictionary a standard transcription of the name where the standard transcription differs from that used in the keypunch format. London, when written in Cyrillic and then transcribed by the system given in Table 1, appears as LONDON, but New York appears as N6H 1ORK, which indubitably needs explication. In addition, a certain amount of biographical material may be advisable in order to help differentiate between people of the same surname or to establish connections between people who work in the same field of research or in the same geographical location.

A great deal of ingenuity has been expended on the structuring of dictionaries, and it will be difficult to describe even the most important dictionary formats here. The following remarks cover certain aspects of the dictionary organization which any dictionary designer will have to take into consideration.

Even slightly inflected languages, such as English, would require enormous dictionaries if every separate text word were given a separate entry, so that forms such as *analyze, analyzes, analyzed* and *analyzing* were treated as if they had no connection with each other. In the case of a highly inflected language, such as Russian, the problem of dictionary size would become much more acute. It is therefore advisable to consider the possibility of listing as entries stems such as *analyz* which may not exist in the text by themselves, but which can be used in conjunction with a morphological routine which will allow the various words which are based on this stem to be looked up by means of the one dictionary entry.

The splitting of forms in this way can be carried further, so that each word is analyzed into a number of rather small morphological components. In practice, it usually turns out that any further analysis than simply splitting off one ending from the stem is inefficient.

Some words show no inflection at all, and thus the practice of splitting them into stem and ending is unprofitable. An English example is *again*.

Other words are inflected, but either the ending is so aberrant or the stem so unusual that splitting the form offers no advantage. An example is *further*; splitting off the ending *-er* leaves the unproductive form *furth*; it is as well to leave *further* unsplit. Another example is *unerring*.

It may be, consequently, that it is desirable to have two separate dictionaries, one containing unsplit forms, and one containing split stems which can only be effectively used in connection with a morphological routine which will recognize the particular value that each ending adds to the stem to which it is attached. It is also possible to arrange both split and unsplit entries in one dictionary listing, and to treat the unsplit entries as having an ending of length zero.

The usual procedure with separate dictionaries is to look up the word first in the unsplit dictionary, and, if it is not found there, to look it up subsequently in the split dictionary. If the first segment of the text word corresponds with a stem in the split dictionary, then the remainder of the text word is looked up in a special subdictionary of endings, and, after tests have been made to ensure that the ending is indeed compatible with that particular stem, the information from the dictionary of endings can be amalgamated with that from the split dictionary to produce a complete listing of dictionary information for the entire form.

If a word is not found in either dictionary, and does not yield any information when analyzed for possible endings in Gap Analysis, it is printed out in transcription both in the translation text and in a list of dictionary errors as a signal that the dictionary needs to be updated. If the word is part of the international technical vocabulary, it may be recognizable even in transcription; Russian words such as METEOROLOGII, IMPRESSIONISTICESKI1 and TRANSFOR-MAQI4 may be quite recognizable to an English speaker even though they are in transcription.

The dictionary constitutes a file. The entries are the individual records, and each entry may contain two or more fields.

In the more expanded dictionaries, each entry contains many fields. One field will record the part of speech of the entry. Another will record its morphological peculiarities. Another field may indicate whether the form governs an object, and what kind of object it governs. Another field may indicate whether or not the item participates in an idiom. Still another field will contain various semantic codes, and these may be quite complex in cases where one and the same form has different meanings in different areas of discourse; for example, the Russian word *jadro* is to be translated as *kernel* in botanical and biological contexts, but as *nucleus* in the context of nuclear physics. Still another field may contain the gloss which is to be used in the target-language output. Each gloss may be accompanied by fields which contain expanded codes to indicate the functional peculiarities of the gloss in the target language.

A greater degree of compactness in the dictionary may be achieved by dividing the dictionary into a number of segments, or code-lists. One way of doing this is to have, following the entry, a small number of fields, one of which is a cover code for the morphological characteristics, another a cover code for the syntactic characteristics, the third a cover code for semantic characteristics, and so on. These cover codes then serve as points of entry to a number of code-lists. The morphological code indicates where a full display of the morphological characteristics can be found in the morphological code-list, the syntactic code leads to the syntactic code-list, and so on. While it is less than likely that any one entry will have exactly the same total set of characteristics as any other, it is extremely probable that many entries will have identical morphological characteristics and can all be channelled to the same entry in the morphological code-list, thus reducing the amount of repetition needed to record all of the morphological information. Similarly, a number of entries will have certain syntactic characteristics in common, and these can be listed in full detail in only one place in the syntactic code-list, again reducing the amount of repetition needed. In this method, the information recorded after each entry in the first dictionary will be simply a list of codes to indicate where the full listing of information can be found in the various subdictionaries.

The most compact dictionary is one where the various codes are coalesced into one field, where a single terse cover code epitomizes the entire range of the morphological, syntactic, semantic, and other characteristics of the entry. In such a case, two entries will have the same terse code only if *all* of their characteristics are exactly the same in all respects. In a viable machine-translation system, the number of such cover codes will be very great indeed. Such codes are usually used in the type of system to be described later as a theoretical system.

The mechanics of the dictionary lookup system can vary considerably.

In the early days of machine translation, when most devices large enough to contain a dictionary (e.g., tapes) permitted only serial access, it was common to read in a large batch of text, to attach serial numbers to each word in the text, to sort the words into alphabetic order, and to match them against the dictionary by proceeding serially through both the sorted text and the dictionary. Whenever a match was made, the dictionary information would be attached to the text word. If the text word occurred a certain number of times, the dictionary information was repeated after each occurrence of the text word. When the lookup was completed, the text was sorted into its original order by means of the serial numbers which had been attached to the text words, and the result was a batch of text in its original order, each word having the dictionary information attached to it, ready for further processing.

More recent developments (e.g., disc packs) allow for other types of lookup, so that it may now seem more desirable to deal with the text one sentence or one paragraph at a time, and to look up the words in a random access listing in the order in which they occur in the text.

Many intermediate stages between these two extremes are possible, of course.

Another lookup device which merits consideration is that which utilizes a small subdictionary of the most frequently occurring words of the language, with the text, however it is batched, being checked first against this subdictionary. The words which remain unmatched can then be looked up by one of the other processes. Since, depending on the individual language, the one thousand most frequent words may constitute up to forty per cent of a running text, a notable saving in the time required for lookup may be achieved by this method.

As each text word is matched in the dictionary, and the dictionary information is attached to it ready for the processing, some provision may have to be made for space in which the processing will generate additional codes as further information is obtained in the course of the analysis. In some cases, the generated codes will simply replace codes originally provided by the dictionary. In other cases, the codes will be added to those derived from the dictionary. As the processing proceeds from level to level, it may be desirable to eliminate certain codes which will not be significant in the levels remaining. If a system operates with only the one terse code for each entry, this generation and suppression of codes is less common.

While in general it seems most efficient to combine the dictionary lookup with the morphological analysis, and to divide each form only once into stem and ending, other processes have been attempted for various reasons, and with varying degrees of success.

Russian is generally capable of multiple analysis of words parallel to such an English word as *retrogression*. Here there are three elements, *retro, gress* and *ion*, all of them clearly recognizable, and all forming components of other words as well. The listing of these separate formants (morphemes) separately in the dictionary is of course quite possible, but the advantage gained thereby is not readily discernible. True, the simple addition of some other forms, such as *di* and *ag*, provides the possibility of looking up such forms as *digress, digression* and *aggression*, thus shortening the dictionary; but the manner in which the various semantic codes are to be attached to these forms, so that a combination of the semantic codes for *ag* and *gress* and *ion* will produce the semantic characteristics of *aggression*, is rather difficult to conceive; nonetheless, such an organization has been attempted in at least one case.

While such an attack on the overall morphology of a language may seem inefficient, there are areas where this approach is more desirable. Certain sciences, particularly chemistry, have immense vocabularies which can both be analyzed in this way and are susceptible to translation into other languages on the basis of operations performed on the individual components, and on the manner in which they are combined. Thus, it is possible to translate the corresponding Russian form into the English *4-halogen-2-chlorobutane-2* precisely by analyzing it into six components, transferring them to their English form, and combining them again in the same order. One can readily think of other examples, perhaps not so complex, which might be handled in the same way, e.g., *Russo-Japanese*.

Another way in which a specialized morphological analysis has proven useful is in dealing with words not found in the dictionary. If these words can be shown to have certain components which indicate that they are part of the international vocabulary of science, there may be excellent odds that the same form can be modified and used in the target language. Studies of this from Russian to English have not been particularly fruitful, but such correspondences can be very useful in French to English translation. Assume that the word *polymeriserait* is not found in the dictionary. A comparison with the entries in the subdictionary of terminations provides matchings for the portion *erait*. This matching provides the information that the form is a third person singular conditional of a verb. Further testing reveals that the French verb probably corresponds to an English verb having the suffix *ize*. The assumption is made that the form may be transferred into English as *would polymerize* and this assumption is well founded.

It would seem that this more detailed morphological analysis is only of value in the case of highly technical vocabulary where little semantic variation between languages is to be expected.

Whatever the nature of the morphological analysis of a highly inflected language, it is extremely probable that some of the forms will continue to be ambiguous. Specifically, in Russian, masculine inanimate nouns, neuter nouns, and certain feminine nouns have the same form in the nominative singular and in the accusative singular. Difficulties of this type can only be resolved during the syntactic analysis, when the interaction of the noun with adjectives, prepositions, or other function classes will resolve the ambiguity.

2 Processing

2.1 Segmentation

Segmentation, or sentence separation, has not always been recognized as a necessary component of a machine-translation system. Some systems have ignored it entirely, others have divided it up in such a way that there is no unified segmentation process. Still other systems have made it so important that it is the first routine to be utilized once the dictionary lookup and any morphological analysis have been completed.

The purpose of segmentation is to divide the text into easily manageable segments. An obvious way to do this is to divide it into text sentences. The text sentences, however, vary considerably in their complexity, and in many cases it is possible to segment the text sentence further into its component main clause and subordinate clauses so that each of these can be treated as a separate unit. Segments of this sort have sometimes been referred to as machine sentences. When the segmentation routine works well, each machine sentence can be expected to contain one subject and one predicate. There may be different kinds of predicate, depending on the structure of the language under analysis. In Russian, for example, the predicate may be a noun structure, an adjective structure, a prepositional phrase, or a verb string, and if it is a verb string, it may or may not be followed by one or more objects or complements in predictable declensional cases, such as accusative, dative, instrumental, and so on. In standard English, it is reasonable to anticipate that the predicate will always contain a verb string, and that the verb string may be followed by an object, by a complement, by two objects, by an object and a complement, or by none of these.

Accurate segmentation of a text sets very definite bounds on the area in which syntactic and semantic searches need be carried out, and so segmentation of some sort is a necessity in any multi-pass system where the processing moves freely back and forth through the text. In a well arranged single-pass system where the processing proceeds in strict sequence, usually from left to right, there is of course no need for setting the left and right boundaries of the area to be searched.

Segmentation may prove disadvantageous in any system if the segmentation boundaries are so rigorously observed that it becomes difficult to go into earlier segments to determine, say, the antecedent of a pronoun, or to establish whether a particular term has already been used so that in building up an English translation the definite article *the* might be preferable to the indefinite article *a*. Again, where semantic matching is used, it may prove misleading to confine the search strictly to the immediate segment.

The process by which segmentation is achieved will probably have many characteristics in common, whatever language is being processed. Marks of punctuation, especially commas, are especially important, as are conjunctions such as *since* or *because*, disjunctives such as *moreover* and *however*, and special verbal forms such as the English participle or the Russian gerund.

One viable segmentation procedure for English operates in the following manner. The search begins at the beginning of the text, or at the last mark of final punctuation which has been recognized as a segmentation boundary. All commas that are passed are recorded, and parenthetical marks of punctuation, such as parentheses, quotation marks, dashes and so on, are coded as boundaries of inserted combinations which are to be regarded as unitary. The search stops moving to the right when a mark of final punctuation is reached. The search then moves to the left through the text sentence which has just been delimited, and tests each comma in terms of its relationship to conjunctions and participles, establishing other segmentation boundaries where certain specified combinations occur. The leftward movement stops when it reaches the mark of final punctuation from which it began. The search then moves to the right again and tests each item which might be a conjunction, and which is not preceded by a comma, and establishes further segmentation boundaries as necessary. For this last pass, it is frequently necessary to call in subroutines which are designed to resolve common types of ambiguity between conjunctions and prepositions; for example, *for* and *since* may have either function. A further check on the distribution of verb strings in the segments already established is necessary to establish the boundaries of those clauses (nominal or relative) in which the conjunction has been omitted, a fairly common feature of colloquial English which is becoming relatively common in written English also.

The segmentation process will not only divide the text sentence into clauses, but will show the interrelation of these clauses among themselves, and so develop essential information for the buildup of an adequate translation in the target language. It will be more easily feasible under these circumstances to have the structure of the target sentence vary from the structure of the source sentence in cases where the target language prefers less complex sentences than are usual in the source language.

2.2 Idioms

Idioms may be defined in various ways. A common definition is that an idiom is a group of words the meaning of which is different from the sum of the meanings of the individual words and of the syntactic pattern which binds them together.

But some machine-translation systems have taken a broader view and have defined as idioms all of those combinations which the system in its present state of development is incapable of translating adequately. With this kind of definition, it is anticipated that the number of idioms will decrease as the system develops, but one must not expect, even so, that the system will be developed to the point where there are no idioms whatsoever.

The basic problem of the idiom is that it is best looked up not as a series of words, but all at once as a group. Various devices have been tried for achieving this effect.

It is much more feasible now than it was earlier to incorporate idioms into the dictionary as individual entries. This presumes that if the first word of an idiom is found in the text, a search will be made to see if the subsequent words of the idiom follow in due order; if they do, the entire collocation is treated as one unit and given whatever dictionary information occurs with the idiom in the dictionary.

Desirable as this may seem from certain points of view, there are difficulties which may make this solution seem less reasonable.

Naturally, idioms may be considerably longer than single words are. If the field provided in the dictionary is of fixed length, and must be extended so as to include the longest idiom, there may be an undesirable amount of empty space in cases where the entry word is quite short. If the field for the entry word is of variable length, this problem does not arise.

Again, the same idiom may occur in a number of forms with different declensional or conjugational endings. If the idiom is to be listed only once, then those items which are inflected must be entered as split stems, and some morphological process must be used to check what inflections occur in the text, whether they are compatible with the various stems and with each other, and how they affect the meaning and function of the idiom. The ordinary morphological analysis found in most systems will not handle idioms of this sort without considerable expansion.

Situations have been tried in which the idiom is listed with some special character indicating the length of the inflections, and their relative position in the idiom. This special character will be matched in the lookup process with any text letter which occurs. If a string of the text matches the idiom perfectly in terms of length of items and spacing, then an attempt is made to establish the inflectional relationships within the idiom. In this case, since the idiom in one form may have longer inflections than the same idiom in another form, it may be necessary to list the idiom as many times as there are variations in the pattern of length of the inflections.

At least one system simply listed every idiom in full in the dictionary in as many different forms as occurred, and lookup would only be achieved if a stretch of the text matched one of these idiom sequences at all points. In this particular case, it seemed inadvisable to try to incorporate the idioms into the general dictionary, and a special dictionary of idioms was set up to hold them.

Another difficulty in the listing of idioms is that an idiom which consists of, say, four words may not necessarily have the four words in immediate sequence in some texts. Extraneous material of one sort or another may interrupt the idiom. Thus, if a system treated *turn off* as an idiom in English, it would have to allow for the contingency where the idiom occurs in a sequence such as *turn the light off*.

These various factors generally conspire to make it seem desirable to have the idioms listed in a separate dictionary, and the usual procedure will then be to look up the words of the text in the general dictionary first and then, if necessary, in the idiom dictionary. The necessity is usually indicated by providing a special field in the general dictionary for a code which will show that that individual word participates in some idiom or other. If, in checking through the information from the general dictionary, a sequence of words is found each of which has an idiom code, then the idiom dictionary is checked to see if the sequence is indeed to be considered as an idiom. In some cases words are given two codes to indicate either that they constitute the first word in an idiom, or that they constitute a subsequent word; recourse to the idiom dictionary would be indicated only where the idiom codes indicated first an initial word followed by a number of possible subsequent words.

Another approach to the problem of idioms involves focusing on one particular word in the idiom, usually the least frequent word, and assigning it a special code in the general dictionary. When this special code is found during the search in the idiom routine, a particular subroutine is called in to test whether the word is participating in any of the idioms in which it is known to take part. The subroutine is so constructed that it is capable of delimiting the idiom and of assigning the appropriate grammatical code to replace the codes found in the general dictionary for the individual words comprising the idiom.

However idioms are handled, it is necessary to have some means of taking certain groups of words, treating them as a unit, and assigning grammatical functions and meaning to this unit.

2.3 Exclusion

In the translation of a natural language text, it may become necessary to exclude certain items from the translation process. This is usually done because these items do not need to be translated. Items may also be excluded because they are in a list, and can be translated item by item, since there is limited syntactic interdependence among the items and the usual analysis need not be carried out.

Other stretches of text which are candidates for exclusion include abbreviations, formulae, numbers, particular signs, such as the per-cent sign or the degree sign, many punctuation marks, the various mathematical operators, Greek letters, Roman numerals, anything in a language other than the source language, single words contained within formulae, and words in lists.

These items may be recognized in various ways. If they occur in the dictionary, they may have special exclusion codes which show that they are simply to be transferred into the target language without change. If they are not written in the alphabet of the source language, the keypunch format will undoubtedly have provided for special signs to indicate this fact, and these signs serve as the basis for exclusion. Words which are simply not in the dictionary, even though they are legitimate words in the source language, cannot be handled by the system, and so are usually excluded.

The source language words which occur in lists, or as isolated items in the midst of formulae, would simply be translated without grammatical analysis.

In a sense, exclusion achieves much the same end as idiom processing, since, in both cases, strings of items which cannot or need not be treated individually are marked off as unitary, and are not analyzed. The idiom processing, however, assigns a grammatical function to the idiom while the exclusion process does not assign a grammatical function to the items which are excluded. This is done by interpolation.

2.4 Interpolation

When a stretch of numerals or formulae or symbols appears in a text, a speaker normally reads it off in words. Many of these words are inflected, and these inflections imply specific function in the sentence in which the numerals and so on occur. Thus, though these items may have been excluded because it is not necessary to translate them, but simply to transfer them unchanged from source to target language, it is nonetheless necessary to give due attention to the way in which they affect the non-excluded parts of the text. This is particularly true with Russian numerals, which tend to force the occurrence of a particular case and number in the noun which follows. The 'equals' sign in Russian is usually followed by a noun in the dative case. Roman numerals in Russian may function as nouns in some cases, such as designations for hours, but as adjectives in other cases, such as designations for centuries.

The interpolation process endeavors to assign to excluded items as much information as is possible about the relationship of the excluded item to the rest of the sentence. This information is necessary in the syntactic analysis, which endeavors to determine the structure of the sentence.

2.5 Gap analysis

It is usually desirable to include with interpolation and exclusion a method of gap analysis. The exclusion process excludes both items that fall into certain recognizable categories and also items which prove to be unrecognizable in that they are not found in the dictionary. While the interpolation endeavors to supply functional information about those items which are recognized and excluded, the gap analysis endeavors to do the same for those items which are not recognized. Gap analysis is usually more successful in highly inflected languages than in others.

If, in a Russian text, the word MARGAETS4 occurs as the result of a mispunching, the word will not be matched in the dictionary. Nonetheless, there is a high degree of possibility that it is an intransitive verb in the third person singular; it is clearly not past, and it is more probably present than future. This information could be derived by matching the form against various endings in the subdictionary of endings that is used in connection with the split dictionary in the dictionary lookup process. This knowledge will not help significantly with the problem of how the form is to be translated, but it may prove very important in establishing the syntactic interconnections in the sentence, and so help significantly with the other items.

The analysis of such forms as *polymeriserait*, discussed previously, would be handled under gap analysis.

In some cases the endings may prove to be more ambiguous than in the case cited, and some sort of disambiguation procedure will have to be included in the gap analysis.

2.6 Syntactic analysis

Once the system has established the boundaries within which the syntactic search is to be made, and has further established which items are to be treated singly and which are to be grouped as idioms, syntactic analysis becomes easier. Of course, single-pass systems endeavor to operate on all of these problems simultaneously. Most multi-pass systems, however, tend to divide them among a number of routines. In such a case, the syntactic analysis is often divided into a number of levels, establishing smaller syntactic groups first, and the overall syntactic pattern later. The establishment of the smaller syntactic groups can be distinguished by the name syntagmatic analysis.

The nature of the syntagmatic analysis will vary considerably from language to language. In Russian, much depends on the case of the noun or adjective and on the form of the verb. A certain amount of information can be derived from the order of the words. In English, on the other hand, much more depends upon the order of the words, and variations in form of nouns, adjectives and verbs are of less help.

Another important factor is the way in which the linguist classifies words into function classes. The traditional grammatical description of English is woefully inadequate and confusing. The same may be said, to one extent or another, of the school grammars of practically any language. The kind of grammatical analysis which is necessary for computational work requires much more subclassification of items than is commonly used in teaching. English nouns, for example, divide into four subclasses, and individual items in each class have their own idiosyncracies. These subclasses are illustrated by the forms *glass* in the following sentences.

I found some glass.	(uncountable)
I found two glasses.	(countable)
I found two pairs of glasses.	(plurale tantum)
I never found Professor Glass.	(particular)

If these sentences are translated into Russian, four quite different forms must be used for *glass* or *glasses*. In the examples given here, syntactic clues clearly differentiate the four types, but ambiguous examples are easy to devise.

The syntactic difficulties exemplified by *glass(es)* are, of course, peculiar to English. Other languages have their own peculiarities, too numerous to be exemplified in this survey.

Certain patterns of syntagmatic combination are, however, sufficiently common in a variety of languages that they may be mentioned specifically here.

Endocentric structures are those in which one word of the structure determines the syntactic function of the entire structure. This word is commonly called the head of the structure. The head can function by it-self, or it can be expanded by various premodifiers and postmodifiers which, however, do not change the function of the entire structure, but form a homogeneous group with it. In Russian, many of the modifiers of the head are in agreement with it, that is, they are in the same inflectional category as the head. If the head is a noun in the accusative case, and is accompanied by two modifying adjectives, these adjectives will also be in the accusative case, and the whole unit can be treated as being essentially a noun in the accusative case. In English, the relationship of the modifiers to the head is generally one of order, and the modifiers fall into a number of order classes which precede or follow the head and each other in regu-lar patterns.

Whatever analysis procedure is used must establish the first item, the head, and the last item of such endocentric structures, and mark each item composing the structure with some code which will show that the structure is cohesive.

Exocentric structures are those which have a grammatical function which is different from that of any of the items composing the structure. Thus, in English, a preposition and a following endocentric noun struc-ture comprise an exocentric structure which functions adverbially. In ex-ocentric structures, there is usually one item, such as the preposition, which is fairly easily identifiable and which is predictably followed by another structure of a particular type, such as a noun or an endocentri-cally expanded noun structure. In Russian, there are some prepositions which typically follow the noun structure; this is not particularly common in English. In English, there are at least four sentence patterns in which the noun structure is removed from its position after the preposition, usually to be placed at the beginning of the sentence. This arrangement is practically non-existent in Russian.

Coordinated structures are those which are composed of a number of items all having the same grammatical function, and linked together by special coordinators such as *and, but* or *or* in English. Coordinated struc-tures of this sort are usually easily recognizable because of the coor-dinator, and once it has been established what the function class of the coordinated items is, the limitations of the coordinated structure are fairly easy to determine. Of course, if the coordinate structure consists of a number of nouns, and each of the nouns is endocentrically expanded, there are certain difficulties in establishing the fact that it is nouns which are coordinated unless the limits of the endocentric noun structures have already been established.

A specific type of structure is that in which a verb, or some form derived from a verb, requires particular structures to accompany it. Some English verbs make no requirement (*sleep, faint*); others require an object (*want, cut*); others require a complement (*be, seem*); others require two objects (*give, promise*); and still others require an object and a complement (*call, make*). Certain forms (*call, make*) may fit in more than one of the above patterns. The object may be a pronoun, a noun, a gerund, an infinitive, or a noun clause; both the infinitive and the gerund are derived from verbs and they may in turn require a fresh assortment of objects and complements; the noun clause is a subordinate sentence which requires its own analysis. Complements may be any of those items which comprise objects, but may be adjectives or certain types of adverb in addition. It is a rare verb which allows for all of these possibilities; most verbs make a specific selection as to what varieties of object and complement they will allow, so that the government patterns of verbs in English are many and varied, and the traditional division of verbs into transitive, intransitive, and copulative is simply insufficient. The patterns for Russian verbs are similarly complex; they are less complex in that Russian does not have a gerund like the English gerund, and they are more complex in that the various objects and complements must be in specific cases for specific verbs, and these may change if the verb is made negative.

All of these types of syntagmatic structure may be interconnected in a multitude of ways, so that an endocentric structure may contain an exocentric structure which may in turn contain an endocentric structure which contains a coordinate structure. It is therefore necessary to devise a method of marking these structures in such a way that their interrelation among themselves will be perfectly clear.

The results of the segmentation process are particularly important in the syntagmatic analysis. No syntagmatic structure should cross a segmentation boundary unless the segmentation boundary marks a parenthetical insertion, in which case the stretches of text before and after the parenthetical insertion must be treated as a unit, and the syntagmatic structure must be recognized as being divided by the insertion.

The proper delimitation of syntagmatic stretches is also particularly important in rearrangement, which will be described later.

Specific difficulties in syntagmatic analysis arise in particular languages.

Corresponding to the English *every decision independent of outside influences* Russian and German may have constructions which would translate literally as *every independent of outside influences decision* or *every of outside influences independent decision*. In each of these two latter cases the endocentric structure *every independent decision* is interrupted by an exocentric structure which postmodifies only one component of the endocentric structure (*independent of outside decisions*). Structures which interlace in this fashion have been called nestings.

Other syntactic structures are even more discontinuous. English examples are: *He* bought *the store* out; What *did you come* for; *that is the man I gave it* to; the last example has the additional difficulty that the prior component of the discontinuity (*who* or *that*) has been omitted from the structure.

Since nestings are frequent in technical writing in German and Russian, the analysis of these languages is thereby more difficult. Since nestings require considerable rearrangement when translated into such a target language as English or French, the proper synthesis of the target language is rendered more difficult. Fortunately, formal written English still does not exhibit as many discontinuities as spoken English.

In a highly inflected language, such as Russian, the syntagmatic analysis is the point at which a great deal of morphological and syntactic ambiguity is resolved. A number of Russian prepositions govern more than one case, with related changes in meaning. One and the same ending may indicate more than one case in particular adjectives and another ending may indicate a different assortment of cases in particular nouns. The morphological analysis can do no more than to demonstrate what cases are possible. It is during the syntagmatic analysis that a definite decision can be made. For example, suppose that the six Russian cases are represented by the digits from 1 through 6. The preposition S may govern one of three cases, 2, 4 and 5. The adjective BOL6WO1 may be any of the six cases in the singular, depending on whether it is masculine or feminine. The noun form RADOSTI may be cases 2, 3 or 6 in the singular or 1 and 4 in the plural. If these facts are lined up, doubling the case possibilities for the preposition, since it may govern either a singular or a plural, we arrive at the following display.

S	020450 020450
BOL6WO1	123456 000000
RADOSTI	023006 100400

From this information it is clear that if these three Russian words constitute a cohesive syntagmatic stretch, the preposition must be governing
the second case, with the result that both adjective and noun will be in the
second case. This also clears up the ambiguity as to whether the noun is
singular or plural, since it can only be in the second case if it is singular.
The translation is 'because of (his) great happiness'. This example has
been chosen because it is a good indication of morphological disambiguation. It is not always possible to disambiguate in this way, unless a
sufficiently long syntagmatic string is developed. If only the noun and the
adjective were compared, it would be clear that they would have to be in
one of three cases (2, 3, 6) but further discrimination is not possible until
they are considered as part of the exocentric prepositional construct.

The major syntactic units are the subject and predicate, along with
those adverbial structures which modify the sentence as a whole. These
are not difficult to recognize once the syntagmatic groupings have been
recognized. In Russian, the subject is usually in the nominative case. Unfortunately, in too many instances, the nominative has the same form as
the accusative, and so other tests must be made. If the predicate contains
a verb in the past, the form of the verb will be masculine, feminine or
neuter, depending on whether the subject is masculine, feminine or neuter. If the verb is not past, it will have a plural form if the subject is plural
and a singular form if the subject is singular. In many cases, the subject
precedes the verb, but not frequently enough for this to be a dependable
criterion. With some verbs the subject is almost invariably animate (this
is a morphological category in Russian), and this fact is helpful, but there
remain a number of instances which can only be resolved by a study of
the meaning of the various components of the sentence, and by a knowledge of what is possible or impossible in the extralinguistic world. Turkish is a fairly highly inflected language, but the analysis can depend very
heavily on the order; the subject precedes the predicate, and the verb is
regularly at the end of the predicate. By far the greatest majority of English sentences have the subject preceding the predicate, and the verb at
the beginning of the predicate. Some languages, like Russian, have pred-
icates without verbs; the predicate may be an adjectival structure or it

may be a noun structure; such adjectives and nouns are in the nominative, the adjectives often being used in the short form. In addition, some languages, and again we may cite Russian, have minor sentence types where the subject may be conceived of as being in the genitive or the dative case, while the predicate is an irregular verb, or, more commonly, apparently an adverb. Minor sentence types in other languages may be formed from other components.

The syntactic analysis must therefore be closely tailored to the characteristics of the source language.

Most of the earliest systems were developed with one particular source language and one particular target language in mind; the result was that these systems addressed certain syntactic problems directly and specifically, and solved them reasonably well; such a solution is not necessarily a general solution, however, and, if the translation process is too closely bound to the interrelationships of one pair of languages, work with any other pair of languages might have to be begun afresh.

Largely as a result of the popularity of the transformational model of linguistic description, some of the later systems introduced the idea of syntactic analysis according to a particular model, with the expectation that the system would be sufficiently general that it could be utilized in dealing with more than one language pair. Such systems are of the general type that will be described later as theoretical systems.

In cases where the syntactic characteristics of the target language are considerably different, the process of generating an acceptable target sentence from the analysis of a widely different source sentence can only be solved if the source sentence is correctly and completely analyzed.

2.7 Semantic analysis

Despite the manifold difficulties and complications of the morphological and syntactic analyses and of the handling of idioms, the biggest problem in machine translation is probably the semantic analysis. There are a number of reasons why this should be so, but one of the chief reasons is that no adequate amount of semantic research has been done in any one language. Linguists have been devoting considerable attention to semantics in the past decade, but many of their results take the form of sweeping and rather shallow generalizations. Such semantic research as has shown depth has been confined to rather narrow areas.

The semantic analysis is undoubtedly very important. With an adequate system of semantic analysis, it might be possible to analyze a text almost entirely at the semantic level, and to have reference to syntactic and other similar levels of analysis only in the case of ambiguity on the purely semantic level.

Certain measures have been taken to reduce the semantic problem if not to solve it. Most of these attempts see, as the chief difficulty, the fact that a particular text word may have more than one meaning in general, and that it is necessary to decide on which of these meanings fits in any particular case.

A rather primitive way of meeting this difficulty is to have the computer print out all possible meanings of such polysemantic words. The user of the translation can then select the meaning which best fits the context and ignore the others. There are at least two difficulties with this procedure. One is that this method of reading is highly artificial and usually highly displeasing to the user. The other is that if there are a number of polysemantic words in a particular sentence it becomes increasingly difficult to follow the train of thought and to decide which possibility to choose; in fact, there might arise cases in which two seemingly valid interpretations or more could be drawn from the same piece of text. Of course a post-editor might alter the text, and so present the user with a single possibility in each case, but this introduces another human factor. While this might be acceptable in primitive machine translation, it clearly must be eliminated from any sophisticated system.

Another principle which has been introduced and used with some success is that of microglossarization. In many cases the text word has different meanings in different areas of discourse, as *plant* means one thing in botany and agriculture, and something quite different in the manufacture of machinery. Since it is expected that any text which is to be translated will confine itself largely to one area of discourse, polysemantic words will either have their various meanings coded to show which meaning is compatible with each area of discourse, or the dictionary will be modified so that there is a separate dictionary for each area of discourse which provides only those meanings which are compatible with that area of discourse.

It is not always the case, however, that differences in meaning correlate with differences in area of discourse. Sometimes the same word has different interpretations depending on the words with which it is associated in the text. Thus, the Russian word which is commonly translated into English as *black*, must be translated as *manual* if it is connected with *labor*, and must be translated as *ferrous* if it is to be connected with such words as *metal* and *metallurgy*. An attempt has been made to deal with this situation by entering a special lexical choice code in the dictionary for each polysemantic word, and by entering an identification code in the dictionary for all words which will trigger one of the specialized meanings. The lexical choice code on the polysemantic word directs the system to a subroutine which will search the environment of the polysemantic word to see if any of the surrounding items have an identification code to which the polysemantic word is sensitive. If such a code is found, then the appropriate specialized translation of the polysemantic word will be chosen. If no such identification code is found, the most generally useful translation of the polysemantic word is chosen. While this system works adequately as long as there are relatively few polysemantic words in the dictionary, when there are many, as there must be in any well developed system, the special lexical choice subroutines grow so numerous that they overbalance the rest of the system and present problems of storage and access. While the buildup of such routines might be justified on the basis that in the course of time they would present recurring patterns which would allow for consolidation, and perhaps lead to a generalized theory for handling the semantic analysis, it cannot be regarded as a viable solution in the long run.

How many different semantic categories would it be necessary to recognize in order to analyze a language adequately? Roget's Thesaurus has attempted such a classification for English, based on just over one thousand categories. It may be possible to argue that there are really only approximately half this number since one category frequently simply contains a list of antonyms to another category. It has been theorized that Roget's classification would be quite adequate for English, but the necessary research has not, I believe, been done.

The use of Roget's categories presumes that every word will be categorized by only one term. This may be feasible, but it also raises the question as to whether the categories themselves do not need to be defined in some way which will show how they interconnect and overlap.

A finely detailed semantic analysis would end up with more items than there are words in the dictionary, since, as has been pointed out, many of the words in the dictionary are polysemantic. However, the meaning of each item would be an aggregate of certain components, many of which would be repeated in other units. Thus, the components of the meaning of the English adjective *yellow* will include visibility and color and hue, the hue probably being defined by naming some object or objects which are typically yellow in color. A definition of *green* would probably use exactly the same terms of definition except that the specification of the hue would be different. Thus, the number of semantic isolates needed to define all terms might be considerably reduced, though it is difficult to say without considerable research to what extent their number could be reduced. When they are finally selected it will be possible also to answer the question as to the average number of isolates necessary for the definition of an English word. If there is any latitude in the number of isolates to be used, it will probably be advisable to choose a number which will keep the complexity of the combinations of the isolates within reasonable bounds.

2.8 Artificial intelligence

Even when the syntactic analysis and the semantic analysis are reasonably efficient, there may be areas which are ambiguous to the computer. We have already discussed the potential ambiguities of the form *glass* in English, citing examples where the syntax gives clues as to how the ambiguity is to be resolved.

It is easy, however, to generate an example where resolution of the ambiguity is considerably more difficult. Let us consider the sentence: *Where did this glass come from?*

In a real situation, the person who hears this question would look to see what is indicated by *this*, and he would know whether he was dealing with *glass* (uncountable) or *a glass* (countable).

If this sentence were found in a book, the ambiguity might be resolved by the following sentence. If the answer were *Tom broke the window*, then *glass* would be understood. If the answer were *Tom had a drink before he left*, then *a glass* would be understood.

While these contexts are definitive for the human being, they present no evidence which can be used in computational analysis to resolve the ambiguity.

If the computer were supplied with a bank of information to which references could be made to establish such information as that windows are made of glass (uncountable), and that a person drinks out of a cup or a glass (countable), a proper analysis, and, consequently, a proper translation could be made.

It has therefore been argued that machine translation will be practical only when the computer is provided with an encyclopedic store of information about the manner in which both the source language and the target language categorize the real world, and about the manner in which the real world is structured, independently of language. If this is so, then it will indeed be a long time before practical machine translation is realized.

There are indications, however, that an information structure of this sort is not invariably necessary.

There are many types of text to be translated. The point has already been conceded that it will be a considerable time before machine translation can deal adequately with various forms of literature. Undoubtedly an extensive information store would be needed for such a purpose.

But many people perceive that the immediate task of machine translation is to achieve good technical translations. There is far less variety in the way in which different languages structure our current, definitely international, science and technology. A speaker of one language will generally look at mathematics or jet engines in essentially the same way as the speaker of another language. A machine translation can therefore rely heavily on the user's understanding a technical translation with comparative ease because, presumably, he has a good understanding of what is reasonable and possible in that technical field. As is pointed out in Part III of this volume, such machine translation as is currently in use depends heavily and successfully on this fact.

It would appear, then, that the need for an information bank might vary depending on the nature and purpose of the translation process, and that, for technical translations, information banks, though helpful, are not strictly necessary.

With the completion of the semantic analysis, the analysis of the source language is at an end. The system can now transfer to the task of synthesizing the target language.

2.9 Synthesis

The raw materials for the synthesis consist of the analysis of the source text, the glosses in the target language which are available in the dictionary against the words of the source language, and the codes which follow these glosses in the dictionary and give indications of their inflectional and syntactic possibilities.

The glosses in the dictionary are presumably in one canonical form. Nouns are in the singular, verbs are uninflected or in some specific inflected form, items which can have more than one case are all in whatever case is considered basic, usually the nominative, and so forth. When a word which may be freely singular or plural in the source language is plural in the text, one can presume that the corresponding form in the target language will also be plural; it thereupon becomes necessary to develop the plural form from the canonical form. In the same way, if the source verb is in the past, the target verb will probably also be in the past, and the past form of the verb must be generated. Among the codes entered against the gloss, then, are those which indicate the manner in which these inflections are to be formed, and the synthesis must contain a routine which will generate the appropriate form.

It may happen that the target language will contain syntactic items which are not present in the source language. English has the definite and indefinite articles, while Russian has neither. If English is the target language and Russian the source, the appropriate articles must be selected and inserted into the output text. If target and source were reversed, the synthesis of the Russian would at worst simply ignore the English articles in translation, and at best, convert them into the rather subtle features of vocabulary selection and word order which Russians use to convey the meanings which the articles have in English. In many cases also, in going from Russian to English, it is necessary to insert prepositions in English where Russian merely uses a particular case form of a noun. Thus, the synthesis must contain special mechanisms for insertion and deletion.

Certain types of conversion may prove to be necessary. In most cases where Russian uses the infinitive of a verb, English may use either an infinitive or a gerund. The choice is not free; it depends on the syntactic function of the item. Turkish does not use forms corresponding to the English adverb of manner. Instead, the sentence is recast so that an adjective is used. Thus, an English sentence such as *She sings beautifully* must appear in Turkish in words which are a literal translation of the English *Her singing is beautiful*. The synthesis must contain a routine which recognizes this kind of difficulty, and makes the appropriate conversion.

There may be considerable discrepancies between the source language and the target language in terms of the order of the various components on the syntactic or syntagmatic levels. On the syntagmatic level, a Russian collocation which would translate literally as *rich with methane gases* must be rearranged in English to *gases rich in methane* if the original meaning is to be preserved. On the syntactic level, a Russian order such as *established was the tendency of the halides of mercury to combine with the halides of alkali metals* must be altered to *the tendency of the halides of mercury to combine with the halides of alkali metals was established*. The synthesis must contain a rearrangement mechanism which can handle such changes. In practical experience, rearrangement proves rather difficult. Unless the syntagmatic analysis is clear and complete, an attempt to move a subject or a predicate may produce unhappy results when only part of the subject or predicate is moved in the rearrangement process and the other part is left where it could not possibly belong. Some machine-translation systems have simply given up on an overall attempt to rearrange, or have confined their rearrangement routine to those cases where necessary rearrangements can be performed with a high measure of success.

In a sophisticated system, it is to be expected that there will not be a rearrangement routine as such, but that instead there will be a routine which will construct viable sentences in the target language instead of merely moving about segments derived from the organization of the source language. Varying measures of success have been achieved in this endeavor, but in most systems it remains a goal to be aimed at rather than an actuality.

3 Post-editing

It will be clear from what has been said previously about pre-editing, that post-editing is undesirable. It introduces the human being into the translation chain, and this results in higher costs for the end product, and also in greater variability in the end product.

The disadavantage of increased costs is obvious.

The disadvantages of variability may not be so readily apparent.

It has been shown that various human translators have their favorite translations for certain words, and that two translations of the same material by different translators will vary stylistically and in choice of vocabulary because of this fact.

A machine-translation system avoids 'elegant variation', and produces the same translation for a given term, presuming that there is no semantic variation, wherever that term occurs. If the machine-translation system produces a term which is not precisely apt, this fact will become obvious to the user much more quickly, because of the consistent use of the term, than it would in a case where a human being was, consciously or unconsciously, varying the vocabulary being used. People who make use of the admittedly imperfect translations which are currently produced develop a familiarity with, and perhaps an affection for, the idiosyncracies of the output text. In the course of time, having learned what is to be expected in output of a specific quality, they are able to interpret quite accurately what is put before them, partly on the basis of what they see in the printout, and partly on the basis of their own knowledge of the topic under discussion. In fact, there may be advantages in having the specialist interpret the translations himself, rather than have them worked over by a human translator who may very well know the language with which he is dealing, but not know sufficiently well the technical field in which he is endeavoring to make sense.

Under certain circumstances, there may be an advantage in having inadequate translations post-edited. Certainly, while a machine-translation system is being evolved, post-editing may be the only way of achieving reasonable output. When a system has largely evolved, however, further progress in its evolution will be achieved much more speedily if those who are building up the system receive feedback from the ultimate user who understands the subject matter thoroughly, rather than from a specialist in translation who does not.

As long as items occur in the text which are not adequately listed in the dictionary, some kind of human intervention will be needed. Such intervention should be held to an absolute minimum, and that minimum will grow smaller and smaller with use.

4 Types of systems

4.1 Empirical vs. theoretical

The problem of machine translation has been attacked in many ways, but it is possible to classify these ways under two chief headings. Machine-translation systems have tended to polarize around the empirical approach or around the theoretical approach.

The empirical approach usually starts with a particular piece of text, and determines what must be done in order to secure a satisfactory translation of that text. Then another text is adduced, and the system is expanded so that it can cope with the new material. By this means, a system is achieved which is capable of translating any text which is presented to it, since, after 200,000 running words in any technical field have been processed, all possible problems are expected to be met and incorporated into the system, and the dictionary is complete, except perhaps for personal and geographic names.

The theoretical approach begins by postulating the adequacy of some particular model of language description, and evolves a rule format appropriate to that model. All aspects of the translation process are then stated as rules of the chosen format.

Both the empirical and the theoretical approaches tend to evolve specific characteristics which are by no means essential to the specific approach, but which are strongly favored by it.

Thus, the empirical approach tends to evolve as a bipartite system, consisting of the dictionary and the procedure (or system). The dictionary is characteristically expansively coded, and contains its information in a series of fields following each entry; any of these may be investigated in the course of the procedure either independently or in combination. The procedure consists of an elaborately programmed investigation of the text, and it is brought into play once the dictionary lookup is completed. Unless due care is exercised to ensure that the procedure is a combination of independent subroutines, each of which can be modified without affecting the others, any change in one area may have such far-reaching ramifications that it becomes necessary to rewrite the procedure periodically in order to preserve its consistency. It is clear that the procedure will in the course of time evolve into a specialized programming language for the handling of the specific translation problem which it was designed to meet, and that, eventually, a series of such specialized programming languages might be combined into a generalized programming language particularly adapted to problems of translation.

Because of its nature, the empirical system tends strongly to evolve as a context-sensitive decision-making system. The fact that it is context-sensitive may seem to limit its breadth of application, but this is no defect to the empiricist, because he sees his task as the development of a system which will actually operate; when it has been discovered what steps are necessary to produce an operating system, or series of systems, a generalized theory of such systems can be evolved. The fact that the empirical system makes decisions at various points in the procedure has an advantage in that the more improbable possibilities are discarded, and what remains is thereby more manageable both in terms of processing and storage; there is a disadvantage, however, in the fact that, if a wrong decision is made, there may be no possibility of backtracking and of checking whether another decision would have produced a happier result; the more sophisticated empirical systems are therefore designed in such a way that it is possible to return to any point of decision and choose some other possibility if there is evidence that the final analysis was unsatisfactory.

There is a strong tendency also for an empirical system to be a multi-level system and a multi-pass system. In a multi-level system, the processing of the text is accomplished at different and separate levels, so that the morphological analysis is completed first, on the basis of the codes found in the dictionary, and the output from this level is used as the input for the basic syntactic level. On the completion of the basic syntax, during which the dictionary endings are used, and other new codes may be generated by the program, the output is used as the input for a more advanced syntactic pass. This process continues until all parts of the operation are completed. The fact that a system is multi-level strongly implies that it is decision-making, since it is economical to close off each level as it is completed, carrying only the coded text to the next level.

A multi-pass system is one in which the procedure scans backward and forward through the text, attacking each problem according to a system of priority which is built into the program, and which depends on the nature of the problem rather than on its position in the text. A problem may be attacked more than once if there is insufficient or ambiguous information generated on the earlier occasions, and the final pass through the text is usually a check to see that everything which is to be handled at that particular level has indeed been dealt with.

The theoretical approach, on the other hand, tends to evolve as a tripartite system consisting of a dictionary, an algorithm and a grammar. The dictionary is characteristically, but not necessarily, tersely coded; the information for each entry consists of one field which is not analyzable in any way, but which must be treated as a unit. The grammar consists of rules which follow the established format, and which have as their components the codes which are found in the dictionary against particular entries. These rules can generally be typified as consisting of a resultant and a number of formants; if in the course of the operations a resultant is found, it can be replaced by the string of formants given in the rule, and conversely, if the string of formants is found, they can be subsumed under the resultant. This system of rules allows the operation to proceed either in the direction of analysis or the direction of synthesis, and one of the advantages of such a system is that the same analysis can serve whether the language analyzed is the source language or the target language. Since all operations are expressed in terms of rules of one possible conformation, the algorithm can be written so as to handle these rules, and, once it is written, it need never be changed in any way, the presumption being that all modifications in the system as the system increases in scope will be achieved only by writing more rules.

The theoretical system tends strongly to evolve as a context-free decision-postponing system. The fact that it is context-free allows it greater breadth of application, so that, once the system has been evolved, additional languages may be added to it, either as source or target languages, by the creation of a dictionary and a grammar. The fact that the theoretical system is a decision-postponing system has the advantage that no possibility, however remote, is discarded until the time comes to make the final decision as to the choice of various interpretations of the text; there is a disadvantage, however, in the fact that, in the typical theoretical system, the number of possibilities developed in one text increases geometrically at such a rate that it becomes extremely difficult if not impossible to keep track of all of them, no matter how capacious the storage facilities of any contemporary computer; if the procedure has had built into it a means of handling only one text sentence at a time, the amount of storage space required is considerably reduced, but there may be theoretical considerations which militate against limiting the procedure in this way.

There is a strong tendency for a theoretical system to be also a single-level single-pass system. All of the processing of the text is planned to be accomplished in one pass through the text, and this pass proceeds in one direction only, commonly from left to right. In actual fact it has been found exceptionally difficult to build a system to such rigorous specifications, and certain modifications of the single left-to-right pass have been introduced. Thus, leftward regressions of one word are sometimes permitted. Alternatively, after the single pass is completed, another pass is made to check whether the entire text has been covered without either gaps or overlaps. Presumably, at a later date, a theoretical system would rid itself of these temporary aberrations, and would achieve its goal of completing all of the work in a single pass.

Given these two widely differing trends in dealing with machine translation, it is clear that two descriptions of the processes involved will be needed. The empirical system will be discussed first, because the various details can be better isolated in an empirical system. A description of a typical theoretical system will follow.

4.2 A typical empirical approach

The empirical system to be described here is essentially that developed at Georgetown University and known as the GAT (Georgetown Automatic Translation).

The typical empirical dictionary contains for each entry the entry codes, the glosses, and the gloss codes. The entry codes are arranged in a number of fields, and they record all desirable information about the entry. Each field can be checked separately, and usually the various positions in each field can also be used separately. The glosses give the acceptable translations of the entry. Usually there is one gloss; if there is more than one gloss, then special codings are required to serve as an indication of the conditions under which each gloss is to be selected. The gloss codes give all desirable information about the morphology and syntax of the glosses in the target language. There may also be, in the dictionary listing, blank spaces in which codes can be generated in the course of the processing. Blank spaces of this sort are usual in fixed length dictionaries, such as the original GAT dictionary; they are not found in variable length dictionaries, such as the SLC dictionary, which is also used in connection with the Georgetown system. On the whole, fixed length dictionaries tend to be uneconomical, since the amount of coding for a preposition is considerably less than that required for a verb; to have the listings of both preposition and verb occupying the same amount of space in the dictionary is clearly wasteful.

The Russian dictionary is largely a split dictionary. This presumes the need for another smaller dictionary of endings, with the result that a great deal of the morphological analysis is performed in the course of the lookup.

Following the morphological analysis there are a number of levels designed to resolve difficulties in the text. These have been covered in the general description of the problem areas of machine translation. There is a level for sentence segmentation, a level for idioms and collocations, a level for exclusion, a level for interpolation and a level for gap analysis. The output for the morphological analysis serves as the input for segmentation, and so on through all of the levels mentioned.

At this point, the main work of the analysis begins. There is a level for syntagmatic analysis followed by a level for syntactic analysis. These are followed by a level which is called Lexical Choice in the GAT, and which is a rudimentary method for dealing with semantic problems. If an entry has more than one gloss, searches are made in the environment of the textword which matches that entry in an attempt to determine whether there are specific other textwords which will give a valid indication as to which of the various glosses is to be chosen.

At this point, transfer takes place, and the emphasis now shifts from the source language to the target language.

There is a level for the morphological synthesis of forms in the target language. There is a level for article and preposition insertion. There is a level for rearrangement, in which the order of items in the target language is made as compatible as possible with the normal word order of that language. As was pointed out previously, this has proven to be one of the most difficult aspects of the work.

After the rearrangement, printout occurs.

The empirical approach has frequently been condemned as *ad hoc*, and as having no underlying and unifying theoretical position. These criticisms are really tantamount to restating the fact that the system is empirical.

The empirical approach has produced usable output of texts selected at random.

4.3 A typical theoretical approach

The ensuing description of a theoretical model of machine translation is based largely on the phrase-structure model of analysis such as that used at the University of Texas Linguistics Research Center. Other theoretical models, such as the dependency grammar model or the predictive analysis model, may differ at points from the phrase-structure model, but these differences are not great when the various theoretical models are considered in contrast to the empirical models. Questions of editing and of transcription are essentially the same for all systems. The ordering of the components of the rule may vary, and the order in which the rules are applied in the text, but these differences are trivial.

The typical theoretical dictionary usually has just one code against the entry, and this code is unanalyzable; if it is used, it must all be used. All of the nouns in the dictionary might receive a code beginning with N, and the N may be of mnemonic advantage to the human being working with the dictionary, but it cannot be read off by the computer as an indication that the item is a noun. Any attempt to analyze the dictionary coding in this way would result in a very considerable complication of the algorithm, and one of the basic principles of a theoretical system is that the algorithm should have one simple well-defined task to perform; once it is built to perform that task, no changes should be necessary. The principle of the indivisibility of the dictionary code results, as we shall see, in a great proliferation in the number of grammar rules necessary; again, a basic principle of the theoretical system is that the bulk of the information stored in the system shall be contained in the grammar, and no limitation is put upon the number of rules in use.

In the dictionary lookup, the unitary dictionary code is set against each item of the text. The processing then is carried out using only the dictionary codes, and without reference to the actual words of the text; the analysis is therefore context-free.

A partial dictionary might look like this:

book	NCI23
man	NCA39
on	P37
saw	VV728
boardwalk	NCI23
the	T2

If one segment of the text reads

The man saw the book on the boardwalk,

the result of the lookup process will be

T2	NCA39	VV728	T2	NCI23	P37	T2	NCI23
The	man	saw	the	book	on	the	boardwalk

(Questions of capital letters and punctuation are handled differently in the different systems, and are ignored in this description. The spatial arrangement of text and codes is chosen to make this explanation clear; it should not be assumed to be the actual arrangement.)

The grammar is written in the form of rules. The rules have a fixed format, which may vary, but which usually indicates that a particular string of codes (the formants) can be interpreted as being equivalent to some other code (the resultant). In each rule there is only one resultant, but the number of formants may vary. There must of course be at least one. It is always possible to reformulate the longer rules in such a way that they can be expressed as a series of shorter rules, and thus a greater uniformity in the length of the rule can be achieved if this seems desirable.

For the purposes of this discussion the rule format will be that the first item is the resultant, and all subsequent items are formants. The presumption is that the resultant is equivalent to the string of formants, and vice-versa, only if the formants appear in the given order and without interruption. Thus, a rule such as

NPA   T2   NCA19

implies that, in the process of analysis, the succession T2 NCA19 can be considered as equivalent to NPA, and also, in synthesis, that NPA is equivalent to and can be replaced by T2 NCA19.

The rules are arranged in alphabetic order, and the order must be different for analysis from the order used in synthesis. In the system described here it proves useful to arrange the rules for analysis with the last formant in alphabetic order. For synthesis, the rules are arranged with the resultants in alphabetic order. A set of rules for the analysis of the sentence given above might look like this:

S	S	D4
NPA	T2	NCA39
NP	T2	NCI23
D4	P37	NP
VP	VV728	NP
S	NPA	VP

The algorithm is so constructed that it begins with a code attached to a textword and tests whether any rules end with that code. If there are such rules, a test will be made to determine whether the code attached to the preceding textword corresponds to the next to last (penultimate) formant of any of these rules. If so, the test is continued in an endeavor to match the antepenultimate formant with the text item preceding that last match, and this procedure is continued until a formant cannot be matched, or until all of the formants have been matched. If the matching is not complete, the rule is abandoned, and any other suitable rules are tested in turn. If there is a complete match, the entire string of formants is subsumed under the resultant. This is done in such a way that the resultant can now be considered the formant in another rule, in which case, none of the formants subsumed by it may take part in that rule. The subsuming of a group of formants under a particular resultant in this manner, however, does not prevent those formants from being tested as formants in some other rule. Nor does the search for applicable rules stop when one rule is successfully applied.

When the first code in the text is tested, no rule can be found to apply to it, either because there is no rule which ends with the formant, or, more probably, because there is nothing preceding it to match the penultimate formant of the rule.

The algorithm then focuses on the next code to the right, and tests whether there are rules in which this code is the last formant. If there are, the preceding code is tested against the preceding formant. If a match is made, the resultant is introduced into the system as a new formant which may be tested in the subsequent application of rules. By continuing in this fashion one or more analyses of the sentence will be obtained, if the rules are adequate, by the time the last code has been tested. Thus the testing moves in one single pass from left to right through the text. Admittedly, the application of the rules is retrograde, but the point at which this retrograde process begins shifts always and only to the right.

Given the brief text being used as an example, the dictionary and the set of rules, the analysis of the sentence would proceed in the following fashion (see Table 2a). Is there a rule which ends with T2? No. (Even if there were such a rule, it could not apply unless T2 were the only formant in the rule.) Move to the right. Is there a rule which ends with NCA39? Yes. Is there another formant to the rule? Yes. Does this formant correspond to the immediately preceding code, whether this is one of the original codes or whether it is a code introduced by the application of a rule? Yes. Is there another formant? No. Then subsume T2 NCA39 under NPA. Move to the right. Is there a rule ending in VV728? No. Move to the right. Is there a rule ending in T2? No. Move to the right. Is there a rule ending NCI23? Yes. Application of this rule leads to the subsuming of T2 NCI23 under the code NP. NP now becomes the subject of a search, and two rules are found which end with NP. The first does not apply. The second does apply and results in VV728 NP being subsumed under VP. Is there a rule which ends in VP? Yes. This rule is also found to apply, with the result that NPA VP is subsumed under S. Is there a rule ending with S? No. Move to the right. Since S now subsumes everything in the sentence up to and including NCI23, the next item to the right is P37. No rule ends with such a formant. No rule ends with the formant T2. Is there a rule which ends in NCI23? Yes. This rule succeeds with the result that T2 NCI23 is subsumed under NP. Is there a rule which ends with NP? There are two. The first of these succeeds with the result that P37 NP is subsumed under D4. Is there a rule which ends in D4? Yes. This rule succeeds with the result that S D4 is subsumed under S. This S now covers the entire text without gaps and without overlaps, and the tree structure which has been generated as emanating from this node S is accepted as a valid analysis of the sentence.

Table 2a

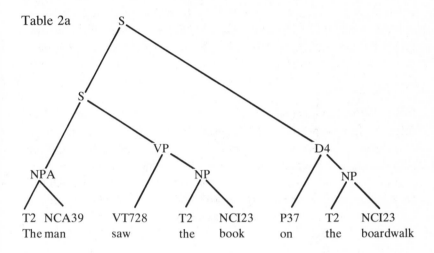

Table 2b

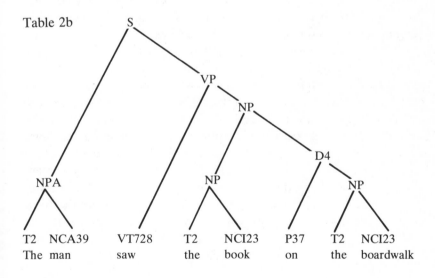

The example given here presents no complications, but it is easily possible to see what complications might arise.

The analysis of the sentence presumes that the man saw the book, and that the place in which this action took place is the boardwalk. At least one other interpretation is possible. Imagine that the man saw the book and that the book described the boardwalk. In this case, *the book on the boardwalk* should be interpreted as a unit at some level in the analysis rather than separated as it would be in the previous interpretation. A new rule could be introduced:

NP   NP   D4

If the first of the original rules were eliminated, the application of the rules would now produce the analysis in Table 2b.

If the new rule is introduced, but no rule is eliminated, the algorithm will develop two overlapping analyses of the same stretch of text. Since both of these analyses are possible, both covering the entire stretch with no gaps or overlaps, the algorithm will show that the text as it stands is ambiguous. Not all sentences have more than one valid interpretation, but, when they do, all possibilities are developed and preserved.

As the number of rules increases, the number of possible interpretations of any stretch of text likewise increases. Not all of these interpretations are valid. They may cover only part of the text because, while rules will associate the items in that stretch, there are no rules to associate that stretch with anything on either side of it, and so a partial analysis is started but comes to nothing. Such partial analyses can be very numerous.

Since the algorithm is built in such a way that it tries every possibility of analysis, and makes no decision among the various interpretations until the end of the processing, when only those interpretations which cover the entire text without gaps or overlaps are printed out, the storage of all of these analytic possibilities until such time as the final decision can be rendered presents a considerable problem. If the text is treated sentence by sentence, the problem is somewhat reduced, but the amount of storage needed may nonetheless be surprisingly large. Systems which endeavor to analyze large batches of text in one pass have on occasion lost many of the items that they were endeavoring to preserve because the information exceeded the storage capacity, with the result that some of the material was lost, with no control over whether the lost material was necessary or unnecessary for the final analysis.

In a system of this sort, where the dictionary contains a minimal amount of coding and the algorithm cannot really be said to contain any linguistic information whatsoever, practically all of the information in the system is included in the grammar. This fact alone would make the grammar very unwieldy, but there are other factors which conspire to increase its size.

It has been pointed out that the dictionary codings are unanalyzable in the usual theoretical system. When many of these systems were originally planned, it was felt that relatively few codes would be necessary for an adequate analysis. Thus, all nouns might simply be coded N, and all verbs V. As more experience was gained, it became obvious that much more subclassification would be necessary so that nouns, for example, must be distinguished as to whether they are countable, uncountable, pluralia tantum, or whether they fall into the category which has been traditionally designated by the term proper noun, and which is actually a complex of at least six different subtypes of noun. In addition, nouns have to be distinguished as to whether they are singular or plural, and this involves a large number of cross-classifications, because not all nouns which are morphologically plural are syntactically plural, and not all noun constructs which are syntactically singular are semantically singular. Nouns must further be distinguished as to whether they are personal or non-personal, and so on. As it became clear that a great deal more subclassification was necessary, the number of codes increased rapidly.

If it becomes necessary to write a rule which involves any of five classes of verb and of six classes of noun, since there is no way of generalizing the rule, separate versions must be written for every possible combination, so that a rule which might conveniently be stated in a few words will appear as thirty separate rules in the grammar. It is for this reason that the grammar threatens to become so enormous that it is very difficult for human beings to monitor it and to know exactly what it is capable of doing. Any monitoring which is done must be done by means of the computer, and this involves more programming than the fairly basic direct algorithm originally projected for this kind of system.

There is another difficulty with the grammar which must be overcome. All of the rules are necessarily of the same format. Otherwise the algorithm will not handle them. Unless this format is very carefully chosen, however, it may not be adequate to analyze all the structures of a language. Most rules deal only with items that are contiguous in the text. Many languages have structures which are not contiguous, such as the English verb *turn off* in such a combination as *Please turn the lights off*. There are ways in which this difficulty can be overcome, but they generally involve a rather artificial approach to the analysis, such as regarding *the lights off* as subsumable under one code which can then be matched with the code for *turn* to produce a structure *Turn the lights off*. Coordinated structures such as *bread and butter, John or Mary* may also be difficult to handle with this kind of rule. There is considerable doubt as to whether it is possible to evolve one single rule which will be pleasingly effective throughout all of the ramifications of a natural language.

It is clear that the rules as given are oriented largely toward syntactic analysis. They can be utilized equally well for morphological analysis. Thus a form such as WALKED in a dictionary lookup which utilizes morphological analysis might have a code such as VV3 assigned to WALK, and a code such as D1 assigned to ED and a rule to join the two which might read VVP3 VV3 D1. As in the case of the empirical systems, the splitting of textwords into much more than a stem and ending as exemplified here tends to be counterproductive.

It is also possible to construct rules which will deal with idioms. One way is to assign special codes to all of the words which compose an idiom, and then to write a rule in which those codes will be the formants leading to a particular and specialized resultant. Unfortunately, if one of the items in the idiom would have some other more general code if it were not in the idiom, it becomes necessary to duplicate all of the rules which have that general code, substituting the special idiom code of that word so that the word can be treated both as a member of an idiom and as a non-idiomatic word. Another manner of handling idioms is the following. Suppose the rule is to be amplified in such a way that the formants may be either codes derived from the dictionary, or pieces of the actual text. The general rules would continue to use the dictionary codes, but the idiom rules would use the text itself. If there is a convention that formants which are to be treated as members of the original text will be preceded by an asterisk, rules of the following type would be possible.

VVA63   *KICK   *THE   *BUCKET

With such a rule, if the idiomatic expression *kick the bucket* appeared in the text, it would be subsumed as one unit under the code VVA63.

Naturally it will be necessary to write a new rule for every inflectional variant of the idiom. Moreover, there is a diminution of the context-free character of the procedure.

We have already seen that the sentence

The man saw the book on the boardwalk

is capable of at least two syntactic interpretations. One of these interpretations, the second one given, is capable of two semantic interpretations depending on the meaning assigned to the preposition *on*. If *on* is equivalent to *about* or *concerning*, then the man saw the book which was written about the boardwalk. If *on* carries the sense of location, then the man saw the book which was in some respect located on the boardwalk.

Any single code which attempted to represent all of the syntactic and semantic peculiarities of *on* would be likely to have no generality at all; it would be specific only to the word *on*. In an analysis of English, it would rapidly develop that almost all of the so-called function words are so idiosyncratic that they would have to have their own code, and these codes would serve less to summarize a class than to identify the individual form. Again there would be a diminution of the context-free character of the procedure.

If the syntactic codes and the semantic codes are listed separately, the generality of the codes would be preserved, but it would no longer be possible to process a text by means of one single pass.

The organizational problem of establishing and maintaining a grammar merely for the syntactic rules is enormous. The development and monitoring of a single comprehensive grammar which would cover the morphological analysis, the syntactic analysis, the semantic analysis as well as such problems as idioms, interpolation, and so forth, would seem to be quite impossible.

It is perhaps for this reason that no theoretical approach has produced usable output of texts selected at random.

4.4 Melded systems

Computers are frequently classified as first-generation, second-generation, and third-generation computers. It has been suggested that the empirical systems of machine translation are first-generation systems, that the theoretical systems are second-generation, and that the third-generation system will be a melding of both the empirical and the theoretical. This is probably too facile an analogy.

There are, of course, various conceivable ways in which the two systems could be melded together, each of them giving up some of its characteristics. An example of such a system is that which is currently being developed for Russian-to-French translation at Grenoble in France.

But there is another way in which the two systems can interact.

One important difference between the empirical approach and the theoretical approach is that the empirical approach is basically oriented towards the human being, while the theoretical approach is oriented towards the computer. In general, the proponents of the empirical approach have been linguists who developed a knowledge of computational processes as their involvement in machine translation made it necessary for them to do so. The typical empirical approach is divided into a number of levels, or a number of modules, each of which can be grasped by the human mind, and controlled by human ingenuity. The interrelation among the various parts is likewise clear to the human being. Hence, it would seem, the empirical system is more advantageous for the human being to work with and to perfect.

The proponents of most of the theoretical systems were people whose primary interest was the computer, and who acquired some knowledge of linguistics as their machine-translation research made it necessary for them to do so. The theoretical systems are computationally efficient, but the simplification of the dictionary and of the algorithm results in the storing of by far the greatest bulk of the system in the grammar. The information in the grammar is expressed in rules which are well designed for the computer, but which carry very little mnemonic advantage for the human being, and they are too multitudinous for any human being to oversee and control. Increasing the number of research workers may only exacerbate the problem of control. Changeovers in personnel will further compound the confusion, unless a strict protocol is enforced on all of those who write the rules.

It seems probable, therefore, that an empirical system will evolve more rapidly and will achieve satisfactory results sooner. When the development of the empirical system is reaching a point of considerable stability, only a bare minimum of human intervention will continue to be necessary. It will then prove economical from the point of view of programming and data manipulation to convert the empirical system into a theoretical system which is equally efficient linguistically, and more efficient computationally. At this point the requirements of an adequate translation system will be clear. It will be possible to devise a rule format flexible enough to be used under all circumstances, rather than postulating that a rule of a certain form is adequate for the purpose, and then discovering, after much work has been done, that the rule is not effective, especially in particular situations. The computer can be programmed to convert the expanded coding typical of an empirical system to the terse coding typical of a theoretical system; the computer will do this much more accurately and consistently than even the most careful of human beings. The necessary rules can be written by the human being in terms of the expanded coding which he understands easily, and can then be reformulated by the computer to the form most convenient for the algorithm. The algorithm can be elaborated once a comprehensive rule format has been devised, and when it has been written, it will never need to be changed; this is the immense advantage of the theoretical system.

The preliminary research on the empirical system will serve the purpose of establishing the nature and extent of the problem of machine translation clearly and definitively. When the nature of the problem has been recognized as fully as possible, a rigorous and elegant solution of the problem can be devised.

PART III

Users' evaluation of machine translation

BOŻENA HENISZ-DOSTERT

Introduction

The conviction that machine-translation research should be directed to the needs of real users had always been part and parcel of the philosophy and guiding principles of the Georgetown Machine Translation Project (Dostert 1963:VII–XVII). It was reflected, on the one hand, in the choice of real texts as sources for deriving grammar rules and vocabulary. On the other hand, the developing methods were applied to real texts, which in turn served as the basis for guiding continued improvements in the translation programs. It was a simple consequence of those principles that the reactions and cooperation of real users should be sought. As early as the spring of 1964, a questionnaire aiming at obtaining users' evaluations had been devised and distributed to scientists who had already made use of the system, some of the results of which are mentioned later on. Work on the further development of the Georgetown Automatic Translation – GAT System (hence usually referred to as the "Georgetown System") – had to be almost totally discontinued as of the summer of 1964 because of lack of financial support. In the years that followed, the Georgetown System, in the form in which it existed in the summer of 1964, was actively used to make translations at the requests of scientists at two centers, one in Europe, and the other in the United States. Documented requests for machine translations exceed 20,000 pages. The translations were from Russian into English, and were made completely automatically, without any linguistic editing of the texts, either in preparation of the computer process or subsequent to it.

The two centers where translation activities were maintained were the Centro Europeo di Trattamento dell' Informazione Scientifica – CETIS (European Scientific Information Centre) – of the European Atomic Energy Community – EURATOM – in Ispra, Italy, and the United States Atomic Energy Commission's National Laboratory at Oak Ridge,

Tennessee. The two installations will hence be referred to as "EURATOM" and "Oak Ridge", respectively. The scientists whose dedication and efforts kept the activity going in view of financial and other problems were Dr. Sergei Perschke and Dr. H. Fangmeyer at EURATOM, and Dr. F. Kertesz at Oak Ridge.

In 1966 a report was published by the Automatic Language Processing Committee which came to be known as the ALPAC report, discussed in Part I, section 3.3, which contained the following statement:

> 'Machine translation' presumably means going by algorithm from machine-readable source text to useful target text, without recourse to human translation or editing. In this context, there has been no machine translation of general scientific text, and none is in immediate prospect. (*Language and machines* 1966: 19).

In view of the documented amount of unedited machine translation that had been made using the 1964 Georgetown System, the correctness of the above statement (and many others) in the ALPAC report needed reexamination. It was clearly important to assess actual users' evaluations of actual translations.

The first opportunity presented itself in the summer of 1971 when a visit was arranged to EURATOM, where, as it turned out, detailed records of machine-translation use had been kept. These led to the identification of some users. Preliminary discussions with a few users proved encouraging, since they were satisfied with the texts they had used, and even interested in machine-translation processes. These discussions provided some ideas for a questionnaire to sample users' reactions and opinions, which was subsequently developed.

Another source of encouragement was a visit to the European Translations Centre in Delft, Holland, which serves as an information and coordination organization for translation activities in several European countries, many of whose customers were users of machine-translation facilities at EURATOM. Numerous users' reactions had been obtained by this Centre and their very positive character served as a further stimulation.

The bulk of the data of users' evaluations was collected through the questionnaire in an interview situation in the summer of 1972 at EURATOM and in January 1973 at Oak Ridge. Section 1 contains an analysis of records of machine-translation activity at both centers, 2 describes the procedures of collecting the data on users' evaluations of translations, and 3 presents an analysis of the results of the questionnaire completed by the users. Much of the statistical data and the Appendix found here were earlier incorporated in the author's report on Users' Evaluation of Machine Translation (Henisz-Dostert 1973).

A grateful word is in order on the users' attitudes, who were most cooperative and friendly, and interested in what was involved in machine translation. They showed their familiarity with the aberrations of the texts, some of which were considered quite amusing 'classics', e.g., "waterfalls" instead of "cascades" (the users asked that this not be changed!). Very commonly, and understandably, they were interested in improvements and offered many suggestions. An example of an extreme attitude on the part of one user in this respect was that of "cheating" on the questionnaire by giving less positive answers than in oral discussions. When subsequently asked about this, he reacted with something like: "I use it so much, I want you to improve it, and if I show that I am satisfied, you will not work on it any more." Users' written comments, both in the form of reactions obtained from the clients of the European Translations Centre and those sent in lieu of a questionnaire or in addition to it, as well as comments inside the questionnaires, overwhelmingly showed quite positive attitudes. The reaction of professional translators was also quite interesting, ranging from an enthusiastic one on the part of a translator who worked with a large amount of machine-translation output, to a ridiculing one on the part of one who was asked to evaluate the translation of one article.

In 1972, prior to the analysis of the questionnaire results, a report came to the author's attention which provided a framework for some of the discussion of the results. The report was that of a conference on machine translation held at the University of Texas in 1971, which contained a statement that by coincidence expressed perfectly not only the philosophy and policy of the Georgetown researchers, but also the motivation for undertaking an investigation of users' evaluations of machine translation. The statement was made by the very influential scholar in the development of machine translation, Yehoshua Bar-Hillel, and it read as follows:

Every program for machine translation should be immediately tested as to its effects on the human user. He is the first and final judge, and it is he who will have to tell whether he is ready to trade quality for speed, and to what degree. (Bar-Hillel in Lehmann and Stachowitz 1971: 76)

The consistent views on the same topic of one of the first and foremost experts in the Georgetown System and machine translation in general, Paul Garvin, were reiterated in his excellent position paper in the Texas report of which this short statement is representative: "Clearly, the question of the quality of translation has to be related to user need: the greater the need, the more it is possible to compromise with quality" (Garvin in Lehmann and Stachowitz 1971: 114).

The results of the present investigation showed that the user is a willing, concerned and competent judge, and that no evaluation of machine translation, whether by linguists or other experts, can be considered complete and valid unless it includes an analysis of the attitudes of actual users.

Several other issues which were discussed in the Texas conference report and in the field of machine translation in general for a number of years, were reflected in, and shed light upon by users' evaluations as elicited through the questionnaire.

The issue of the correctness of a translation was discussed in the report with quotations from one of the leading authorities on the theory of translation, Eugene Nida, especially the following two: "... even the old question: Is this a correct translation? must be answered in terms of another question, namely: For whom?", and "In fact, for the scholar who is himself well acquainted with the original, even the most labored, literal translation will be correct, for he will not misunderstand it" (Nida and Taber 1969: 1, quoted in Lehmann and Stachowitz 1971: 2). In view of the users' opinions the latter quotation could be modified to read: "... for the scholar who is himself well acquainted with the subject matter...", since the results show that understandability of translation depends primarily on familiarity with the subject matter. Not unlike many other matters, the obvious importance of context becomes more obvious and convincing when supported by direct experience. In the case of machine translations what was quite understandable and clear in spite of imperfect rendition to, say, a specialist in heat transfer in fluid rod bundles, who had requested the translation, was not at all clear to the present author even though some language puzzles could be resolved. Correctness ties in, of course, with the problem of ambiguity which might present a source of misinformation. The judgments of the users indicate that mis-informativeness of machine translations is quite unlikely, the main reason being again the user's familiarity with the subject matter. With respect to scientific texts, the problem of ambiguity was dealt with by Bross *et al.* (1972: 1303–1307). They pointed out that surgeons would never interpret the commonly used sentence in surgical reports that "the patient left the operating room in good condition" to mean that the patient put away the instruments, mopped up the floor, and so forth.

The problem of the correctness of a technical translation has other facets, however, and in some of them machine translations appear to fare definitely better than human translations. One of these is the question of consistency, as was pointed out in the Texas report in the following statement: "Among the advantages of machine translation is consistency... any technical term need never be varied, unlike practice of many translators" (Lehmann and Stachowitz 1971: 10). Experiences with such and similar practices must have led the users of machine translations to make comments such as "machines do better than humans", "the machine is more honest", "machine translation is more intelligible [than human translation]" and that "... the translations sound like the computer just got off the boat, and they need to be improved. However, I have found that human translators frequently give the same translation as the machine for passages that don't make sense. The problem, of course, is jargon." Statistical analysis of users' answers in the questionnaire shows that human translations were considered far from perfect, and users even stated their clear preference for machine translations, in spite of the fact that these were said to require about twice as much time to read as original English texts.

Probably the most important two issues with respect to machine translation are its speed and quality. The users' evaluations showed that speed still left much to be desired. However, another factor connected with rapidity of access to translations is of considerable importance, namely the possibility of using texts only for scanning purposes, because, as one user put it, machine translation means "less labor than human", and so, as another user said, one can read it "like a newspaper". Garvin pointed this out (Lehmann and Stachowitz 1971: 114) by saying that "For many purposes, machine translation output will be only casually scanned rather than carefully read." Although the majority of users in this particular investigation indicated that they treated the texts as sources of information rather than scanning, it would undoubtedly be a fact that machine translations could help solve the problem of keeping up with literature if they were regularly and speedily available to scientists.

Quality, of course, is the crucial problem, but one, however, that is likely to remain without an optimal solution. The users' evaluations seem to indicate, though, that in spite of many imperfections, the quality of machine translations is already such as to make them a usable product. The controversy over this issue between two linguists with a long history of involvement in machine translation, Michael Zarechnak and Y. Bar-Hillel in which the former's estimate was that machine-translated texts were 80 percent complete and the latter's that they were 35 to 40 percent complete (Lehmann and Stachowitz 1971: 36) can perhaps be resolved by the users' evaluations of the degree to which machine translation was informative, which was stated to be 93 percent, and readable, which was said to be almost 60 percent. As Rolf Stachowitz pointed out, "Quality is in the eye of the user", and the users judged the quality of machine translations that they had experience with to be over 90 percent good or acceptable. This, of course, does not mean that the translations do not need improvements, all it means is that there seems to be something worth improving in view of the fact that the users have expressed their judgments in rather clear ways.

Before entering the detailed discussion of the users' evaluations as elicited by the present questionnaire, it may be worthwhile to compare some summary results with those obtained through an earlier one, even though the results were not analyzed along the same lines and only a rough picture can be derived (Henisz-Dostert 1967: 77–81). A short questionnaire was responded to at EURATOM in the spring of 1964 by 20 scientists, some of whom had used even earlier, more inferior machine-translated texts. Among the results, 16 users (80 percent) answered "no" to the question whether difficulties of the translation were such as to prevent the general understanding of the text, which could be compared with the judgment as to completeness of texts in the present case, which was rated at over 80 percent, or intelligibility, which was said to be almost 80 percent. The degree of accuracy of information transfer was considered adequate or sufficient in the 1964 questionnaire by 13 users (65 percent), which would compare rather low with informativeness as rated by present respondents at over 90 percent, or general quality judged to be over 90 percent good or acceptable. Revision of the translation was considered desirable by 10 (50 percent) of the respondents, which would indicate a lower quality of translations. The areas where improvements were most desirable were, first of all, technical vocabulary, with 17 votes, and the grammar, with 9 votes, which results coincided with the desires of the present respondents. The earlier users were almost unanimous in responding "yes" to the question whether speed of access could compensate for inadequacies of machine translation (19 out of 20), and were willing to wait for the translations about 17 days, both results corresponding very well with the statements made by the present respondents.

The Texas report discussed earlier contained several statements pertaining not only to the need for paying attention to users' requirements with respect to translations, but also to the necessity of studying their judgments of them. On pages 39–40 the statement is found that "As several participants in the study pointed out, a convincing analysis of the usefulness of machine translation will result only from a well-designed experiment determining reactions to its output" (Lehmann and Stachowitz 1971: 39–40). It is followed by one of the Conclusions, reading that "Investigations of user–translation interaction should be carried out, especially in view of the highly divergent estimates of Zarechnak and Bar-Hillel" (Lehmann and Stachowitz 1971: 45). Another of the Conclusions was that

> The usefulness of translation depends on various factors: cost, timeliness, comprehensibility. In locations where imperfect, lexically-based machine translations are available, scientists have selected these over human translation when they could be made available the following day and human translations only after a week. In view of this situation, studies should be performed to measure the extent to which comprehensibility of a translation is dependent on the knowledge available to the actual user. (Lehmann and Stachowitz 1971: 46).

Although the present questionnaire was designed before the publication of the Texas report, it was directed at many points discussed in it. It carried out the recommendation on conducting an experiment to determine users' reactions to machine translations. The results certainly elucidated user–translation interaction in many of its aspects, including that of quality and completeness. They also showed the users to be considerably more patient and stating more preference for machine translations than appeared earlier. And, perhaps most importantly, they showed what a large role is played by context as evidenced by the very extensive contribution to comprehensibility of translation by the users' knowledge of the universe of discourse.

1 Machine-translation activity at Euratom and Oak Ridge

EURATOM and the AEC Oak Ridge National Laboratory were the centers where the translations were actually made and used by the scientists on the premises. However, translation requests have also been processed for organizations and individuals from outside.

At both centers the translations were made with the Georgetown system in a virtually unchanged form. Some improvements were made in the dictionaries, namely 5,000 to 6,000 words were added in each center. The most noticeable improvements were in the format of the translations since both lower and upper case were introduced as well as other features giving the general impression of a normal printed page. This had a positive influence on readability, and even led the users to believe that more substantive improvements had been made.

With respect to computers, at EURATOM the translations were run on the IBM 7090 till the beginning of 1972 and then on the IBM 360/65 in emulation through a conversion package. At Oak Ridge they were still run on the IBM 7090 in early 1973 and conversion to the IBM 360 systems was in process.

The cost of machine translations, which constitutes such an important consideration in discussions and comparisons of machine translation with human translation was still based on estimates. Dr. Perschke at EURATOM quoted the figure of $ 7.00 per 1,000 words on the 7090 computer and estimated it to be somewhat higher on the 360/50. Dr. Kertesz at Oak Ridge estimated the cost at about $ 20.00 per 1,000 words on the 7090. In both centers, the cost was primarily due to keypunching.

The users of machine translation were not aware of the cost in most cases. At EURATOM the service was free of charge and the cost borne by CETIS. At Oak Ridge users payed, but not in any direct form and if they were aware of the cost it was mostly hearsay.

Machine translations both at EURATOM and at Oak Ridge were made strictly on a request basis, i. e., translations were not made unless a scientist asked for one. The service was not advertised and users learned about its existence in a variety of accidental ways, mostly by word of mouth. The procedure followed most commonly was that a user sent in a request for a translation, sometimes accompanied by the Russian original which may have been, for instance, sent to him from a Russian colleague, to the office responsible for the service either directly or via an intermediary, which in the case of EURATOM was the library. The materials whose translation was requested, which ranged from short papers to whole books, got keypunched and run on the computer, usually several at a time, when computer time was available. The translation process itself on the computer is very fast, so that theoretically translations should be given to the user in a very short time. A number of factors, however, contributed to delays. This is discussed in the analysis of users' reactions to Question 26 concerning the length of time in which a translation reaches the user.

1.1 Analysis of records

Records of translation requests and performance of the service have been kept both at EURATOM and Oak Ridge and these constitute a rich source of information on the service. The information included in both sets of records is on the date of the request, the date of mailing out the translation and the name of the requestor or source of request. This yields facts about the beginning of the service and the time intervals of use, and, more importantly, the length of time between the request and the translation. The total number of translations made is also thus recorded, as well as their distribution over the years. To the extent that the name of the user was decipherable, the number of users could be deduced. The EURATOM records also show the total number of words in a given translation text for some years, so that the total number of words translated in those years could be calculated. Some of the results of calculations along these lines are summarized in the tables below. They include information on the dates of records, the total number of requests, the distribution of translations over the years, the number of words translated and the time lag from request to the mailing of the translation.

Table 1. Dates of service and number of translations

	First record	Last record	Number of translations
EURATOM	Feb. 65	Aug. 72	~ 900
Oak Ridge	Feb. 67	Jan. 73	~ 600 + Documentation service

Some comments need to be made about these data. As for the beginning of the service, it clearly was started before the records themselves were, since users quote the years 1963 and 1964 in the case of EURATOM an 1964 in the case of Oak Ridge as the dates when they first used machine translation. Even the records bear some evidence of this since the Oak Ridge records contain a note saying "10 requests from January 1–February 17, 1967". As for EURATOM, the author knows from personal presence there that the system was available in late 1963. With respect to the last date, this is simply a reflection of the time at which the survey was completed at each place, i.e., September 1972 for EURATOM and January 1973 for Oak Ridge.

The figures for the number of translations are somewhat rounded since in the case of EURATOM the records were a little unclear in a few places. At Oak Ridge, the recorded number was exactly 612, but translations were also made at the request of "documentation service". This refers to three abstractors and one translator who had used an amount of machine-translation output about twice as large as all the scientists at Oak Ridge combined. Two of the abstractors were at the Atomic Energy Commission's Technical Documentation Center located in Oak Ridge. The third was at the Laboratory, but had used machine translation while at the Documentation Center. Machine-translated abstracts were used for the preparation of abstracts for inclusion in the publication *Nuclear Science Abstracts*. The total of machine-translated texts used amounted to the equivalent of 1,400 pages.

The translator worked on about 6,000 pages of texts which were translated by machine and subsequently edited by the translator. One text was a 5,000-page request by NASA (National Aeronautics and Space Administration) and the remainder were five scientific books.

The data on the distribution of the use of machine translations over the years shows some fluctuation, and as can be seen from Table 2, a considerable increase in the number at EURATOM, which is due to the extension of the service to other centers and organizations in Europe.

Table 2.   Number of translations over the years

Year	66	67	68	69	70	71	72	73
EURATOM	62	128	122	93	108	186	176 (Aug.)	
Oak Ridge		87	113	171	85	74	67	4 (Jan.)

The total number of words in the texts might be of interest to indicate the volume of translation, but only some figures were available for EURATOM, which are summarized in Table 3.

Table 3.   Number of words translated (EURATOM)

Year	1969	1970	1971	1972 August
Words	335159	330578	630705	419111

As in Table 2, an increase is indicated in 1971, almost doubling the volume, to reach over two-thirds of a million words translated. The trend seemed to hold for 1972.

One of the central issues in discussions of machine translation is that of its speed. The records at both centers give information on the amount of time that the whole process (including keypunching) required. Table 4 shows that the overall average time lag for both centers was twenty days.

Table 4.   Records of time lag from request to translation

Place	Year	Number of days
Oak Ridge	1967	10
Oak Ridge	1968	14
Oak Ridge	1970	14
Oak Ridge	1972	18
EURATOM	1969	21
EURATOM	1972	44
	Average =	20

The analysis of users' impressions on the length of time involved shows that the two estimates do not quite coincide, the users' estimate being the longer. It is therefore important to add here that the dates in the records from which the average time lag for a given year was computed are those of the receipt of the request and the mailing of the translation. Since the time lag was primarily due to two factors – keypunching and the mail – both the users and translation offices realized that the second factor lengthened the actual waiting time for the user. On some occasions when texts were handcarried and keypunching was done immediately, translations were delivered to the users overnight. Needless to say, those users enjoyed a privileged status in the organizations.

1.2 Requests from outside

It was mentioned above that in addition to providing translations for scientists at the centers, requests from outside had also been processed. In the case of EURATOM this resulted in a considerable increase of activity, as can be seen from Tables 2 and 3. At the time of the survey, EURATOM had connections with three organizations on a firm and regular basis. Those were the European Translations Centre (ETC) located in Delft, Holland; the Centre National de Documentation Scientifique et Technique (National Center for Scientific and Technical Documentation) in Brussels, Belgium; and M.A.N. (Maschinenfabrik Augsburg-Nürnberg), a major motor vehicle factory in Germany. Table 5 summarizes the activity for each of these organizations.

Table 5.   Outside service provided by EURATOM

	Starting date	Number of requests	Number of pages
ETC	1969	350	2500 *
NCSTD	1971	120	963
M.A.N.	1968	81	~530

* Not available directly, but the figures in Tables 2 and 3 for the number of translations and the number of words in the years 1969–1972 allow this calculation, assuming pages of about 350 words (1,715,000 words/~660 translations yields about 2,600 words per translation; that divided by the number of words per page yields about 7 pages as the average length of a translation; that multiplied by 350, the number of requests, gives close to 2,500 pages.)

The European Translations Centre was founded in 1960 to serve as a coordinating service for translation activity in Europe by maintaining and providing information on the availability of human translations. At the time of the author's contacts with the Centre in 1972, its director was Mr. D. Van Bergeijk and the personnel responsible for machine-translations activities were Mr. C. M. A. Knul and Mrs. J. A. Trijssenaar. The cooperation between ETC and EURATOM was initiated in 1968, with an experimental period following until 1969. The typical mode of operation at ETC was that a user would send in a request for a translation to the Centre; if one was on file, it would be forwarded to him; if not, the requestor was referred to the holder of the translation if one existed elsewhere. If a translation did not exist, machine-translation service was offered to the prospective client. Between 1969 and early 1971 over 100 requests had been received. As seen from the figures through the summer of 1972 (350 requests), the service was enjoying growing popularity. The number of individual users is very difficult to estimate. Even a partial list of users shows a great variety of organizations and countries. As such, it may be of some interest and is therefore included in the Appendix. The users of machine translations provided through ETC did not pay for them, but they were requested to submit comments on the translation. A large number of these (in hundreds) were on file at ETC and a few are included here (in the Appendix). The comments are generally very positive, and often quite detailed. What might at first be suspected is that the positive nature of the comments is due to the fact that they constitute the only payment for the translation, so the principle of not looking a gift horse in the mouth might be in operation. While it is a fact that users in EURATOM also obtain translations without any charge and those in Oak Ridge do not pay for them directly (see responses to Question 16 of the questionnaire in the Appendix), those users may expect the service since it comes directly from their installations. The users who contact ETC with requests for translations expect to pay for them, and if they are provided with human translations, they do pay for them. The laudatory nature of their comments on the quality of machine translations might therefore be attributed, in part at least, to the free nature of the service. However, there are two counter-arguments to this reasoning: first, in most cases, it is their organizations, and not the users themselves that would have to bear the costs of translation; and second, the users must find the translations indeed of sufficiently acceptable quality to be willing to bother with writing comments (one can presume that they do that because they wish to continue using the service). Moreover, it was reported by the director of ETC that no complaints about the machine-translation service had been received. The positive nature of the users' reactions who obtain machine translations through ETC is in agreement, of course, with the general attitude of the users of the machine-translation services.

The requests to the service at Oak Ridge by outside users were not as extensive as in the case of EURATOM, but they included one major user – NASA – and several requests came from NOAA (National Oceanic and Atmospheric Administration), and the AEC Technical Documentation Center, which was mentioned above (section 1.1). NASA made a request for 5,000 pages of translation. According to Martha Gerrard, the professional translator who post-edited the machine-translated text, the final translation could not possibly have been achieved in the allotted time if the text had not been machine-translated first. The director of NOAA, Dr. F. A. Gifford, and his colleagues used the machine-translation service at Oak Ridge on several occasions. One was a 1968 book on "Turbulence in free atmosphere" which in slightly post-edited form was also used at the AEC establishment in Denmark.

This concludes the picture of machine-translation activities as documented in the records on the service maintained by those involved in it at a number of places. It is a necessary background for the examination of the users' reactions although it is the latter that are of foremost interest. We turn to the discussion of the results of the survey of users' evaluations which was made with the use of a questionnaire, which is included in the Appendix.

2 How the data were collected

The bulk of the data consists of the results of a questionnaire which the users were asked to complete, and these are analysed in great detail. However, there exists also a large body of data of users' reactions and opinions in the form of their letters. These comments came mainly from the clients of ETC, who were routinely asked to supply them, as was mentioned in section 1.2 above. Some came from the users at Oak Ridge who responded to a request for evaluation. Occasionally, a letter with comments was sent along with the questionnaire or instead of the questionnaire. The shape that the comments take is quite varied, from short expressions of opinion to extensive detailed lists of corrections and suggestions, and even one angry outburst from a professional translator. They constitute very interesting reading since they are quite positive and in many cases very constructive and informative. The general tone is that of satisfaction with machine translations and serious interest in it. However, they are obviously totally unstructured and would require a highly specific set of techniques to analyze them, if any methical study is possible at all. In order to give an idea of them, some representative ones have been selected for inclusion in the Appendix.

2.1 The nature of the questionnaire

The questionnaire, which was aimed at eliciting users' reactions and opinions about the machine-translated texts they had used, is included here in the Appendix in its entirety since it might be serviceable in other investigations of similar nature. It consists of fifty-one questions, including the optional one about the respondent's name. Although this may seem to be a rather long questionnaire, and as is only too well known, filling out questionnaires is not an exactly thrilling activity, it turned out not to be too much of a burden on the respondents. This may be partly due to the fact that several questions are of the multiple choice type and can be answered quickly. But mainly it was clear that users had little hesitancy in answering and no reluctance.

The information that the questionnaire was intended to elicit falls roughly into two categories: facts and opinions, and can be summarized as follows:

Facts:	Opinions:
Language familiarity	Informativeness of machine
Field of work	translation
Use pattern of machine	Understandability
translation	Correctness
Cost of machine translation	Mental correcting
Purpose for using machine	Unintelligibility
translation	Time for reading
Human translation use	Harmfulness
Wait time	Improvements
	Recommendability

Of the 51 questions all in all, the first few questions are aimed at gathering information about the user: nationality and native language (these do not alway coincide: in one case, for instance, nationality was French, but native language was German), familiarity with English and Russian, principal field of work and place of employment. The next group investigates the respondent's use pattern of machine translation: when use was made first and last and the approximate amount of translations requested, and also the reason for using machine translation. The following two questions deal with paying for translations, both human and machine. Next, the user is asked whether he gets enough information for his purposes from the machine-translated text. It might be expected that if this is not the case, the user would request retranslation of at least some of the materials by a human, and the next two questions are addressed at that. The question that follows asks whether the Russian original is consulted while using the machine-translated text, and for what purpose. Length of waiting time for a translation both human and machine is investigated next, including a question about the acceptable period of waiting, and one that asks the user to state preference for either human or machine translation if he had to wait three times as long for human as for machine translation. This question was based on an earlier observation, from informal talks with users, that the waiting time for human translation is much longer than for machine translation. The next three questions try to establish the percentage of literature in a given user's field that is written in Russian, and how it comes to the user's attention.

So far, mostly factual information has been requested. The remainder of the questions primarily seeks to establish the user's opinion about machine translation and his personal evaluations. Thus, he is asked to rate the quality of machine translation and comment on what affects and determines the understandability of the translations. Next, the user is asked to estimate the percentage of sentences in translations that fall on the scale from unintelligible to correct and the percentage of technical words on a scale from untranslated to correct. The two questions that follow attempt to establish the importance of context: if Russian words are untranslated, can they be understood from the transliteration into Latin script, together with the surrounding English words? The next four questions request comparison, in terms of percentages, between the unintelligibility of machine-translated texts as against texts originally written in English on the one hand, and machine-translated texts as against texts translated by humans on the other, as well as comparisons of the amounts of time required for reading the three categories of texts. The next three queries ask for a judgment on whether inaccurate translations result in complete distortion of meaning; whether distortions in translation could lead to a meaning opposite to that of the original; and whether misleading conclusions could be drawn from unclear translations which could have harmful effects on the user's work. The remaining questions probe the user's opinions and desires with respect to improvements in machine translation: first, were any noticed, can one get used to the style of machine translation as one reads more translations, would the user recommend machine translation to his colleagues, and, finally, what improvements would he like to see. A detailed statistical analysis of the answers, as well as some comments on them, follow in Chapter 3.

2.2 How the users were reached

An attempt was made to interview personally as many users as possible, and this was achieved both at EURATOM and Oak Ridge. That method was considered the most interesting both for the interviewee and the interviewer, and the least taxing for the former. In most cases the questionnaires were filled out during a general discussion of machine translation. That also yielded many comments on the part of the user which of course cannot be reconstructed, but which led to the general impression that the users were much more positive (in some cases outright enthusiastic about and very much interested in machine translation) than is apparent at times from the questionnaires. The reason for this may be either that the questionnaire was not constructed in such a way as to elicit the most positive response or that people in general tend to be more cautious and conservative with the written than with the spoken word.

The attempt was made not only to reach as many users as possible, but also to interview those who might be called "heavy" users. A heavy user was first defined in terms of frequency of his requests and the length of time (number of years) in which he made requests. It later turned out that these are not the only significant criteria since some users who appeared "light", having only asked for two or three translations, were indeed "heavy" users in terms of the number of pages they had requested. Typically, a translation of a whole book would be involved, and such users were quite knowledgeable and helpful. In the case of EURATOM, "heavy" users were identified by an investigation of the records of machine-translation requests and Dr. Fangmeyer was helpful in setting up some interviews. In Oak Ridge, Dr. Kertesz helped make contacts with the users.

A number of expected and unexpected problems hampered the interviewing process. People were on vacation, at meetings, or just simply out of their offices, or no longer employed there. This last factor was particularly important at EURATOM, where the changes in personnel had been very considerable over the years, and thus many "heavy" users were irretrievably lost. In Oak Ridge security regulations required an escort inside the laboratory, thus limiting freedom of movement.

Some questionnaires were obtained not in connection with interviews, but from individuals outside of the two centers. Some clients of ETC were contacted and responded. About twenty questionnaires together with translation samples were sent out by a user in EURATOM to his fellow geologists in a number of countries. A few responded and sent in evaluations.

3 Analysis of questionnaire results

Responses to each question were analyzed separately and the analysis is presented in this form. In some cases the results are summed up for some questions dealing with related topics. Some particularly salient results are highlighted in the Summary and conclusions. First, however, a brief look at some characteristics of the respondents and their attitudes is in order.

3.1 The users

All in all, evaluations were obtained from 58 users, although only 57 questionnaires were returned. One was filled out by two users jointly and in most calculations that was treated as one response since most of them were identical. That, however, was probably an error. Table 6 gives a picture of the number of respondents in terms of the center whose translations they used.

Table 6. The respondents

	Number of users	Number of questionnaires	Number of users interviewed
EURATOM	36	35	19
Oak Ridge	22	22	21
Total	58	57	40

The actual number of those persons who have used machine translations over the decade that was studied is rather difficult to establish. EURATOM records showed about 100 inside users, but far from perfect legibility of the entries made it sometimes impossible to establish the identity or nonidentity of a name entered. Oak Ridge records were even worse in this respect, but the number appeared to be somewhat less. It was even more difficult to estimate the number of outside users, but the discussion in section 1.2 above gives an idea of the activity.

The respondents (excluding documentation services) seem to have used about one-third of all the translations made, since the number of translations requested by them (the heavy users) was quoted to be 500 and the total number of translation-request entries was about 1,500.

The majority of users who responded were scientists or engineers in a variety of fields (see Question 6). In reality, all users were scientists or engineers, but some did not deal with the machine-translation services directly, going instead through a documentation service handling translations. Thus a few of the respondents were the personnel who processed translation requests at these documentation centers. Especially important here were the reactions of a translator who edited 6,000 pages of machine-translated texts. The other documentation specialists were a translation-service coordinator who handled requests totaling 963 pages in basic and applied science, and three abstractors who worked with machine-translated texts mostly in nuclear physics, totalling some 1,400 pages. The volume of translation requested by the two types of respondents is summarized in Table 7.

Table 7.   Types of respondents

Type	Number	Number of pages	Field
Scientists and engineers	54	5465	(see Question 6)
Documentation service	4	8363	Basic and applied sciences

3.2 Analysis of the answers

A detailed analysis of the answers to each question, and the presentation of the results in that form was considered the only adequate way of conveying an objective picture. As an introduction, however, a few summary results give an overall characterization of the attitudes of the respondents, which were quite positive, as the figures indicate. The users considered the quality of machine translation acceptable and even good (91.4

percent for the two categories, see Question 31), and informativeness and readability both received high ratings (over 90 percent and 60 percent, Questions 19–20, 36–37). The waiting time for translations was considered somewhat too long, the desirable time being about one-third less than the actual (Question 26). However, 70 percent of the sample (87 percent of the respondents) would prefer machine to human translation if the waiting time for the latter were three times as long as that for the former (Question 27). Most users were sufficiently satisfied to recommend the machine-translation service to colleagues since 85.9 percent of the sample (96 percent of the respondents) either had done so or would be willing to do so (Question 50).

The results on the individual questions speak for themselves, so it did not seem necessary to provide lengthy comments. The phrasing of each question appears below exactly as it was in the questionnaire.

Question 1   Your name, last and first (omit, if you prefer to)

The name was usually supplied automatically by the user, without even reading the whole line. In a few cases, it was simply omitted, but no hesitation was ever observed. This was probably mostly due to the fact that in an interview situation the name of the user was known anyway. The knowledge of the name made the work with the questionnaires much more interesting since the users had acquired distinctive personalities for the investigator both from the records and interviews. But it is, of course, recognized that in general this is not a desirable question to include.

Question 2   Nationality

USA	18	French	3	Turkish	1
German	10	Belgian	2	British	1
Italian	9	Czech	2	Israeli	1
Dutch	6	Swedish	1	Indeterminate	1

This question was mainly dictated by curiosity as to the identity of the users. In general, it is doubtful that the nationality of a user would influence his evaluation of machine translation. The large number of United States nationality users is of course due to the location of one of the centers (Oak Ridge). The large number of German respondents among the European sample is in part due to the M.A.N. group of users, that of

Italians to the location of EURATOM, and that of Dutchmen to the location of ETC.

Question 3   Native language

English	20	Czech	2
German	13	Swedish	1
Italian	9	Turkish	1
Dutch	6	Polish	1
French	4	Indeterminate	1

Not surprisingly, the data on native language do not coincide with the data on nationality. The inclusion of this question is much better justified, since a comparison of attitudes of users with different language backgrounds might be of linguistic interest. Especially the question whether non-native speakers of English would be more likely to be more tolerant of the imperfections of machine English or vice-versa was deemed of interest. The general impression was that it made no difference, but no specific correlations were made.

Question 4   Please rate your familiarity with English

Here, a scale was provided (excellent, good, fair) both with respect to speaking and reading and the answers are presented accordingly.

Table 8.   Familiarity with English

	Speaking	Reading
Excellent	25	32
Good	24	23
Fair	9	2
Indeterminate		1

This question is also motivated by linguistic interest as to whether there is a correlation between the degree of familiarity with English and tolerance of imperfections in the machine-translation type of English. The general impression was that the greater the familiarity, the more tolerance there was. One of the only two negative answers to the question on recommendability of machine translation was from a respondent who filled out the questionnaire in his native language, not English, and rather spottily at that. But no definite results are available on this issue.

Most users rated their English as excellent (that, of course, included the 20 native speakers) or good, with figures somewhat higher for reading ability, as might be expected. What this seems to indicate is that at least a good knowledge of English is necessary to use machine translations, or at least that only scientists with such knowledge use them.

Question 5   Your familiarity with Russian

A scale was provided again in this question, but different from the one in Question 4, where it was assumed that a user had to have a reasonable knowledge of English to want an English translation. Here, excellent knowledge of Russian was excluded on the obvious grounds that such scientists would not request a translation, and the ratings of "poor" and "none" were included. The answers showed that this latter inclusion was particularly relevant.

Table 9.   Familiarity with Russian

	Speaking	Reading
Good	0	4
Fair	5	3
Poor	9	14
None	43	36
Indeterminate		1

Some familiarity with Russian, and therefore an awareness of the difficulties it presents to non-Slavic speakers, might be expected to con-tribute toward a more positive attitude toward machine translation. But since most users have no knowledge of the language, all that can be said is that this group needs translations most and that that need might influence their positive attitudes. Primarily, however, the significance of these results is that in spite of the heavy "Russian accent" of the transla-tions, no knowledge of Russian is needed to use them.

Question 6   Your principal field of work

A large variety of fields were represented, from cancer research to Diesel motor engineering at the extremes. A proper classification of the fields would require extensive knowledge of the fields themselves, and the list-ing that follows undoubtedly shows many overlaps. It was considered of interest, however, to show the variety of fields in which machine transla-tion had been used successfully, with a dictionary that was by no means suited to many of the areas. Another point of interest may be in what areas translations seem to be needed most. In the listing below specialities are combined only if they appear to overlap; otherwise, the users' exact wording is quoted without any attempt at inclusion in a broader category. Many users seem to be in physics, but the spectrum is broad. Thus: physics (7), geology (4), Diesel engine (4), nuclear physics (3), fusion research (plasma physics) (3), physics information (3), theoretical physics (2), reactor technology (2), metallurgy (2), biology (2), soil science (2), chemistry (2), meteorology (2), neutron physics, high temperature technology, high energy nuclear reaction, heat transfer fluid dynamics, heat transfer in fluid rod bundles, heat transfer, high temperature mass spectrometry, materials research, microbiology, geochemistry, ecology, pharmaceutics, chemical and biological engineering, engineering, nuclear safety, process control and instrumentation, numerical analysis, applied mathematics.

Question 7   Your department at EURATOM, AEC, or other place of employment

As discussed elsewhere, the majority of respondents were employed at EURATOM and the Oak Ridge National Laboratory. A large group of users, of whom only a few were contacted, was scattered throughout Europe. Some of those are shown in the partial list of ETC clients in the Appendix. The reconstruction of a full list could be attempted, but it does not seem of sufficient interest even though a great variety of institutions are represented. Within the two centers themselves, the information on what departments the requests came from might perhaps be useful.

Question 8   How did you come in contact with MT?

This question did not yield any particularly interesting results, due undoubtedly to the fact that the service was handled in rather centralized ways. Thus "the library" or someone's name in the information or documentation center would be the typical reply.

Question 9   Why do you use MT?

Answers to this question were necessarily unstructured and precise analysis is impossible. The word "quick" in one form or another appeared in several answers (14), "cheap" also, but less often (3); other

reasons quoted were simply lack of knowledge of Russian or just translation of Russian literature (11). Some of the answers may be of interest, so
the full list is quoted below.

"Quick translation of articles and translation of books"
"Quick"
"To obtain more rapid and occasionally unique access to Russian
  literature"
"Quick translations"
"Early awareness of scientific papers and books"
"Quick translation"
"Fast"
"Cost and expediency plus experimental program"
"Convenience and speed"
"It is faster than human translation"
"Cheaper – fast"
"The only one available in short time"
"Cheap"
"Impossible to meet requests with traditional methods"
"Less work than human"
"Easier access"
"No knowledge of Russian"
"Translation of Russian literature"
"Because I need some Russian papers to be translated"
"Much work in my area done in Russia"
"For translating Russian literature not yet available in English"
"Translation of author abstracts in Russian language"
"To prepare materials for Nuclear Science Abstracts"
"Preparing input to nuclear information systems"
"Unique translation"
"Because no translation was available"
"No other possibility for translation"
"I have no other means to get Russian papers translated"
"It's available"
"Yes, why?"
"It is a useful tool for my job at Ispra"
"To determine if the publication contains material that is pertinent
  to my work"

"Makes it easier to read long articles"

"Through present job"

Questions 10–11 When did you first use MT? When did you last use MT?

The earliest date quoted was 1963 by one respondent, then 1964 by three, and 1965 by five. The latest date was 1973 quoted by six respondents (EURATOM users were last contacted in summer of 1972). Calculations show that the average number of time of machine-translation use per respondent is 3.8 years.

Question 12 Approximately, how many translations have you requested?

The total figure computed for these data does not include requests from or through documentation services (Brussels Documentation Center, and translator and abstractors at Oak Ridge). Thus, the total number of requests quoted directly by scientists was 500. (Since about 1,500 translation requests were recorded, the sample constituted one-third of the total.) The average number of translations per respondent, again excluding documentation services, turn out to be 10.6. The users' memory as to the number of translations they requested coincided amazingly well with the records for the individual users. In only one case, a considerably lower figure was quoted.

Question 13 On the average, how many translations a year have you requested?

From the data on the average number of years of machine-translation use per user (Questions 10–11, answer being 3.8) and the average number of translations per user (Question 12 with answer 10.6) we find that the figure sought here is 2.8, and this was corroborated by the responses.

Question 14 Approximately, how many pages of translations have you requested?

The answers here provide the best idea as to the volume of translations used by the respondents who had requested about one-third of all translations made. But it would probably be incorrect to guess that the total number of pages would be about three times the total amount shown below for the respondents, since some of the translations included here were of exceptional length, especially those requested by the documentation services. Partly for this reason, the figures are shown separately for the scientists. The comparison of the two centers also seemed of interest, but it must be borne in mind that this is a picture only for the respondents and not for the general activity.

Table 10. Number of pages requested

	Scientists	Documentation service	Total
EURATOM	1,780	963	2,743
Oak Ridge	3,685	7,400	11,085
	5,465	8,363	13,828

These figures indicate that the respondents at Oak Ridge were considerably "heavier" users in terms of the volume, this being primarily due to the fact that some books were translated. It is interesting to look at the total number of pages in terms of how many books that would constitute. Assuming a book of 200 pages, all the requests of the respondents amounted to about 70 books.

Question 15   What is your primary reason for using MT?

This question clearly overlaps with Question 9, "why do you use MT?", however, the purpose here was to elicit answers to one of the following choices supplied on the questionnaire: "cost", "rapidity of access to translation", "reliability", "accuracy". The chief interest was in comparing cost and rapidity of access as reasons for use, and the answers to those (compared in Table 11) clearly show that rapidity of access was the chief reason. However, cost was not a very important factor in general for these groups of respondents, as will be seen from Questions 16–17, even though it was given as a primary reason for use. "Reliability" and "accuracy" did not, as expected, get any votes, but some other reasons were supplied and those are listed below. The most important, and obvious, conclusion to be drawn from the answers here is that machine-translation service must be as fast as possible to be of maximum usefulness.

Table 11.   Primary reasons for using machine translation

	Number of respondents*	% for sample**
Rapidity of access to translation	37	64.7
Cost	10	17.5

*   "Number of respondents" will from here on be abbreviated to "Number".
** "Sample" means the total number of users who answered the questionnaire; "respondents" means the users who answered a given question.

As other reasons for using machine translation, the following were given: "availability (2), unique source, loss of fulltime translator, only way to get translation, impossibility of meeting the rising volume of requests by traditional methods, testing only, impossibility of getting a human translation, testing how it works, only alternative, not yet translated articles."

Some of these answers indicate that machine translation was used because of unavailability of human translation, and this is a reality that machine-translation developers and services must take into account.

Question 16   Do you pay for MT?

In addition to this 'yes' or 'no' question, the user was asked "How much", and "Do you know how much it costs to translate 1,000 words by machine translation?" Since the issue of cost is such an important one in almost all discussions of machine translation, the answers to all three parts are given, with the latter two parts being combined.

Table 12.   Paying for machine translation

	EURATOM	Oak Ridge	Total	% for sample
Yes	0	21	21	36.7
No	32	1	33	57.4

Table 13.   Knowledge of cost of machine translation for 1,000 words

	EURATOM	Oak Ridge	Total	% for sample
Yes*	3	3	6	10.6
No	20	12	32	56.0

* The "yes" answers are: EURATOM – "$7", "$7–8", ~$7"; Oak Ridge – "about the same as human", "60 % keypunching, 15 % IBM 7090", "$8".

It is clear from the answers, which tested users' awareness of the cost, that they have only a vague idea of it, including those who are certain that they do pay, i. e., the Oak Ridge group. Also, these answers seem inconsistent with those to Question 15, where 10 users stated "cost" as the primary reason for using machine translation. One must conclude that when the service was provided by the institutions, the users were not directly subjected to the costs. The accurate figures quoted by the three EURATOM users doubtlessly reflect the knowledge of the official estimates.

Question 17   Do you pay for human translation? How much?

The motivation for this question was to continue the assessment of the importance of the cost of translation, this time by testing the awareness of human translation costs. Since these are generally known to be high, it was reasonable to suppose that they might influence the users' choices. However, Table 14 shows that there is not too much awareness of the actual costs and thus no conclusions could be drawn on whether machine translation offers the users advantages in this respect.

Table 14.   Paying for human translation

	EURATOM	Oak Ridge	Total	% for sample
Yes	"$5 a page of 300 words" "$.50 a line" no amount shown (3)	"short paper $ several hundred" "$20/1000 words" "$8–9/abstract" "$3–12.50/abstract" "$10–12/abstract" no amount shown (9)	20	35.0
No	23	7	30	52.5

Question 18   What is your primary use of machine-translated texts?

As examples of an answer, choices were provided: "details of experiments" and "surveys of experiments", and also a blank box. The main purpose was to determine whether machine-translated texts were merely scanned or whether they constituted a source of important information in themselves. The latter turned out to be the case, since the two choices combined received, in about equal distribution, 82 percent of the votes, as shown in Table 15. "Other" answers were not very interesting on the whole, citing literature consultation or surveys, but also "theoretical results" occasionally as the reasons.

Table 15. Primary use of machine-translated texts

	Number	Total	% for sample
Details of experiments	24		
Surveys of experiments	23		
		47	82

Only one respondent indicated using machine translation to determine if a human translation was warranted (quoting him, "to determine if article is of sufficient interest to justify human translation"). Thus, Garvin's prediction, noted in the Introduction to Part III, that "for many purposes, machine translation output will be only casually scanned rather than carefully read; from a great mass of documents so perused a few may then be selected for later, more careful, human translation" is only partially supported by answers to this question, although the "surveys of experiments" choice might, at least in part, fall under the category of scanning. But it seems that for this group of respondents machine-translated texts were used more as a tool of information than as a tool for the selection of information. The reason for this may be the overall low key of the machine-translation activity. It can very well be imagined that under the conditions of a regular, vigorous service, requests for translations for scanning purposes only would become routine.

Question 19   Can you decide on the basis of a machine-translated text whether the work described is important to you?

The answers to this question together with those to Question 20 serve to establish a measure of "informativeness" of machine-translated texts. First, the results for each question are given (Tables 16 and 17), and then the combined results (Table 18), followed by a brief discussion.

Table 16.   Answers to Question 19

	Number	% for sample
Yes	57	100
No	0	0

Question 20   Do you get enough information about the work described?

Table 17.   Answers to Question 20

	Number	% for sample
Yes	49	85.7
No	3	5.3

Table 18. Combined positive answers to Questions 19 and 20

	Number	% for sample
Question 19	57	100.0
Question 20	49	85.7
Average	53	93.0

Questions 19 and 20 deal with what might be called "information transmission" in some admittedly undefined sense. Question 19 merely asks whether it is possible for the user to judge as to the importance of the work. It may be argued that one can decide that even on the basis of understanding only a small portion of the text. This may be true, but it is rather irrelevant. The question as it stands does inquire about the information value of machine-translated texts, and thus the answers can contribute toward the measurement of informativeness. Question 20 serves as a much clearer measure of informativeness, since it probes the problem directly. The answers to both questions are not far apart, but the slightly lower results for Question 20 show that it was felt to be more specific. Still, the questions, and answers, seemed close enough to warrant combining the results, and computing averages. These, as shown in Table 18, are considered a measure of "informativeness" of machine-translated texts. This is contrasted with "readability" measured through Questions 36 and 37, and discussed following those.

Question 21 Have you asked for human translation of articles translated by MT?

In a more remote way, the answers to this also throw light on how well the machine-translated texts carry information, and since Table 19 shows that two-thirds of those who answered did not ask for retranslation by a human, the rate of transmission must be sufficiently high – even if it serves only as a basis for discarding a given text. The answers also seem to conflict with Garvin's prediction that a human translation would be requested subsequently to machine translation. However, the same reasoning applies as in the case of scanning versus reading (see Question 18 above).

Table 19. Requests for human translation of machine-translated texts

	EURATOM	Oak Ridge	Total	Combined % for sample
Yes	4	9	13	22.7
No	26	12	38	66.5

In the second part of this question the user was asked to estimate what percentage of the total volume was thus retranslated for him, and for EURATOM the answer turned out to be 3.6 percent, at Oak Ridge considerably higher – 24.2 percent – yielding an average of 14 percent. It is not clear why the volume of retranslation was so much higher at Oak Ridge, but it must be remembered that the use of machine translation was higher there, as was the use of human translation in general.

One user's answer to this question of retranslation was particularly interesting and illuminating: "once in the very beginning when machine-translation was not clear and unambiguous." This came from a very "steady" user, one who had regularly requested translations since 1965, and since the translations themselves had not improved substantially, we must draw the conclusion that the user "improved" in the sense of getting accustomed to the style of the output. This issue is discussed more extensively in connection with Questions 48 and 49.

Question 22   Have you compared human translations with machine translations of the same articles?

This question, it was hoped, would merely continue Question 21 and try to find out if actual comparisons were made and for what purpose. The results, however, showed that several users at Oak Ridge had compared translations even though they had not requested them. What the source of the human translation was remained obscure, since the discrepancy in the results was not noticed for some time. Why would a machine translation be consulted when a human one existed is also not clear.

Table 20.   Comparing human and machine translations

	EURATOM	Oak Ridge	Total	Combined % for sample
Yes	4	17	21	36.7
No	30	5	35	61.2

The purpose of making a comparison was then inquired about with the provision of choices: "clarification of language", "missing words", "missing formulae, etc.". The priorities in answers were marked in the order of the categories as above. A few "other" answers were given and they are of interest: "to answer this questionnaire", "accident", "to understand what the machine was trying to do", "cross-checking".

Question 23   When reading a machine-translated text, do you look at the Russian original?

"Yes" answers were expected here since some parts of the original are simply not included in the translation, i. e., formulae and diagrams of various kinds. Those users who answered "no" either must have scanned rather than really read the texts, or dealt with texts which did not include such material.

Table 21.   Consulting Russian original text

	Number	% for sample
Yes	47	82.4
No	10	17.5

The purpose of the consultation was also inquired about in order to weigh the choices supplied, which were: "missing words", "incorrectly translated words", "incorrectly translated sentences", "missing formulae, diagrams, etc.". Not surprisingly, "missing formulae, etc." scored highest at 46.8 percent, indicating the obvious importance of this portion of a scientific translation. Items 1 and 2 were next, and item 4, "incorrectly translated sentences", scored lowest, thus providing more evidence for the conlusion that sentence structure of machine translations is not a major deterrent in its usefulness (see discussion of Question 36 below).

Question 24   Have you requested human translations?

It was considered important to gather some information on the users' experiences with human translations in general for the sake of the necessary comparisons with machine translation.

Table 22.   Requests for human translation (in general)

	EURATOM	Oak Ridge	Total	Combined % for sample
Yes	12	14	26	45.6
No	21	8	29	50.7

The next two questions included here, "More often than machine translation?" and "Less often than machine translation?" were each answered by eight users, thus indicating no trend. Generally, half of the users had experience with human translations, slightly more among those at Oak Ridge.

Question 25   On the average, how long have you had to wait for a human translation?

The EURATOM users responded with an average of 50 days, users at Oak Ridge showed a longer time, 84 days, which gives an average of 67 days for both groups. Just over two months seems to be a rather short time compared to the general knowledge, and complaint, that the human translation process is a very slow one. However, these results were very strongly influenced by the interpretation of some of the answers, namely those that read simply "months" or "several months". Such answers suggest a protracted period of time, and it was probably a mistake to interpret that for statistical purposes as '3 months'. The impression from oral interviews was that the waiting time was very long. As is known, and also was the case for the scientists interviewed, the longest time lag is in the translation of whole journals and other large official translations. Since the answers do not reflect this fact, it must be concluded that the users probably referred only to translations they themselves requested. It must be noticed that slightly less than a half of the users answered, which closely follows the figure in Question 24 for those who had requested human translations. The remaining users either wrote "not applicable" or simply left the space blank. The user was also asked whether he considered that period of waiting as too long, and 20 users (35 percent of the sample) answered "yes" while only 5 (8.7 percent of the sample) said "no".

The motivation for Question 25 was, clearly, to compare the waiting time for human with that for machine translation and that is discussed next.

Question 26   On the average, how long have you had to wait for a machine translation?

For the users at EURATOM it was 41 days, for those at Oak Ridge 17, yielding an average of 29 days. The computation of this average may not be very meaningful, but it is useful for some general comparisons. Begging the question, the user was next asked to say whether this period of waiting was too long. Table 23 shows that the users are rather patient.

Table 23.   Is waiting time for machine translation too long?

	Number	% for sample	% for respondents
Yes	15	26.2	33.3
No	30	52.5	66.3

Finally, the user was asked to state the period of waiting acceptable to him. EURATOM users answered with 22 days, the Oak Ridge ones with 14 days, which gives an average of 18 days.

It is interesting to compare the results of the examination of the official records at the two centers with the users' responses concerning the length of waiting time for machine translation. Six different year-records showed an average waiting time of 20 days, yet the average for the users was longer, i.e., 29 days. This discrepancy is partly accounted for by the fact that the date marked as the delivery of a given translation was the day it left the office rather than the day it reached the user. Since the factors accounting for most of the waiting time were keypunching and mail, it is not surprising that the users experienced a longer time lag due to the mail. As has been noted, machine translations could be (and were) supplied overnight. It is felt that this time lag was largely due to the fact that machine translation was a marginal and sporadic activity, especially at EURATOM, where texts were keypunched when operators were not otherwise busy and translations run when the computer was not. Under such circumstances the speed of machine translation, its crucial advantage, could not be adequately felt by the users and therefore evaluated. Thus, it is even more significant that translations were used so extensively despite the fact that the user did not really have an opportunity to "tell whether he is ready to trade quality for speed".

Question 27   If you had to wait for human translation three times as long as for MT, which would you prefer?

This question was formulated on the basis of an impression, backed by initial conversations with users, that human translation required considerable waiting time, at least three times that required for machine translation. This was not supported by answers to Questions 25 and 26, which show 67 days as against 29 for human and machine translation respectively, but as was pointed out, that figure for human translation is deceptively low. The results here show a definite preference for machine translation.

Table 24.   Preference for human or machine translation

	Number	% for sample	% for respondents
Machine translation	40	70.0	87
Human translation	6	10.6	13

Particularly noticeable was the case of Oak Ridge, where the waiting time for human translation averaged 84 days as against 17 days for machine translation, or five times as long. It might be expected that those users would state a larger preference for human translation when the waiting time would be only three times as long, and yet only six respondents in all stated such a preference.

Question 28   What percentage of the literature that you read in your field is written in Russian?

The answer for the whole sample turned out to be 16.5 percent, but it is not certain whether this figure is meaningful because of the faulty phrasing of the question which was realized through the comment of one user which was: "I read only a small [portion] because I can't read it." Leaving out the phrase "that you read" would have undoubtedly resulted in a higher figure.

Question 29   What is the primary field in which you requested machine translation from Russian?

It was hoped that the answers might yield a few broad categories which might point the directions for vocabulary development, but users were quite narrow and the answers coincide pretty well with the users' field of work (Question 6).

Question 30   How do Russian articles come to your attention?

This was clearly not an important question from the point of view of the users' evaluations of translation, and the answers were uninteresting, being mostly "References in journals" and "Abstracts", and also "Reviews" and "Colleagues". The motivation for the question was the assessment of the ease of obtaining the original, but there is no direct answer to that.

Question 31   How do you rate the quality of machine translation in general?

Preceding this query, the user was told in a note that "your answers to the questions below will be of particular importance and value". Several of the questions that follow were complex, so it was significant that the users cooperated so well. Question 31 is general, but some of the following ones probe a number of details in a multiple-choice format. The choices selected by the respondents appear in the tables below.

Table 25.   Judgment of quality of machine translation

	Number	%
Good	9	15.5
Acceptable	44	75.9
Poor	5	8.6
Total	58	100.0

Some users put a bracket over the two top categories, one comment was "acceptable or better", another (after a bracket linking the top two and check in the middle) "for my purposes, and could easily be improved". Those two figures combined yield 91.4 percent "good or acceptable" as an overall evaluation of machine-translation quality.

Question 32–33   What affects understandability of machine translation most?

The discussion of the answers is combined since it was really one question in two parts. The choices supplied were:

sentence structure
untranslated words
lack of diagrams, formulae, figures, etc.
incorrectly translated words
other

and the user first could simply check them, but then was asked to "assign numbers in descending order of importance, i. e., 1 to most important, 2 to the next most important, etc.". The results proved difficult to present in a clear manner. Table 26 shows all the ranks of importance for each factor in descending order of importance from (1) to (4), together with the number of respondents assigning a given rank to a given factor. The highest number of votes for each of the ranks (or 'no response') is italicized. The table is arranged from top to bottom according to the highest number of votes for ranks (1) and (2).

Table 26.   Factors affecting understandability of machine translation

| | Number of responses | | | | |
| | Rank of importance | | | | |
	(1)	(2)	(3)	(4)	No response
Untranslated words	*18*	*23*	6	7	4
Sentence structure	15	15	15	5	8
Incorrectly translated words	13	9	7	2	*27*
Lack of diagrams, etc.	8	6	*17*	*14*	13

All the factors given as choices could contribute adversely to the understandability of machine translation since all those areas had flaws; it was therefore quite important to obtain relative evaluations. What seems clear from Table 26 is that untranslated words affect understandability most since this factor received the highest number of votes in the top two ranks. The factor "incorrectly translated words" received the highest number of 'no response', but that was unfortunately biased by the format of the questionnaire, since it was not repeated in the second part of the query (see Appendix). It is quite likely that under different circumstances this factor would also receive a fairly high rating. "Lack of diagrams, etc." seems to be the least important factor, receiving the lowest number of responses in the top two ranks, and the highest number in the bottom two ranks. "Sentence structure" appears to be the second most important factor, with the number of responses high across the first three ranks, but never appearing as the highest number. What is perhaps most significant about these results is that the semantic factor (untranslated words) dominates over the syntactic one (sentence structure). Much clearer results along these lines emerge from the answers to the next two questions.

Questions 34–35   What does understandability of MT primarily depend on?

The discussion is combined here for the same reasons as in the case of Questions 32–33. It may seem at first that this question is very close to those two, but the purpose here was to elicit different information by providing different choices. Primarily, the aim was to obtain reactions on the importance of extralinguistic context, i.e., familiarity with the subject matter of a given translation for understanding the text as compared with linguistic factors. The choices supplied were: "familiarity with subject matter", "sentence structure", "translation of words", "format", "general style". The results were analyzed and presented along the same principles as for Questions 32–33 where those are discussed.

Table 27   Understandability of machine translation depends on:

	(1)	(2)	(3)	(4)	(5)	No response
			Rank of importance			Number of responses
Familiarity with subject matter	45	6	1			6
Translation of words	4	20	18	1		15
Sentence structure	4	23	20	1	1	9
Format			3	17	3	35
General style				5	5	45

The results unequivocally show familiarity with the subject matter as the primary factor in understanding machine-translated texts, and this should come as no surprise, not because machine-translated texts are involved here, but because much of our understanding of any phenomenon, and especially linguistic ones, depends on context. In reference to translations this has been pointed out by Eugene Nida, some of whose statements were quoted in the Introduction to Part III above. It should be mentioned that in the second part of the question the order of presentation of the choices was deliberately reversed, thus "familiarity with subject matter" was put at the bottom of the listing. This rearrangement, however, did not distract the users, since out of 52 responding, 45, or 88.5 percent, ranked that category as being of primary importance. Those very definite results have important implications in pointing out the relative significance of the semantic factor, which is also confirmed by the users' assignment of the second place in importance to the category "translation of words" which received the highest number of responses in the second and third rank. Syntactic factors, i. e., "sentence structure", scored below those semantic ones, "sentence structure" receiving responses somewhat lower than "translation of words" in the second and third rank and as low ones in the first rank, which is very considerably lower than the responses for "familiarity with the subject matter" in the first rank (4 as against 45). It is also interesting to notice the relatively high number of no responses in the case of "sentence structure". These results confirm those of Questions 32–33, but are much more definite and conclusive. The remaining choices supplied, "format" and "general style" received little attention as evidenced by the high number of no responses. In the case of the latter, this may have been influenced by the fact that it was not repeated in the second part of the question, but that is doubtful in view of a similarly high number of no responses for "format" which was repeated.

The results concerning the relative importance of the semantic and syntactic factors in the comprehension of translations, or texts in general, suggest a particular advantage of machine-translated texts in their imperfect form, since the very fact that they are syntactically deficient makes them into interesting material for the study of the interplay of semantic and syntactic factors. One might investigate the question of how much bad grammar one can get away with and yet retain comprehension and usefulness of texts through, for instance, deliberately making the grammar worse on the one hand, and also attempt to determine if comprehension is increased through the improvement of grammar on the other, and in what areas.

The next two questions probe the users' views of the imperfections of the texts they dealt with in the area of translation of sentences and technical words.

Question 36   Approximately what percentage of MT sentences are
unintelligible
badly distorted
understandable with difficulty
understandable
correct

This question was aimed at getting direct information on sentence structure, both from the point of view of their form and comprehensibility. The results are shown in Table 28 in the reverse order from the listing of choices above. This, however, is of no consequence and only serves the ease of comparisons in the following discussions.

Table 28.   Evaluation of translation of sentences (in percentages)

	Mean	Standard deviation	No response
Correct	17.10	20.9	(11)
Understandable	49.20	25.8	
Understandable with difficulty	20.90	21.5	
Badly distorted	9.70	12.7	
Unintelligible	5.39	5.2	

The results of this question are discussed after the analysis of results of Question 37 and a combined analysis of both those questions since, jointly, they are considered to provide some measures as to aspects of "goodness" of machine-translated texts. What is significant to notice with regard to Table 28, even though some standard deviations are high, is that two-thirds of the sentences (66.3 percent) were judged by users to fall into the top two categories, i.e., "correct" and "understandable", and also that the three top positive categories account for over 87 percent of all sentences.

Question 37   Approximately what percentage of technical words are
untranslated
incorrectly translated
unintelligible
badly distorted
understandable with difficulty
correct

As in the case of the previous question the results presented in Table 29 are in reverse order, for the same reason as before.

Table 29.   Evaluation of translation of technical words (in percentages)

	Mean	Standard deviation	No response
Correct	52.40	23.5	(13)
Understandable with difficulty	23.50	19.5	
Badly distorted	8.30	10.8	
Incorrectly translated	6.47	7.6	
Untranslated	6.40	7.2	
Unintelligible	4.20	4.4	

The discussion of these results is deferred until after the analysis of combined results of Questions 36 and 37, which follows. It should be noticed in Table 29 that more than half of the technical words were said to be "correct" and thus the two top categories, which are the positive ones, include almost 80 percent of all the technical words.

Table 30 below shows the combined results of Questions 36 and 37 in the positive categories in order to convey a feel for users' evaluations of the "goodness" of translations on the basis of their judgments of sentences and technical words of the texts in a summary manner.

Table 30   Combined results: Evaluation of translation of sentences and technical words

	Question 36	Question 37
Correct	17.1	52.4
Understandable	49.2	
Understandable with difficulty	20.9	23.5
Total	87.2	75.9
(Average:	81.5)	

One of the reasons for this joint analysis of the positive judgments as to the translation of the essential ingredients of a scientific text, i. e., sentences and technical words, was to make a comparison with the users' overall impressionistic assessment of the quality of translations. This, as may be recalled, was judged to be over 91 percent "good or acceptable", and while the figures here are somewhat lower, they certainly confirm the general evaluation.

Those three positive categories in Table 30 are considered to provide a measure of "completeness" of machine-translated texts, since adequate rendition of sentence structure and the essential vocabulary would clearly make the text accessible. The term, however, stems from the Zarechnak – Bar-Hillel controversy (Introduction) on the completeness of machine-translation output, and it is therefore considered desirable to go back to it and compare the results obtained here with figures quoted by them. The measures of completeness as used here may of course be somewhat different from what they and others had in mind; nevertheless, a comparison of figures is of interest, especially in view of the disparity of the figures quoted by the two scholars. It may be recalled that Zarechnak stated that machine-translation output was 80 percent complete and Bar-Hillel that it was 35 to 40 percent complete. To judge from the users' positive evaluations in Table 30 they seemed to agree with Zarechnak, the average being over 80 percent. The objection might be raised that the category "understandable with difficulty" should not be taken as a measure of completeness. If those figures are left out and only the categories "correct" and "understandable" used, the results are clearly somewhat lower, the average for the two categories for both questions being 59.3 percent. This figure would thus be right in between the estimates of Zarechnak and Bar-Hillel. It was pointed out that Bar-Hillel's estimate had to do with *readability*, while Zarechnak's dealt with *informativeness*. In terms of the results here, it is felt that the average of 59.3 percent obtained for the categories "correct" and "understandable" constitutes a measure of "readability". As for "informativeness", it can be measured in terms of the results of Question 19, "Can you decide on the basis of a machine translation text whether the work described is important to you", and Question 20, "Do you get enough information about the work described". As may be recalled, the combined number of "yes" responses to both questions amounted to 93 percent. Finally, the average for the combined results of the three positive categories of Questions 36 and 37, i. e., percentages of sentences and technical words evaluated to be "correct", "understandable" and "understandable with difficulty" and which was over 81 percent, can provide a measure of "completeness". The three concepts and the figures characterizing them are summarized in Table 31.

Table 31. Informativeness, readability and completeness of machine-translation output (in percentages)

	Question	Rating	Average
Informativeness	19	100.0	93.0
	20	86.0	
Readability	36	66.3	59.3
	37	52.4	
Completeness	36	87.2	81.5
	37	75.9	

The results on "informativeness", "readability" and "completeness" as shown in Table 31 seem to provide a fairly definitive portrayal of the goodness or adequacy of machine translations. The users' contribution to reading them is investigated in the next four questions.

Question 38   If the style of MT is awkward, can you correct it mentally?

Table 32 summarizes the overwhelmingly positive response, which was somewhat of a surprise, in view of some of the criticisms contained in the results of other questions.

Table 32. Correcting machine-translation style mentally

	Number	%
Yes	56	98.3
No	1	1.7

These results could also be considered as a measure of "readability" to the extent that reading machine-translated texts appears not to be a problem. They could likewise be related to the results of Questions 34 and 35 on the role of the nonlinguistic context, i.e., knowledge of the subject matter, and to the lesser importance of sentence structure. The ability to correct mentally was, not surprisingly, connected with familiarity with English. The only negative answer came from a user who filled out the questionnaire not in English and rated his speaking familiarity with English as 'fair', which, however, was a slight exaggeration.

Question 39   If words are untranslated, can you understand them from context?

Question 40   If words are untranslated, can you understand them from the transliterated Russian words?

These two questions make sense only in view of the machine-translation practice that words which are not found in the dictionary during the process of translation are not simply abandoned. Rather, as explained in Part II (sections 1.5, 2.6) they are subjected to as extensive a grammatical analysis as possible, the untranslated portion being transliterated, i.e., printed in (nearly) Latin script, within the body of the text. Most of these words are technical words and their Russian form usually closely resembles the English form, thus facilitating comprehension.

Table 33   Understanding untranslated words from linguistic context

	Context		Transliteration	
	Number	% for sample	Number	% for sample
Quite often	23	40.3	19	33.3
Sometimes	31	54.4	25	43.9
Never	3	5.3	12	21.1

This joint presentation of the results would indicate that transliteration was not quite as helpful as general context; however, it is possible that the users included the contribution of transliteration in their evaluation of the role of context. The results undoubtedly stress the importance of the users' knowledge of the subject matter, but also point out the contribution to understanding of the linguistic context, since the negative answers are a definite minority (94.7 positive versus 5.3 negative and 77.2 versus 21.1 for the two questions respectively).

The next four questions deal with comparisons between machine-translated texts and those originally written in English on the one hand and human translations on the other, in terms of relative unintelligibility and the amount of time required for reading. In each case the user was asked to state his estimate in terms of a scale of percentages. One set of figures was given for the first two questions and another for the remaining two. They are discussed separately. The phrasing of the questions proved rather difficult, and more hesitation was observed in answering. A good deal of valuable information was nevertheless revealed, some of which is summarized below, including a few comparisons of results across questions.

Question 41   What percentage of MT texts is unintelligible as compared with texts originally written in English?

The answer was 21.4 percent. The scale of percentages supplied was 80, 50, 30, 20 and 10. It was assumed that if a machine-translated text were more than 80 percent unintelligible it would not be used, and also that none would be nearer to perfection than 10 percent. The scale seemed to serve the purpose well, although the assumption about the 10 percent limit proved not quite correct since a few users indicated "less than 10 %". The figure for unintelligibility of machine translation obtained from the answers, i. e., 21.4 percent, coincides amazingly well with the measure of completeness as used here, which showed machine-translated texts to be 81.5 percent complete (see Questions 36 and 37).

Question 42   What percentage of MT texts is unintelligible as compared with texts translated from Russian by humans?

The answer was 18.7 percent. The scale provided here was the same as in Question 41. Although the difference in results is very small it tends to show that human translations the users had experience with were not quite as good as texts written originally in English. Far stronger evidence is supplied by Question 44, below. One of the users went so far in this respect as to comment: "machines do better than humans".

Question 43   Does reading MT texts require significantly more time than texts originally written in English?

The answer was 96.5 percent. The scale provided for estimates was 200 percent, 100 percent, 75 percent, 50 percent, 20 percent and 10 percent.

Some clarification was occasionally necessary as to what those figures meant, but in general the intended meaning was assumed, i.e., that "100 %" meant 'once again as much time'. The result thus shows that the reading time for machine-translated texts is almost twice that for texts originally written in English. The extra time, however, was ascribed by users primarily to the lack of formulae, diagrams, etc., which were absent from the translations, necessitating reference to the Russian original. No matter what reason, though, it is a fact that reading machine-translated texts required a good deal of time.

Question 44   Please make the same comparison for texts translated by humans

The answer was 32 percent. The scale provided was the same as in Question 43. The result shows that texts translated by humans require one-third more time to read than texts originally written in English, and thus are much better in this respect than machine-translated ones, which is not surprising. What is less expected, though, is that they are also quite far from perfect. It seems that this is an important result to bear in mind when evaluating the advantages and disadvantages of machine translation, in addition to all the other factors taken into consideration, such as quality, speed, cost, availability of human translators, etc. The experience of one steady machine-translation user with human translations, as recounted by himself, provides an informative story. Having requested a human translation of one of his papers into English for presentation at a conference, he expected the arrival of the text within a reasonable time. Instead, while the translation was being executed in a nearby big city by two translators, he received almost daily telephone calls for several weeks about terminology, etc. After the final product reached him, it had an even more unexpected result: he decided to either translate into or write in English himself, inferior though his English might have been in grammar and style to that of a professional translator. Incidentally, this scientist had also used machine translation a great deal following that experience. Since it is seldom possible for a translator to specialize in some rather specific field, it is not surprising that terminology poses a great problem. It is well known that dictionaries cannot keep up with the often rapid developments and changes in scientific fields. The advantages of machine-translation dictionaries become clear in view of the ease of updating them and avoiding the lengthy publication process.

The comparisons of unintelligibility and length of time required for reading machine-translated texts and human translations, and of both these with English texts are summarized in Table 34 (in percentages).

Table 34   Summary of Questions 41–44

	Unintelligibility	Extra time for reading
Machine translation versus English	21.4	96.5
Machine versus human translation	18.7	
Human translation versus English		32.0

Now that some of the negative aspects of using machine translation have been exposed, namely the inconvenience of the length of time required for reading it, partly due to the lack of essential portions of a scientific paper, the extent to which the text is unintelligible, and the longer waiting time for the translation than acceptable (29 versus 18 days), it becomes particularly interesting to recall that users expressed overwhelmingly (87 percent to 13 percent) a preference for machine over human translation if the latter were to require three times as long a waiting time (that being the usual case). The conclusion is rather obvious that speed compensates for inconveniences and imperfections and that at least some users were "ready to trade quality for speed", or at least convenience for speed, since those particular users judged the quality to be over 91 percent "good" or "acceptable" anyway.

The next three questions, 45 through 47, investigate another controversial issue about machine translation, and one that is of great importance, namely the danger that might result from inaccuracies of various types of machine-translation output. The three questions are graded, as it were, from inquiring about mere occurrences of distortions in meaning through the possibility of meaning opposite to that of the original to potential misleading and harmful effects on the scientist's work. Jointly, the results are considered as providing a judgment of the potential "misinformativeness" of machine translation, which is of course a fundamental problem, perhaps of even greater importance than "informativeness", "readability", or "completeness". The users' reactions, as will be seen from the results below, make it clear that fears about "misinformativeness" are unfounded.

Question 45   Do inaccurate translations of words, phrases or sentences result in complete distortion of meaning?

The choices supplied were "often", "sometimes" and "never". The category "rarely" was added by the respondents.

Table 35.   Occurrence of complete distortion of meaning

	Number	% for respondents
Often	1	1.8
Sometimes	44	80.0
Never	7	12.7
Rarely	3	5.4

The most frequent answer was, as expected, "sometimes", this being the most cautious and vague reply. What is significant about the results, and what was really the purpose of the question, is that only one respondent marked "often", and that as many as 7 said that complete distortion of meaning never occurs.

Question 46   Can distortions in MT lead to opposite meaning from the original?

This question and the following one contain a very unfortunate ambiguity which was pointed out by the respondents. The two interpretations at which the response can be aimed are either the conjectural one, something like: "is it in the realm of possibilities that..."; or the factual one, which might be paraphrased as "has it been your experience that...". One user summed it up very well in his comment which read: "in principle: yes; in practice: no. The context is no *tabula rasa* for the reader." The real intention, which was the factual interpretation, was indicated during the interviews if the user was in doubt. For a while, however, the ambiguity went unnoticed, and the questionnaires completed outside of personal interviews may very well reflect the ambiguity. Table 36 shows the answers to Question 46.

Table 36.   Possibility of machine-translation inaccuracies leading to opposite meaning

	Number	% for sample	% for respondents
Yes	10	17.5	25
No	30	52.5	75

Some comments qualifying the answers or taking the place of one also refer to the ambiguity discussed in conjunction with Table 36. They were: "of course it is possible", "possible", "possibly, yes", "yes if word in the dictionary is wrong", "never had this experience", "no if familiar with the subject". The first four of these answers were counted as "yes" answers in spite of the qualifying words, and the latter two as "no". As can be seen from Table 36, the results are overwhelmingly negative (75 percent versus 25 percent) as to the possibility of opposite meaning in machine-translated texts, and the existence of the ambiguity allowing the conjectural interpretation might only have had the effect of inducing more answers to the possibility of "misinformativeness". Thus the fact that its likelihood is considered so low is quite significant.

The role played by familiarity with the subject matter and the context is again underscored here, even in direct statements by the users.

Question 47   If the translation is unclear, could you reach misleading conclusions as to the nature of the work described? Could that have harmful effects on your work?

The phrasing of this question is by far the strongest of the three, especially in its second part, and this fact is reflected in the results which turn out to be more definitive. The same ambiguity, however, was involved here as in the previous question and it had a similar effect on the answers. Table 37 shows that the respondents were quite certain (over 85 percent) that misleading conclusions which might have a harmful effect on one's work could not result from the imperfections of machine-translated texts.

Table 37.   Potential misleading and harmful effects of unclear machine-translated texts

	Number	% for sample	% for respondents
Yes	7	12.3	13.8
No	44	77.0	86.2

Some of the comments accompanying answers or different phrasings of the answers reflect the ambiguity in the question which allowed the interpretation as to abstract potentiality as well as actual existence of such misleading and harmful effects, some answers being: "it is quite possible", "it's possible", "sometimes yes", "on rare occasions", "remote possibility", "rarely", "improbable", "not likely", "hardly", "in my cases up to now: no", "no case known to me", "not at all". In order to include these answers in the statistical results, the first four responses were counted as "yes", and the rest as "no", even though "on rare occasions" is probably just as negative as "hardly" and should have been counted as "no". The inclusion of the first four answers quoted above in the "yes" group inflated it somewhat, while in reality there were only three unambiguously "yes" answers.

The results of Questions 46 and 47 are combined in Table 38.

Table 38.   "Misinformativeness" of machine-translation output (Questions 46 and 47 combined)

	Number	% for sample	% for respondents
Yes	8.5	14.9	19.4
No	37.0	64.7	80.6

Thus, in the overall picture, "misinformativeness" was ruled out by 80 percent of the responding users, and that sheds fairly definitive light on a very important issue.

Question 48   Have you noticed any improvements in the quality of MT?

This question and the following one, which is "Was it more difficult to read first translations than later ones? Do you feel that you can get used to the style of MT?" attempt to establish whether "practice makes perfect" also in the case of reading machine-translated output, since it was observed in discussions with users that they were under the impression that improvements had been made during the time they had used machine translation. Since no substantial improvements had been made other than the addition of a few thousand dictionary words, the only plausible explanation for the users' impression was that they gained practice in reading the texts, and Question 49 was included to check that out. Question 48 had two parts, the second being an inquiry as to what areas were observed as having been improved, with the choices: "vocabulary", "sentence structure", "diagrams, etc.", "format" having been provided. Table 39 shows the result of the main question and Table 40 the ratings of the areas.

Table 39.   Judgment of improvements in machine-translation output

	Number	% for sample	% for respondents
Yes	20	35.1	51
No	19	33.3	49

Table 40.   Judgment of areas of improvement

Area	Number	% for respondents
Vocabulary	16	59.2
Sentence structure	8	29.6
Format	3	11.1

These results are quite surprising since half of the respondents answered in the affirmative about noticing improvements in the quality of machine-translation texts. The improvements are primarily credited to the vocabulary, but it is difficult to imagine that 5000 or 6000 additions to the dictionary could improve the quality so perceptibly, especially since machine translation was used in a wide variety of fields, and the additions could not have been significant in all of them. Especially surprising, however, was the impression that sentence structure was improved, since there were no actual improvements in that area. As mentioned above, the most likely reason for the general impression of improvements is that the quality "grows" on the user as he becomes familiar with the style of machine translation and even its imperfections. But in the particular case of the impression of improvements in sentence structure, another clue may have been provided by a respondent with the following comment: "sentence structure – when words are improved". This may be a reference to morphological analysis which can provide information about the function of a word in a sentence or it may point to the dependency of syntax on the semantic component – even the structure of a sentence may seem better if the choice of the words is better. Another factor which may have led to the impression of improved sentence structure was general format, which had been improved, thus facilitating readability on the whole.

Question 49   Was it more difficult to read first translations than later ones? Do you feel that you can get used to the style of MT?

It was expected that continued use of machine-translated texts would result in a certain degree of adaptation, and the aim was to establish that degree. The answers are presented separately for the two parts of the question.

Table 41. First translations more difficult to read than later ones

	Number	% for sample	% for respondents
Yes	25	43.7	75.7
No	8	14.0	24.2

Table 42. Getting used to the style of machine translation

	Number	% for sample	% for respondents
Yes	37	64.7	97.4
No	1	1.7	2.6

It is clear from the above results that "readability" increases with continued use, since 75 percent of the respondents found it easier to read later translations than earlier ones, and almost 100 percent felt that they could get used to the style. These facts should be taken into account in evaluating users' reactions in the sense that the reaction of a first-time user is likely to be different from that of a veteran. Once again, we are confronted with the contribution that the user himself brings to his interaction with machine translation, whether it be in his familiarity with the subject matter, his use of context, his correcting the imperfections mentally, or his accommodation to the peculiarities of the texts.

Question 50   Have you, or would you, recommend the use of MT to your colleagues?

The user's reaction to this question was expected to reflect his overall satisfaction or dissatisfaction which he might hesitate to express more directly. This purpose was achieved rather well, since almost all users responded, and almost all answered affirmatively. Table 43 gives the results.

Table 43. Recommending machine translation to colleagues

	Number	% for sample	% for respondents
Yes	49	85.5	96.1
No	2	3.6	3.9

It is rather clear that users did not hestitate to recommend machine translation, which is a good measure of their overall attitude. Throughout the answers, there was at least one negative vote and that came consistently from one user who was mentioned before as having had rather limited knowledge of English. One of the negative answers here was also his, and the other was followed by a somewhat cryptic comment stating that his must remain a personal opinion.

Question 51   What improvements in MT would you like to see?

The answers, not surprisingly, do not yield themselves to any precise statistical analysis, but certain areas keep recurring in a variety of phrasings. To some extent, they may have been suggested by earlier questions, since the frequently mentioned areas are: vocabulary, sentence structure, formulae, diagrams, format, but that fact in itself is unimportant. What is significant is the relative frequency of these areas. A count of references to vocabulary (or dictionary, technical terms, words, etc.) shows that they are at least twice as frequent as sentence structure (syntax), with 34 mentions of the former and 15 of the latter. Formulae, diagrams, etc. on the one hand, and format on the other, are mentioned only 12 and 6 times respectively and consequently seem to be of lower importance than the other two areas. Some opinions are contradictory, one user stating: "I would rate sentence structure as more important than word interpretation"; another: "Don't feel that sentence structure is enough of a problem to worry about – in any case, would put it low as a priority." Among other comments, the full list of which is given below, two users expressed that they were satisfied, two asked for faster service, one for translation into German, and one concluded that "machines do better than humans". In the list of comments that follows the original wordings of the users were preserved.

1. "am rather satisfied"
2. "words on the diagrams"
3. a. "more double translations of 'homonyms'"
   b. "elimination of all formulae and symbols from the text; for each: 'long formula'"
   c. "list with figures and tables at the end; no open space for figures, etc."
4. "better vocabulary"
5. "A partial translation of only 1) the conclusions, 2) the literature list, 3) the fig. subscripts should be possible."

6. "I. An English grammar in order that it isn't English words with a Russian grammar
II. A good translation of technical words, that is to give the computer a possibility to know when to use a 'common' meaning and not when it must use the technical meaning."
7. "vocabulary, sentence structure, untranslated words"
8. "cover to cover translation"
9. "improve structure of the sentences"
10. "faster service, correct translation of technical words, increased vocabulary"
11. "I was satisfied"
12. "(1) no untranslated words, (2) technical terms (eg. solution of an equation instead of decision, etc.), (3) sentence structure, (4) formulae and equations"
13. "sentence structure"
14. "improve the sentence structure, widen the vocabulary"
15. "format"
16. "translation into German"
17. "better sentence structure"
18. "regular inclusion of new words in the dictionary"
19. "figures and diagrams"
20. "(1) diagrams, formulae and figures"
21. "the sentence structure has to be considerably improved"
22. "expanded and improved technical vocabulary; formulae included in machine-translated text; less repetition of lines."
23. "vocabulary; sentence structure; diagrams, etc.; format."
24. "less distortion and more vocabulary"
25. "split up translation into two possibilities:
1) abstract, tables, graphs
2) MT–translation
one should have possibility to ask for one, or two of them"
26. "better computer output of tables"
27. "vocabulary"
28. "technical vocabulary for a specific field"
29. "dictionary – for different subject contexts"
30. "better coverage of soil science terms could be helpful"
31. "(1) optical character recognition or other input

(2) dictionary for my field

(3) sentence structure"

32. "A translation that more nearly resembles a human translation; I would rate sentence structure as more important than word interpretation"

33. "better translation of technical words"

34. "better vocabulary"

35. "better sentence structure"

36. "syntax and vocabulary"

37. "choices of meanings given when various ones are possible"

38. "dictionary refinement and expansion. Don't feel that sentence structure is enough of a problem to worry about – in any case, would put it low as a priority"

39. "better sentence structure"

40. "more words in dictionary; corrections of those that are now wrong; omission of all articles (this is one of the biggest problems), and work on such words as 'by' with the Russian verb for 'is' which takes instrumental case"

41. "keying to specific vocabularies for specific fields"

42. "if formulas and diagrams were put into the printout, it would make it simpler to use."

43. "expanded vocabulary"

44. "in technical words"

45. a. "faster service"

b. "more precise translation of technical text"

c. "reproduction of formulas"

46. "specialized vocabulary for individual fields"

47. "machines do better than humans"

48. "improved vocabulary in my field"

49. "better physics output; more compact output"

50. "diagrams and formulas in text"

This concludes the detailed analysis of the users' answers to the questionnaire, some results of which are summarized in the conclusions.

3.3 Summary and conclusions

The Georgetown Machine Translation System has been used extensively at the EURATOM Research Center in Ispra, Italy, and the Atomic Energy Commission's Oak Ridge National Laboratory at Oak Ridge, Tennessee (U.S.A.), between 1963 and 1973. Translations made with this system were the basis for the study of users' opinions and reactions to their experience with unedited translations from Russian to English over that period. Information is presented on the activity of the machine-translation services in terms of usage patterns, the volume of texts, the type of users, the cost and the speed. Users' evaluations were elicited by means of a questionnaire, often in conjunction with an interview. The questionnaire is included in the Appendix, together with a partial list of one group of users and a sample of users' evaluative letters. Fifty-seven questionnaires were received from fifty-eight users who represented over thirty scientific and engineering fields.

Among the most important results of the study are the facts that the quality of machine translation was judged to be "good" and "acceptable" by over 90 percent of the respondents, and that machine-translated texts were considered to be 93 percent informative, 59 percent readable, and 81 percent complete. Also significant is the fact that the possibility of misinformativeness was rated low, since only 19 percent acknowledged its possibility, while 80 percent never experienced it. On the other hand, that aspect of machine translation which is universally admitted to be its potential advantage, i.e., speed, was found to be much lower than could be expected and desired (29 days as against desired 18). The reason, however, was not machine aspects, but rather the human factors involved (keypunching and mail).

The users presented a rather satisfied group of customers, since 96 percent of them had or would recommend machine-translation services to their colleagues, even though the texts were said to require almost twice as much time to read as original English texts (humanly-translated texts also were judged to take longer to read, but only about a third longer), and that machine-translated texts were said to be 21 percent unintelligible. In spite of slower service than desired and a high demand on reading time, machine translation was preferred to human translation by 87 percent of the respondents if the latter took three times as long as the former. The reasons for the preference were not only earlier access, but also the feelings that "the machine is more honest", and that since human labor is not invested it is easy to discard a text which proves of marginal interest. Getting used to reading machine-translation style did not present a problem as evidenced by the answers of over 95 percent of the respondents.

From the linguistic point of view the most important finding was that semantic factors (vocabulary, linguistic context) were considered more important for understanding machine-translated texts than syntax, and it was in those areas that improvements were particularly desirable. The most important factor in understanding, however, was familiarity with the subject matter (extralinguistic context) which the user himself contributes.

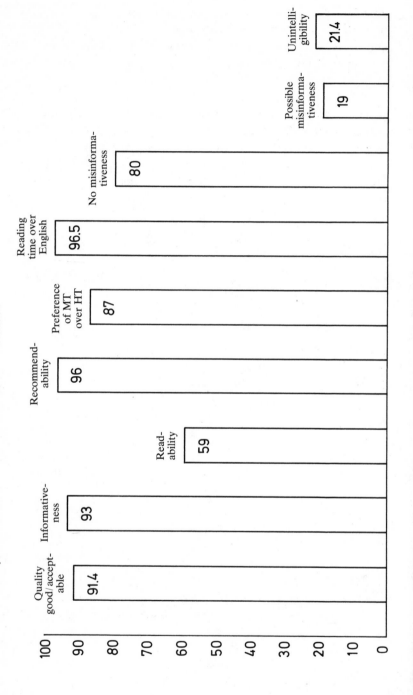

Table 44.   Summary of results of users' evaluations of machine translation

Appendix

The Appendix contains three items: (1) the questionnaire which was distributed to the users of machine translations in order to obtain their evaluations, which are discussed in Chapter 3; (2) a partial list of clients of the European Translations Centre which by 1972 had handled some 350 requests utilizing machine-translation services at EURATOM. Seven European countries are represented even in this small list; and (3) a sample of solicited and unsolicited users' letters evaluating machine translations. Only a few out of hundreds on file have been included, merely to illustrate users' attitudes. The first eight are reactions of the users of the Oak Ridge machine-translation service. The next eight come from the clients of ETC. Finally, a few assorted comments were selected, including one from a professional translator.

   It was considered informative to include this sample of users' letters, but unfortunately the originals were not available and consequently some of the copies are not completely legible.

1. Questionnaire

QUESTIONNAIRE ON THE USE OF MACHINE TRANSLATION (MT)

1. Your name, last and first (omit, if you prefer to)

2. Nationality

3. Native language

4. Please rate your familiarity with English
   Speaking   Reading
   ☐ Excellent   ☐ Excellent
   ☐ Good   ☐ Good
   ☐ Fair   ☐ Fair

5. Your familiarity with Russian
   Speaking   Reading
   ☐ Good   ☐ Good
   ☐ Fair   ☐ Fair
   ☐ Poor   ☐ Poor
   ☐ None   ☐ None

6. Your principal field of work

7. Your department at EURATOM, AEC, or other place of employment

8. How did you come in contact with MT?

9. Why do you use MT?

10. When did you first use MT?

11. When did you last use MT?

12. Approximately, how many translations have you requested?

13. On the average, how many translations a year have you requested?

14. Approximately, how many pages of translations have you requested?

15. What is your primary reason for using MT?
    for example:
    ☐ cost

☐ rapidity of access to translation
☐ reliability
☐ accuracy

16. Do you pay for MT?
☐ yes   ☐ no
How much?
Do you know how much it costs to translate 1000 words by MT?

17. Do you pay for human translations?
☐ yes   ☐ no
How much?

18. What is your primary use of machine translated texts?
for example:
☐ details of experiments
☐ surveys of experiments
☐

19. Can you decide on the basis of a machine translated text whether the work described is important to you?

20. Do you get enough information about the work described?

21. Have you asked for human translation of articles translated by MT?
☐ yes   ☐ no
What percentage of the total?

22. Have you compared human translations with machine translations of the same articles?
☐ yes   ☐ no
☐ frequently
☐ infrequently

If yes, for what purpose?
for example:
☐ clarification of language
☐ missing words
☐ missing formulae, diagrams, etc.
☐

23. When reading a machine translated text, do you look at the Russian original?
☐ yes   ☐ no
☐ frequently

☐ infrequently

If yes, for what purpose?
for example:
☐ missing words
☐ incorrectly translated words
☐ incorrectly translated sentences
☐ missing formulae, diagrams, etc.
☐

24. Have you requested human translations?
   ☐ yes   ☐ no
   ☐ frequently
   ☐ infrequently
   ☐ more often than MT
   ☐ less often than MT

25. On the average, how long have you had to wait for a human translation?
Is this too long?

26. On the average, how long have you had to wait for a machine translation?
Is this too long?
What period of waiting is acceptable to you?

27. If you had to wait for human translations three times as long as for MT, which would you prefer?
   ☐ human   ☐ MT

28. What percentage of the literature that you read in your field is written in Russian?

29. What is the primary field in which you requested MT from Russian?

30. How do Russian articles come to your attention?
for example:
☐ references in journals
☐ colleagues
☐ abstracts
☐ reviews
☐

NOTE: Your answers to the questions below will be of particular importance and value.

31. How do you rate the quality of MT in general?
    ☐ good
    ☐ acceptable
    ☐ poor

32. What affects understandability of MT most? Please comment.
    ☐ sentence structure
    ☐ untranslated words
    ☐ lack of diagrams, formulae, figures etc.
    ☐ incorrectly translated words
    ☐

33. Please assign numbers in descending order of importance, i.e. 1 to
    most important, 2 to next most important, etc.
    for example:
    (1) untranslated words
    (2) lack of diagrams, etc.
    (3) sentence structure, etc.

34. What does understandability of MT texts primarily depend on? Please
    comment.
    for example:
    ☐ familiarity with the subject matter
    ☐ sentence structure
    ☐ translation of words
    ☐ format
    ☐ general style
    ☐

35. Please assign numbers in descending order to the above problems for
    example:
    (1) format
    (2) untranslated words
    (3) sentence structure
    (4) familiarity with subject matter, etc.

36. Approximately, what percentage of the MT sentences are
    – unintelligible
    – badly distorted
    – understandable with difficulty
    – understandable
    – correct

37. Approximately, what percentage of technical words are
    – untranslated

- incorrectly translated
- unintelligible
- badly distorted
- understandable with difficulty
- correct

38. If the style of MT is awkward, can you correct it mentally?
   ☐ yes   ☐ no
   ☐ often
   ☐ infrequently

39. If words are untranslated, can you understand them from the context?
   ☐ quite often   ☐ sometimes
   ☐ never

40. If words are untranslated, can you understand them from the transliterated Russian words?
   ☐ quite often   ☐ sometimes
   ☐ never

41. What percentage of MT texts is unintelligible as compared with texts originally written in English?
   80%   50%   30%   20%   10%

42. What percentage of MT texts is unintelligible as compared with texts translated from Russian by humans?
   80%   50%   30%   20%   10%

43. Does reading MT texts require significantly more time than texts originally written in English? If so, how much?
   200%   100%   75%   50%   20%   10%

44. Please make the same comparison for texts translated by humans
   200%   100%   75%   50%   20%   10%

45. Do inaccurate translations of words, phrases or sentences result in complete distortion of meaning?
   ☐ often   ☐ sometimes   ☐ never

46. Can distortions in MT lead to opposite meaning from the original?

47. If the translation is unclear, could you reach misleading conclusions as to the nature of the work described? Could that have harmful effects on your work?

48. Have you noticed any improvements in the quality of MT?
    ☐ yes   ☐ no

    If yes, in what?
    for example:
    ☐ vocabulary
    ☐ sentence structure
    ☐ diagrams, etc.
    ☐ format
    ☐

49. Was it more difficult to read first translations than later ones?
    Do you feel that you can get used to the style of MT?

50. Have you, or would you, recommend the use of MT to your colleagues?

51. What improvements in MT would you like to see?

2. Partial list of ETC clients

1. LUMMUS NEDERLAND N.V.
   Kalvermarkt 9
   The Hague, The Netherlands

2. N.V. Nederlandse Staatsmijnen DSM
   Centraal Laboratorium (Mr. G. Fritschy)
   Geleen, The Netherlands

3. Technische Universitätsbibliothek (Frau Schilling)
   Welfengarten 1 B
   3 Hannover, West Germany

4. Studiëcentrum voor Kernenergie SCK
   Mol-Donk, Belgium

5. Koninklijke Nederlandse Gist- en Spiritusfabriek N.V. (Mr. Ch. L.
   Citroen)
   Postbus 1
   Delft, The Netherlands

6. Scientific Periodicals Library (Mr. A. B. Britton)
   Benett Street
   Cambridge, United Kingdom

7. NV Koninklijke Nederlandse Zoutindustrie
   Boortorenweg 27
   Hengelo (0), The Netherlands

8. F.O.M. Instituut voor Atoom– en Molecuulfysica (Mr. A. P. M. Baede)
   Kruislaan 407
   Amsterdam-Watergraafsmeer, The Netherlands

9. Laboratorium voor Analytische Scheikunde der Universiteit van Ams-
   terdam (Mr. E. Abeling)
   Nieuwe Achtergracht 125
   Amsterdam-C, The Netherlands

10. Instituut voor Plantenveredeling
    Landbouwhogeschool (Mr. H. Bouter)
    Lawickse Allee 166
    Wageningen, The Netherlands

11. Technische Hogeschool
    Bibliotheek van de Afdeling Metaalkunde
    Rotterdamseweg
    Delft, The Netherlands

12. Mr. J. W. van Lingen
    Oosteinde 139a
    Delft, The Netherlands

13. Mr. J. van Brakel
    Laboratorium voor Chemische Technologie
    Julianalaan 136
    Delft, The Netherlands

14. AKZO ZOUT CHEMIE N.V.
    Boortorenweg 20
    Hengelo (0), The Netherlands

15. Mr. M. ten Voorde
    Jacoba van Beierenlaan 29
    Delft, The Netherlands

16. Erik T. Jonsson
    Technical Librarian
    Fostfatbolaget
    S-840 10 Ljungaverk, Sweden

17. Dr. F. G. Moers
    Catholic University
    Nijmegen, The Netherlands

19. Th. G. A. Boevenbrink
    Noury & Van der Lande
    Deventer, The Netherlands

20. Randi Gjerrsik
    Norges Tekniske Hogskole
    Hovedbiblioteket
    Trondheim, Norway

21. Drs. H. van den Berg
    Rijksuniversiteit
    Lab. voor Technische Scheikunde en Polymeerchemie
    Groningen, The Netherlands

22. Drs. H. J. Boorsma
    Rijksinstituut voor Drinkwatervoorziening
    Parkweg 13
    's-Gravenhage, The Netherlands

23. K. P. Riswick
    De chef van de afdeling Documentatie en Bibliotheek
    MEKOG

24. K. Delcour Central Laboratory
    Dow Chemical (Nederland) N.V.
    P.O. Box 48
    Terneuzen, The Netherlands

25. Ph. de Wijn
    Hollandsche Draad- en Kabelfabrik
    Amsterdam, The Netherlands

26. Dr. E. W. Lindeijer
    Technologisch Laboratorium RVO-TNO
    Postbus 4545
    Rijswijk, The Netherlands

27. J. D. Gilbert or Miss J. W. Bijl
    Unilever Research Laboratorium Duiven
    Helhoek 30 – Groessen
    Postbus 7
    Zevenaar, The Netherlands

28. HTS St. Virgilius (Mr. M. Kerstens)
    Sibeliuslaan 13
    Breda, The Netherlands

29. S. M. Lemkowitz
    Laboratorium voor Chemische Technologie
    Julianalaan 136
    Delft, The Netherlands

30. Blackwell's (attn. Mr. P. J. Molloy)
    Broad Street
    Oxford, England OX1 3 BQ

31. Mr. A. W. Verburg
    Van der Lelijstraat 11
    Delft, The Netherlands

32. Mr. J. A. Feijter
Van 't Hoff-Laboratorium der Rijksuniversiteit Utrecht
Utrecht, The Netherlands

33. Mr. J. G. van Berkum
Laboratorium voor Algemene en Anorganische Scheikunde
Julianalaan 136
Delft 8, The Netherlands

34. H. G. Freie
Houttuinen 2
Delft, The Netherlands

35. Taioloi-Menabeni
Via Chiaramonti 65
Asena, Italy

36. Th. de Ruiter
Bibliotheek Farmaceutisch Centrum
Rijksuniversiteit
Utrecht, The Netherlands

37. Mr. Nusselaar
Dirk Kosterplein 170
Delft, The Netherlands

38. P. Falk
Bibliotheek Metaalkunde
Rotterdamseweg 137
Delft, The Netherlands

39. F. J. M. Wensveen
Friesestraat 7 A
Rotterdam, The Netherlands

3 A sample of users' letters of evaluation

 INTERNAL CORRESPONDENCE ━━━━━━━━━━━━━━━━

NUCLEAR DIVISION   POST OFFICE BOX Y, OAK RIDGE, TENNESSEE 378█

To (Name) Fred Hutton	*Date* October 27, 1965
Company K-1007	
Location	*Originating Dept.* C. F. Barnett
	Answering letter date
	Subject Machine Translation Evaluation

I am sorry to be so long in sending you a note concerning evaluation of machine translation of Russian papers. We have found them to be of great use and the short time that it takes to get the translation is more desirable. Being familiar with the specific field enables one to digest all the information with very little trouble. The five reports from the Culham meeting were given to Dr. A. H. Snell and his opinion was solicited as to their usefulness. He was very impressed that one could take the reports and, not knowing any Russian, make a literal, smooth report with little effort. Dr. L. Branscomb, Head of the Joint Institute for Laboratory Astrophysics, looked over the translation of Russian abstracts from a collision conference and his opinion was that one should make more use of this type translation and wants to know if we can provide a service to them. Dr. E. W. McDaniel of Georgia Tech. thinks the translations are great. I have surveyed approximately a dozen people and they are all enthusiastic about the translations.

There does exist a general criticism in that the program should be updated into a more scientific language. Would it be possible for us to go through some of these translations marking and changing words and phrases and then changing the program to give a better translation?

Also, there is some question about relative costs. From one of the ·first translations I determined that the cost of machine translations was one-fourth of the literal translation. Is this a fair comparison?

I do think that this is an excellent service and we hope to make much use of it in the future.

CFB:mw

.INTRA-LABORATORY CORRESPONDENCE
OAK RIDGE NATIONAL LABORATORY

o: Miss Betty Olinger   Date: March 18, ·1966

rom: A. P. Malinauskas

ubject: Machine Translations from the Russian Language

opy to: S. Zimmer (ORGDP)

            File

Let me first apologize for the rather lengthy delay in getting this
eport to you. I had withheld my comments initially in order to likewise obtain
he opinion of one of our consultants who was also interested in the papers.
fter speaking with him, however, I had completely forgotten about it until
our phone call.

Below is a composite of both of our observations:

Service: excellent, rapid

Cost: very reasonable

Product: Highly recommended, if the reader has a knowledge of the
         subject. Not recommended, however, if the subject matter
         is foreign.

A. P. Malinauskas
Reactor Chemistry Division

PM:cap

INTRA-LABORATORY CORRESPONDENCE
OAK RIDGE NATIONAL LABORATORY

To: Fred Hutton   Date: October 29, 1969
        K-1007, Rm. 209

From: O. L. Keller, Jr.
        Bldg. 5505, X-10

The Joint Institute of Nuclear Research at Dubna under the direction
of G. N. Flerov publishes preprints of their nuclear and chemical work on
superheavy elements, transactinides, and actinides. They do the same
sort of work carried out at ORNL and Berkeley. This work represents the
frontier, the cutting edge, of nuclear science. The ordinary journal
publication route would involve a six month to a year delay before the
Dubna preprint would appear in Russian, then, of course, there is another
six month to a year delay before the journal is translated. By that time,
the information is too "cold" to be very useful to us. The machine translations of the Dubna preprints have proved most valuable in circumventing
the time delay problem. The translations are about 95% understandable
to the specialist. For the remainder, a linguist spends a few minutes
translating for us. The translations sound like the computer just got
off the boat, and they need to be improved. However, I have found that
human translators frequently give the same translation as the machine
for passages that don't make any sense. The problem, of course, is
jargon.

    To sum up:

    1. The machine translations are extremely valuable at their present
stage of development.

    2. They can and should be improved.

    3. An expert in the field must go over the translation to
check it for accuracy whether the original is done by a human or
a machine.

                                        O. L. Keller, Jr.

OLK:jh

INTRA·LABORATORY. CORRESPONDENCE
OAK· RIDGE NATIONAL LABORATORY

March 17, 1966

To: Francois Kertesz

From: J. S. Olson, Health Physics Division

Re: Frank evaluation of Russian computer translation

I am pleased with results of two .successive trials of translating a chapter text and table footnotes from a geobotanical book which included a large number of technical words which were missing from the original dictionary of the computer program.

Even the first try, containing many untranslated words, placed these words so that their meaning could be inferred from context, or from cognates, or from a modest amount of dictionary work. My slight (night school) background with Russian made this much effort possible and highly rewarding, whereas I simply could not have allocated enough time to do the translation completely, even with expert help. I recommended that the book be published in translation, but even if this is done , promptness has had great value for decisions regarding our own research program and reviews of literature.

As a gratified user, I was pleased to return some suggested word translations and corrections in addition to those detected by the computer programmer, for use in his first test of dictionary revision. This test shows that some awkward features of initial output can be overcome. Similar feedback from a number of articles or users in a new field should bring results calling for little personal dictionary work or help from experts, even for scientists having no exposure to Russian. The "foreign accent" of grammatic construction is amusing, but rarely troublesome for comprehension. This can surely be tolerated as a price for tapping a wide field of literature that might never warrant personal translation and publication at all!

.For both advantages (speed; probing specialized fields) the questions of added effort required for reaching publication quality hardly seem pertinent. Reference to original text for figures, tables and "long formulas" can be accepted, even in material (like mine) in which such material is extensive.

Obviously users would be pleased if the amounts and speeds of personal translation and publication of Russian could be increased severalfold. However, instead of making the computer translation obsolete, the widening familiarity with neglected and new literature probably would increase the cases of need — perhaps exponentially. There may be increasingly urgent need for computer screening with user participation, in order to gain more effective channeling of the limited manpower than can be foreseen as available for personal translation and formally edited publication.

J. S. Olson

JSO:mb

INTRA-LABORATORY CORRESPONDENCE
OAK RIDGE NATIONAL LABORATORY

March 17, 1966

To: Translation Office, C. R. Library, Bldg. 4500

From: George M. Van Dyne, Bldg. 2001

Re: Russian Transliterator

I believe that computer transliteration of Russian will become a valuable tool in many phases of our research. I have used it on papers in Ecology, so many of the words we require are not at present in the computer dictionary. However, I understand it is now possible to add to the dictionary; this should improve this tool for our use. To this end I will recommend the following reference as an aid in improving the system:

Dumbleton, C. W.   1964.   Russian-English biological dictionary. Oliver and Boyd. Edinburgh. 512 pages (ORNL Library PG,2640,D8).

I am not competent in the language so I have sent a copy of some transliterations to two colleagues at the University of California for their recommendations. They have good ability with Russian and read and review many biological, ecological, and agricultural books in that language. I would recommend them as consultants if the laboratory is interested in further improving the transliterator.

In summary, this is a good tool, we should use it more, and I hope it can be continued and improved. It makes possible much further contact with Russian science than we would be able to make by conventional translation methods.

Sincerely yours,

George M. Van Dyne (mb)

George M. Van Dyne

GMVD:mb

INTRA LABORATORY CORRESPONDENCE
OAK' RIDGE NATIONAL LABORATORY

March 17, 1966

To: F. Kertesz

From: N.B. Gove

   I used the local Mechanical Translation service to obtain a translation of a ten-page paper, Levels in ^{168}Er Excited by (n, γ) Reactions, L.V. Groshev et al, Kurchatov Institute of Atomic Energy Report 644 (1964).

   I used the computer print-out without post-editing. The English was awkward but quite adequate for my purpose. I was taking data from the tables in the paper and wanted mainly a guide to understand the tables.

   Thus, the Mechanical Translation was useful to me. I am not in a position to compare the cost of this method with that of other methods of obtaining translations.

NBG/sjb

INTRA-LABORATORY CORRESPONDENCE
OAK RIDGE NATIONAL LABORATORY

To: F. Kertesz   Date: March 16, 1966
       Bldg. 4500

From: Harold W. Kohn

Dear Dr. Kertesz:

    Betty Ollinger has asked me to send you an evaluation of the machine translation done for me at K-25. I found the machine translation entirely adequate for the purpose for which I needed it. The article itself was reasonably straightforward in its description of some experimental measurements. It seems to me that anyone who is familiar with the material of the articles should be well satisfied with the machine translation unless the subject with which it deals is extremely complicated or if the writing style is very subtle indeed.

    The machine translation is also, from my standpoint, rapid, cheap, and lacking in temperament or capriciousness. I would be pleased to see it continued.

                                          Harold W. Kohn
                                       Harold W. Kohn

HWK:jh

cc: Betty Ollinger

INTRA-LABORATORY CORRESPONDENCE
OAK RIDGE NATIONAL LABORATORY

October 12, 1964

TO: F. Kertesz

FROM: J. G. Moore

SUBJECT: Machine Translation of Russian Article

I was most favorably impressed with the machine translation of the article, "The State of Protactinium in Nitrate." Most people could probably decipher the translation of an article in their field in a few hours. If the text were not completely understood, at least it could be determined if the article was of interest or pertinent to one's work and returned for editing. This alone would be of great value. I'm afraid we often spend many hours translating a paper only to find it either useless or a rehash of an older work.

Although I'm sure my knowledge of Russian helped considerably, it required about 3 to 4 hours to prepare a fairly understandable text from the machine translation. I'm most anxious to receive your edited copy for comparison.

If I can be of any further help in this matter, please don't hesitate to call me.

John G. Moore

JGM/rw
cc: R. E. Blanco
    D. E. Ferguson
    J. G. Moore

**NV HOLLANDSE
METALLURGISCHE INDUSTRIE
BILLITON**

European Translation Centre
T.a.v. Dr. J.M.A. Biesheuvel
Doelenstraat 101,
DELFT

*atta. dr. S. Perschke
Euratom
M-T's*

uw ref.   onze ref. MvdZ/ml   ARNHEM, 20 april 1971

Dear Sir,

Thank you very much for the clear translation of the
Russian article about the electrolytic dissolution of
lead, you sent us on March 3rd, last.
It is a pity that sometimes technical words were not
translated but we could understand them from the context. Besides this we remarked that the sequence of
the words was not exactly right but that was not dis-
turbing.
The whole translation has been of great value to our
investigations.

                    Yours sincerely,

N.V. HOLLANDSE METALLURGISCHE INDUSTRIE BILLITON.

LABORATORIUM
VOOR CHEMISCHE TECHNOLOGIE
DER TECHNISCHE HOGESCHOOL

DELFT, 22 maart 1971
Julianalaan 136
Telefoon 33222

Attn. Dr. Sergei Perschke,
(reaction from ETC client
Jacob M Bushlow

Dear Sir,

First I want to thank you for the trouble you have taken in translating
the articles. The readability of the translation was surprisingly good. A good
understanding of the text, however, always costs quite a lot of time. In any
case it was nearly always possible to get the right interpretation. When the
authors used sentences that were not too complex, the understanding of the
articles was even very easy.

I got the impression that I became used to some errors introduced by
the translation, although I think that it was to my advantage that the subject,
chemically speaking, was not very difficult to understand and rather descriptive.
It was sometimes like putting together a word puzzle, of which some words were
a little bit wrong and a few missing. Now I shall discuss the three articles
after each other.

First article: J. Phys. Chem. (U.S.S.R.) $\underline{16}$ (1940) p 1428-1446, G.K. Boreskov
V.V. Illarionov: The kinetics of interaction of anhydrous sulfur dioxide and
nitrogen dioxide.

This article brought quite a lot of difficulties. The introduction
consist of summaries of work done by some previous investigators and was not difficult to understand. The description of the apparatus and the methods, by which
the results were achieved caused however, many troubles, that could only be resolved by very carefully considering the design of the apparatus. Indeed it
was always possible to get the exact meaning. Wrong translations were for instance:
'harmful space' must be 'dead space'
' gray' must be 'sulfur'

pag.: 2
dat.: 22-3-1971

'elasticity'must be 'pressure'
furthermore quite a lot of prepositions were incorrectly translated and
sometimes twice translated.

Second article: J. Applied Chem. (U.S.S.R.) <u>19</u> (1946) p 217-230,
J.N. Kuzminikh: The kinetics of the chamber process of sulfuric acid.

This article caused the biggest problems. In my view principally
because the author has written his article in a too complicated manner, dis-
regarding the need for clearness. Also in this article the description of the
equipment and the writers own opinions brought the biggest dificulties, and
I only could understand about 70% of this part of the article. In any case
it was always to get either the good interpretation, or no interpretation at
all. I have never met an apparently good translation that was in contradiction
with the rest.
Some typical errors are:

'to advantage'	must be	'by preference'
'nothing unknown'		'nothing known'
'not places and requirements'		'does not take place necessarily'
'than above...this succesful'		'the higher...the more succesful'
'dampness'		'moisture'
'with the friend of side'		'on the other hand'

much prepositions were wrong or twice translated

'as' must often be	'often'
'even for'	'if only for'
'upon'	'by', 'with', 'at'
'reactions between with'	'reactions between'

The third article: Journal of general Chemistry 16 p 1553-1562,
Kh. B. Medinsky,: Concerning the reactions between sulfurdioxide and nitric
oxides.

This article is a very descriptive one and does not present very big
difficulties. The steps taken by the author are very logical and a misunder-
standing of the text is always corrected by reading what is coming after. Like
the other articles, the tables, introduction and summary are most easily readable

pag.: 3
dat.: 22-3-1971

Suggestions :

    Perhaps it would be useful to enclose a sheet of paper on which
are indicated the kind of typical problems which confronted the reader.
For instance:
    - Problems concerning the word sequence
    - The often wrong translated prepositions
    - The difficulties occurring by using some verbs., for instance
      the verbs to be, to have, to become.

    I hope these remarks will help you to improve your system and thank
you for translating our Russian literature.

                                        Sincerely yours,

                                        (P. Rieff)

VRIJE UNIVERSITEIT
SUBFACULTEIT DER SCHEIKUNDE
ANALYTISCH-CHEMISCH LABORATORIUM
—
De Boelelaan 1085, Amsterdam-Buitenveldert
Telefoon 48 4783   of 48 91 11

AMSTERDAM, **25 februari 1971**

Uw ref.:

Onze ref.:

Dear Sirs,

Some time ago we received English translations of two articles
from Russian journals. As regards the readability and comprehensability of
the text we should like to make the following remarks.
1) Generally there were no problems in reconstructing the original Russian
sentence structures from the English translation. By far the greater part
of the text was therefore easily understood.
2) Incidentally we had some difficulties with translations of Russian
words with more than a single meaning (e.g. НАСТОЯЩИЙ , which means 'right',
'present', 'this'), and a word such as ПАР , which indeeds means 'vapour',
but in the present Russian text obviously must be translated as 'species'.
3) In a single case we found a word, which was translated incorrectly, namely
СОБЛЮДАТЬ   which does not mean 'preclude', but 'satisfy'— a
rather serious mistake, since these words have an opposite meaning.
Summarizing, we can say that the translations are of good quality.
However, some knowledge of the Russian language is advantageous, since it
enables one to look up words, the translation of which is not easily
understood.
Lastly, we should like to express our gratitude for the two translations received. Study of the contents of the Russian papers has contributed
to the progress of our present research.

Yours sincerely,

(H.R.Leene)

Reaction of Prof. Bogdanovich A'dam

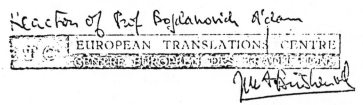

EUROPEAN TRANSLATIONS CENTRE
GENERE EUROPEEN DES TRADUCTIONS

attn. Dr.S.Perschke

The ~~association~~ translation on Neutronnyj
Aksivatsionnyj Analiz ~~fox~~ was of excellent use and
help to me. When using a dictionnary and
with just a slight knowledge of russian it was
very easy to understand and read the article,
I have no remarks on the translation at all. As
to me it is a wonderfull invention. These
machine-translations are, even when sometimes
not entirely perfect, ~~ag~~ as to me, of great use
for ~~x~~ every scientist!
Thank you very much for your efforts!

Prof.Dr. Ir. Ar. Bogdanivich
University of Amsterdam.

Telex 31673   Giro 522178
Bankers: Pierson, Heldring & Pierson The Hague

KNZ

NV KONINKLIJKE NEDERLANDSE ZOUTINDUSTRIE

Boortorenweg 27 Hengelo(O) Postbus 25
Telefoon (05400) 5 32 41
Telex 4 43 12
Telegramadres Zoutindustrie Hengelo
Giro 87 08 63
Banken:
ABN bankgiro 59 02 31 138
AMRO bankgiro 47 46 43 387

The European Translations Centre,

Doelenstraat 101,

DELFT.

Att.: Mr. C.M.A. Knul.

Uw kenmerk	Uw brief van	Ons kenmerk	Hengelo(O).
Konzout MR 265	June 25, 1970	POtw/KD	October 13, 1970

Onderwerp

Dear Sirs,

We received the mechanical translation made by the Centre Européen de Traitement d'Information Scientifique d'Euratom of the Soviet article: An Kaz. S.S.R. Inst. Khim. Trudy 23 (1969), 53 - 79.

In our opinion this translation is very well understandable. We have only one remark: The computer reads "times" instead of "pores".

We thank you very much for the opportunity you gave us to get this translation.

Yours faithfully,
N.V. KONINKLIJKE-NEDERLANDSE
ZOUTINDUSTRIE

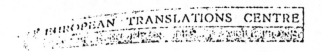

101 Doelenstraat DELFT (The Netherlands)

01730-33222-ext. 5657
Telephone   01730-32597

Telex: 31673

Dr. S. Perschke
Euratom (CETIS)
Ispra (Varese)
Italy

Your ref.   Our ref.   Date
                                                         23rd February 1970

Commentary by Mr. L.S. Ammerlaan-Ziekman of Delft Technical University

On behalf of the receiver of the machine translation:

    Khimicheskaya Promyshlennost,
    1961 art. by N.K. Filatova

I would like to thank you for the speed with which the request was
handled. According to your request I note his reactions to the
translation:

well ordered; passable English translation; a few mistakes in verb
tenses; some words have not been translated; this does not, however, detract from the clearity of the whole.

I hope I have been of some help and wish you the best of luck with
all further experiments.

                                 Faithfully yours,

PRINS MAURITS LABORATORIA
RIJKSVERDEDIGINGSORGANISATIE TNO

TECHNOLOGISCH LABORATORIUM RVO-TNO

European Translation Center
Doelenstraat 101,

DELFT

Uw brief:

Onderwerp:

Bijlage(n):

Ons nummer: 5439

RIJSWIJK (Z.H.), 23th October 1969.
Postbus 4545
Telefoon Delft 01730-20330

Dear Sirs,

The quality of the translation of the Russian article
(The zone of exothermic reaction in one-dimensional striking
wave in gas, by R.I. Solankhin) into English by your computer
is remarkably good. Although, of course, the style is somewhat
distorted, the text is well readable.

In answer to your request for comments, in our opinion
the following points could be observed.
- The typing of the Russian text (computer feed) should be
done with extreme care since any mistake in typing leads to
a non-translated Russian word.
- It would be convenient to print out more or less complicated formulas in stead of the word "formula".

In this way the translated article can be read without
too much consulting the orginal text.

- The translated text shows open spaces on places of diagrams in the original text. This is most useful in order to
complete the entire article with the original diagrams.

We thank you for the opportunity to test the possibility
of automatic translations. We hope the above suggestions will
be of any use to you,

Yours sincerely,

Dr. E.W. Lindeijer.
(Director)

Typ.: IH
copy : Bibliotheek PML.

NV KONINKLIJKE NEDERLANDSCHE ZOUTINDUSTRIE

Boortorenweg 27 Hengelo(O) Postbus 25
Telefoon (05400) 5 32 41
Telex 4 43 12
Telegramadres Zoutindustrie Hengelo
Giro 87 08 63
Banken:
ABN bankgiro 59 02 31 138
AMRO bankgiro 47 46 43 387

The European Translations Centre,

Doelenstraat 101,

D e l f t.

To the attention of Mr. C.M.A. Knul.

Uw kenmerk	Uw brief van	Ons kenmerk Otw/KD	Hengelo(O). 14th October 1969

Onderwerp

Dear Sirs,

We received the mechanical translation made by the Centre Européen de
Traitement d'Information Scientifique of Euratom of the Russian article:
Ukrainskii khimicheskii zhurnal
35 (1969) 422-425
T.V. Kiyazkova and L.A. Kulski.
The investigation of phase equilibrium upon the extraction of water from
solutions NaCl by the triethylamine.

In our opinion this translation is very well understandable.
The untranslated word "solesoderzhania" - salt content - is very common
in literature of this type.
We do not understand why the Russian capitals ТЗА (abbreviation for
TriEthylAmine) are represented in the translation by TNA.

In spite of these details of minor importance; the translation as a
whole is quite satisfactory.

We thank you very much for the opportunity you gave us to get this
translation.

Yours faithfully,
N.V. KONINKLIJKE NEDERLANDSCHE
ZOUT INDUSTR IE

c/o Dipl.-Ing. O. Voigt
MASCHINENFABRIK AUGSBURG-NÜRNBERG AKTIENGESELLSCHAFT

Maschinenfabrik Augsburg-Nürnberg Aktiengesellschaft
8900 Augsburg 1, Postfach

Dr. Bozena Dostert
Senior Research Fellow
in Linguistics
California Institute
of Technology
PASADENA, California 91109
U. S. A.

Ihre Zeichen	Ihre Nachricht vom	Durchwahl/Hausruf	Unsere Abteilung/Zeichen	8900 AUGSBURG, Stadtbachstraße
		322	GFKD/Vo/fü	6.2.73

Betreff:

Dear Dr. Dostert:

Re.: Machine translations Russian - English

Please, excuse my late reply to your letter of the 2nd October,
1972. The delay is partly due to my idea that I should not only
give you my own opinion, i.e. the opinion of the head of the
department for scientific information in an industrial enterprise,
on the problem of machine translation, but also that of a few
users of this kind of service; besides, I was deeply engaged,
for the past two months, in current activities for the set-up
of central information banks for the mechanical engineering
and automobile industries so that I had to let you wait until
now.

Enclosed please find four questionnaires filled in by users of
the MT service (Enclosures 1 - 4) - sorry, unfortunately not
all of them are in English. I myself would like to add the
following remarks on the question of MT:

1) As I personally know Dr. Lustig who was then the head
    of CETIS we tried in July 1968 to have machine translations
    of Russian texts in the field of mechanical engineering
    (internal combustion engines and printing presses) into
    the English language prepared by CETIS although their
    computer was programmed in linguistics for the vocabulary

Encl.

                                                              ./.-2

Vorsitzender des Aufsichtsrates Dietrich Wilhelm von Menges.   Vorstand: Karl Schott, Vorsitzender;   Hans Fischer, Siegfried Meurer, Hans Moll, Alfred Roth, Gerhard Stein, Gerd Wollburg;
Stellv.: Herbert Redlich, Hugo-Bernard Saemann.
Sitz der Gesellschaft ist Augsburg.   Handels-Reg. Augsburg B 6106.   Werke in Augsburg, Hamburg, Penzberg, München, Gustavsburg.

of nuclear technology only. The success was really
surprising for us so that up to now we have had
81 publications in total, each comprising an
average of 6 - 7 pages (DIN A 4), translated from
the Russian language.

2) Every user is furnished by us with a copy of the
                              Russian text
                    the MT text   and
                    instructions for use (Enclosure 5)
                        indicating how to supplement
                        the MT text with regard to
                        formulae, tables, diagrams
                        and the like.

   (NB.: Some of the colleagues interviewed seem
   to have overlooked that: they complained that
   such information is missing in the MT).

3) I doubt whether it would be advisable to mix words of one
   technical terminology, e.g. nuclear technology, with those
   of another, e.g. internal combustion engine technology.
   It would obviously be better to develop a separate programme
   for every technical sector because many mistakes simply
   caused by synonyms and homonyms and others could thus
   be eliminated with certainty - to give an example:

$$par(a) \Longleftarrow \begin{array}{l} pair \\ vapour \end{array}$$

4) I think it is improbable that MT will ever be able to fully
   replace intellectual translation because every improvement
   in quality causes an excessively large increase in
   expenditure for programming and computer time; besides,
   a computer cannot be programmed to allow for inaccuracies
   in linguistic usage that are especially frequent in
   technical texts and are, in many cases, not noticed until
   the full text has been read or even illustrating figures
   have been studied.

It should be realized, however that a very high redundancy will
have to be tolerated in the information sector, which would

M.A.N.

Werk Augsburg

Dr. Bozena Dostert   - 3 -
California Institute
of Technology
Pasadena, California 91109   6.2.73

entail enormous costs if an intellectual translation had to
be prepared of every publication whose title seems to suggest
that its content is of interest. According to our experience,
the quality of MTs furnished by CETIS is adequate to permit
the decision whether the respective publication is relevant
or not, irrespective of the fact that sometimes these
translations resemble Pidgin English. The decisive point is
that such provisional translations are cheap.

I hope this information is of assistance to you for your
further activities.

Yours sincerely,

Prof. F. LEUTWEIN

MINISTÈRE DE L'ÉDUCATION NATIONALE

—

CENTRE NATIONAL DE LA RECHERCHE SCIENTIFIQUE

CENTRE DE RECHERCHES PÉTROGRAPHIQUES ET GÉOCHIMIQUES

54500, Vandoeuvre-Nancy, 26 Février 1973

Mrs. Bozzena Dostert •
Californian Institute of Technology
PASSADENA
California 91109
U.S.A.

Dear Mrs. DOSTERT,

It was Dr. HUBAUX from the Euratom-Center at Ispra - Italia - who sent us a machine translation of a russian publication from A.E. BABINETS et al. from the XXIII International Geol. Congress, vol. 17, 1968. He proposed us to send the questionnaire directly to you. I feel necessary to give you some additional explications. It was my very first confrontation with a electronic traduction - so I am not able to answer to all questions of your questionnaire. For people like me, having rather poor knowledge of the russian language, such a M.T. is an excellent help - but a reader without such knowledge will have, as I fear, difficulties to understand the text - and erroneous interpretation seems to me possible. I feel, that this is a more important danger than the quality of the machine's english. This is rather poor, but quite understandable. In a not english speaking country as ours, there will rise the following problem : most of my colleagues have poor to fair reading knowledge of the english language - and none of russian. So, we should charge a colleage to put the M.T. in a readable english (not french) text. Reinterpretation of the text, putting formulae and diagrams on the right place - all this demands time. For me, the problem is quite clear - with the aid of a M.T., I could make correct and readable translations, from russian texts - without an M.T., I could not. But, if we take an example of a foreign language, which I know better - I would abandone the M.T. and dictate directly a translation from M.T. on the magnetophone. But as regards the problem of translation from russian publications, the M.T. seems to be an excellent help even in its actual state of evolution.

With kind regards, sincerely yours,

F. LEUTWEIN

YAVNE, ISRAEL
Telephone 952075

הוועדה לאנרגיה אטומית
ISRAEL ATOMIC ENERGY COMMISSION
SOREQ   NUCLEAR   RESEARCH   CENTRE

In Replying Please Refer To No.

July 25, 1972

Dr. H. Fangmeyer,
Commission des Communautes Europeennes,
C.E.T.I.S.
Euratom, Ispra,
Italy

Your Reference: HF/IB 3.02/689/72

Dear Dr. Fangmeyer,

I wish firstly to thank you for the mechanised translations sent.

Without correcting or adding anything to the computer printouts
I sent the articles to the scientists who had ordered them.

They were very satisfied with the results and according to their
evaluation it was a 80% success.

There are though a few things they found could be mended to provide
a faster reading of the material:

1. To have, if possible, the English version closely follow the
pagination of the original - in this way the reader could quickly elucidate
any obscure point in the translation; that means, have a new translation
page for any new original page - or at least a numbering of the Russian
pages on the English computer printout.

2. To find a way of translating more accurately certain scientific
expressions - there was for instance the expression "dielectrikcheskoi
pronitsaemosti" which in the translation appeared as "dielectric porosity"
this brought the customer back to me to be told that the English expression
was "dielectric constant".

3. The italicized "a" is being translated by the computer like the
regular Russian "a" by "and" which impedes upon the understanding of the
text.

On the whole - a big success - especially if the mechanized
translation is being intended for reading by a specialist in the field
translated - although I, a chemist and not an expert in the field had no
difficulty in understanding at a first reading without the help of the
original about 70% of the content.

- 2 -

And I do think that you are on the way to prove to Professor Bar-Hillel of the Hebrew University (who after having been an enthusiastic initiator and fervent believer in mechanised translation became a sceptic and a non-believer) that his first enthusiasm was right - at least in so far as scientific material is concerned.

I sincerely congratulate you and your associates and wish you further successes.

Sincerely yours,

B. Gill-Gilbert

P.S. I am sending for translation two more articles in the same field - but, please send them back if you are too overcrowded - I would not like to inconvenience you in any way -.

7/2/1973.

re: California Institute of Technology.

  The translation from Russian into English of
a hydrological subject of high technicality is not precisely
ideal on which to base one's appreciation of the usefulness
of computerised translations in general. Without a good
knowledge of Russian (and mine extends little beyond deci-
phering the letters of the Cyrillic alphabet) I submit it is
hard to produce a reasoned criticism of the attempt on which
our opinion is being solicited. Would it not have been better
to have selected a couple of languages which are in more

current use in America and Western Europe? This would, no
doubt, have elicited a more thorough and dependable expression
of opinion as to the proposals on which criticism has been
invited.

  I would feel inclined to say that the attempt
to produce something worth while has miscarried. One is
reminded of the little story told about a couple of experts,
concerned with computerised translation, testing a machine.
They asked it to translate "Out of sight out of mind" into
French. The machine obyed, but without further ado they
reversed the operation by getting the computer to translate
into English once again. This was duly effected and gave
cause to no little enjoyment: "Invisible lunatic" was the
answer. Need one say more?

Bibliography

ALPAC = Automatic Language Processing Advisory Committee
  1966 *Language and machines; computers in translation and linguistics.*
         A report by the Automatic Language Processing Advisory Committee (AL-
         PAC). Division of Behavioral Sciences, National Academy of Sciences, National
         Research Council Publication 1416 (Washington: NAS/NRC).
Austin, W. M. See *Papers*
Bar-Hillel, Yehoshua
  1960 "The present status of automatic translation of languages", *Advances in Com-
         puters,* edited by F. L. Alt (New York: Academic Press), 1: 91–163.
  1971 "Some reflections on the present outlook for high-quality machine translation",
         Feasibility study of fully automatic high quality translation, edited by W. P.
         Lehmann and R. Stachowitz (Austin: University of Texas, Linguistic Research
         Center, Report No. RADC-TR-71-295), I: 72–76.
Booth, Andrew D., L. Brandwood, J. P. Cleave
  1958 *Mechanical resolution of linguistic problems* (London: Butterworths Scientific
         Publications; New York: Academic Press).
Booth, A. D., K. H. V. Britten
  1947 "Coding for A.R.C." (2nd ed.) (Princeton: Institute for Advanced Study).
Bross, I. D. J., P. A. Shapiro, B. B. Anderson
  1972 "How information is carried in scientific sub-languages", *Science* 176:
         1303–1307.
Chafe, W.
  1971 *Meaning and the structure of language* (Chicago: Chicago University Press).
Corbé, M.
  1960 "La machine à traduire française aura bientôt trente ans", *Automatisme* 5:
         87–91. Cited in I. A. Mel'čuk, *Avtomatičeskij perevod 1949–1963* (Moskva:
         VINITI, 1967), 27.
Delavenay, Emile
  1960 *An introduction to machine translation* (New York: Praeger).
Dostert, Léon E.
  1957 "Brief history of machine translation research", *Research in machine translation,*
         edited by L. Dostert (Georgetown University Monograph Series on Languages
         and Linguistics No. 10) (Washington, D.C.: Georgetown University Press),
         3–10.
  1963 "Machine translation and automatic language data processing", *Vistas in infor-
         mation handling,* edited by Paul W. Howerton and David C. Weeks, 1:
         92–110.

Edmundson, H. P., K. E. Harper, D. G. Hays
1958   *Studies in machine translation – 1: Survey and Critique* (Santa Monica, Calif.: RAND Corp., Research Memorandum RM 2063).
1959   *Essays on and in machine translation* (Cambridge: Cambridge Language Research Unit).
1961   *First International Conference on Machine Translation of Languages and Applied Language Analysis* (National Physical Laboratory, Symposium No. 13) (London: Her Majesty's Stationery Office).

FBIS Seminar
1976   "Summary Proceedings", *American Journal of Computational Linguistics*, edited by David Hays (Microfiche 46).

Garvin, Paul L.
1967   "The Georgetown-IBM experiment of 1954: An evaluation in retrospect", *Papers in linguistics in honor of Léon Dostert*, edited by W. M. Austin (The Hague: Mouton), 46–56.
1971   "Operational problems of machine translation: a position paper", in *Feasibility study of fully automatic high quality translation*, edited by W. P. Lehmann and R. Stachowitz (Austin: University of Texas, Linguistic Research Center, Report No. RADC-TR-71-295), I: 94–118.

Harper, Kenneth E.
1953   "The mechanical translation of Russian: Preliminary report", *Modern Language Forum* 38: 12–29.
1963   "Machine translation", *Current Trends in Linguistics* 1: 133–142 (The Hague: Mouton).

Harris, Z. S.
1962   *String analysis of a sentence structure* (The Hague, Mouton).

Hays, David G.
1964   "Dependency theory: formalism and some observations", *Language* 40: 511–525.
1967   "Computational linguistics: research in progress at the RAND Corporation", *T. A. Informations* 1: 15–20.

Henisz-Dostert, Bozena
1967   "Experimental machine translation", *Papers in linguistics in honor of Léon Dostert*, edited by W. M. Austin (The Hague: Mouton), 57–91.
1973   *User's evaluation of machine translation, Georgetown machine-translation system, 1963–1973*, Final Technical Report, RADC-TR-73-239 (Rome Air Development Center, Griffiss Air Force).

IBM = International Business Machine Corporation
1960   *Final report on computer set AN/GSQ-16 (XW-1)* (Rome, New York: Information Processing Laboratory, Rome Air Development Center [AFSC].

Ivanov, I. I.
1961   "Some problems of machine translation in the USSR", translated by JPRS: 13439. *Doklady na konferencii po obrabotke informacii, mašinnomu perevodu i avtomatičeskomu čteniju teksta* [Proceedings on automatic information processing, machine translation and automatic reading] 10: 1–29.

Jakobson, Roman
1959   "On linguistic aspects of translation", *On translation* (Harvard studies in comparative literature no. 23) (Cambridge, Mass.: Harvard University Press), 232–239.

Joos, Martin
1956 "Machine translation of languages, edited by William N. Locke and A. Donald Booth" (review), *Language* 32: 293–298.
Jordan, Sara R., A. F. R. Brown, F. Hutton
1975 *Computerized language translation at ORNL* (Oak Ridge, National Laboratory, mimeographed).
Josselson, Harry H.
1971 "Automatic translation of languages since 1960: a linguist's view", *Advances in Computers* 11: 1–53.
Kay, Martin
1969 *Computational linguistics at RAND – 1967* (Santa Monica, Calif.: RAND Corp.).
Klein, Wolfgang
1971 *Parsing: Studien zur maschinellen Satzanalyse mit Abhängigkeitsgrammatiken und Transformationsgrammatiken* (Frankfurt a. M.: Athenäum).
Kotov, R. G.
1976 "Lingvistika i sovremennoe sostojanie mašinnogo perevoda v strane" [Linguistics and the contemporary state of machine translation in the USSR], *Voprosy jazykoznanija* 1976, 5: 37–49.
Kulagina, O. S., I. A. Mel'čuk
1971 "Avtomatičeskij perevod" [Automatic translation], *Moskva Progress*. Also in *Problemy strukturnoj lingvistiki* 1971: 3–25.
Language and machines; computers in translation and linguistics.
See ALPAC.
Lehmann, Winfred P., Rolf Stachowitz
1971 *Feasibility study of fully automatic high quality translation* (Austin, Tex.: University of Texas at Austin Linguistic Research Center, Report No. RADC-TR-71-295).
1972 "Machine translation in Western Europe: a survey", *Current Trends in Linguistics* 9: 688–701 (The Hague: Mouton).
Ljudskanov, A.
1963 "Njakoi beležki otkosno obščite principe za sŭstavjane na rečnik za russko-bŭlgarski mašinen prevod" [Certain considerations on general principles relating to the construction of a Russian-Bulgarian dictionary for machine translation], *Slavistični studii*, 251–260.
1966 "Pervyj opyt mašinnogo perevoda v Bulgarii" [The first machine translation experiment in Bulgaria], *Naučno-texničeskaja informacija*, No. 4.
1972 *Mensch und Maschine als Übersetzer* (Halle: Max Niemeyer Verlag).
Locke, W. N., A. D. Booth (eds.)
1955 *Machine translation of languages* (New York: Wiley).
1957 *Mašinnyj perevod* [translation of *Machine translation of languages*] (Moskva: Izd. inostrannoj literatury).
McCulloch, Warren S., Walter Pitts
1943 "A logical calculus of the ideas immanent in nervous activities", *Bulletin of Mathematical Biophysics* 5: 115–133.
Macdonald, R. R. (ed.)
1955 *Machine translation of languages: fourteen essays*, edited by William N. Locke and A. Donald Booth (New York: Wiley).
1963 *General report, 1952–1963*, Georgetown University Machine Translation Research Project, Occasional Papers, No. 30 (Washington, D.C.: Georgetown University).

Masterman, M.
1962   "Semantical message detection for machine translation using interlingua", in *1961 International conference on machine translation of languages and applied language analysis*, National Physical Laboratory Symposium No. 13 (London: Her Majesty's Stationery Office), 2: 438–474.
Mel'čuk, I. A.
1974   *Opyt teorii lingvističeskij modeli "smysl-tekst"* (Moskva).
Mel'čuk, I. A., P. A. Ravič
1967   *Avtomatičeskij perevod 1949–1963* [*Automatic translation 1949–1963*] (Moskva: VINITI).
Mološnaja, T. N., T. M. Nikolaeva
1961   "Trojanskij, P. P., Perevodnaja mašina" [Translation machine] *Problemy kibernetiki* 5: 287–288 (review).
Mukhin, I. S.
1956   "An experiment of the machine translation of languages carried out on the BESM", *Proceedings*, IEE, Part B. Suppl. No. 3, 463–475.
Oettinger, A. G.
1954   *A study for the design of an automatic dictionary* (doctoral thesis, Harvard University) (Cambridge, Mass.).
Pankowicz, Z. L.
1967   *Draft of a commentary on ALPAC report, Part I* (Rome, New York: Rome Air Development Center, Griffiss Air Force Base).
Panov, D. Ju., A. A. Ljapunov, I. S. Muxin
1956   "Avtomatizacija perevoda s odnogo jazyka na drugoj" [Automatization of translation from one language to another] (Moskva: Izdatel'stvo AN SSSR). English translation by JPRS: DC-379, CSO DC-1528.
Papers in linguistics in honor of Léon Dostert, edited by William M. Austin.
1967   (The Hague: Mouton).
Pendergraft, E. D.
1967   "Translating languages", in *Automated language processing: the state of the art*, edited by Harold Borko (New York: Wiley).
Plath, W.
1963   *Mathematical linguistics and automatic translation* (National Science Foundation Report 12) (Cambridge, Mass.: Harvard University).
Proceedings of the First International Conference on Machine Translation
1962   *of Languages and Applied Language Analysis* (London: Her Majesty's Stationery Office).
Quine, Willard Van Orman
1953   *From a logical point of view* (Cambridge, Mass.: Harvard University Press; 2nd ed., 1961, New York: Harper and Row, reprint, 1963).
Reformackij, A. A.
1961   "In place of a preface", translated by JPRS: 13444, *Preliminary publications of the sector of structural and applied linguistics*, AN SSSR, Institut jazykovedenija (Moskva: Izdatel'stvo AN SSSR).
Reichenbach, Hans
1947   *Elements of symbolic logic* (New York: Macmillan, Free Press, paperback; hardcover edition, 1952).
Reifler, Erwin
1950– *Studies in mechanical translation, Nos. 1–8* (Washington, D.C.: mimeo-
1952   graphed).

1954   "The first conference on mechanical translation", *Mechanical Translation* 1: 2, 23–32.
Reitwiesner, G. W., M. H. Weik
1958   "Survey of the field of mechanical translation of languages" (Ballistic Research Laboratories Memorandum 1147) (Aberdeen Proving Ground, Maryland).
Richens, R. H., A. D. Booth
1952   *Some methods of mechanized translation* (mimeographed).
Sherry, M.
1962   "The identification of nested structures in predictive syntactic analysis", *Proceedings of the First International Conference on Machine Translation of Languages and Applied Language Analysis*, Teddington, England (London: Her Majesty's Stationery Office), 143–145.
Taube, Mortimer
1961   *Computers and common sense* (New York: Columbia University Press).
Tesnière, L.
1951   *Eléments de syntaxe structurale* (Paris: Klincksieck).
Toma, Peter Paul
1970   *Probleme der linguistischen Datenverarbeitung am Beispiel der automatischen Übersetzung*, (inaugural dissertation) (Bonn: Philosophische Fakultät der Rheinischen Friedrich-Wilhelms-Universität).
Walkowicz, Josephine L.
1963   *A bibliography of foreign developments in machine translation and information processing* (National Bureau of Standards Technical Note 193) (Washington, D.C.: National Bureau of Standards).
Wall, Robert
1972   *Introduction to mathematical linguistics* (Englewood Cliffs, N.J.: Prentice-Hall), 282–283.
Weaver, Warren
1949   *Translation* (New York: mimeographed).
Yngve, Victor H.
1954   "The machine and the man", *Mechanical Translation* 1: 2, 20–22.
Zarechnak, Michael
1961   "Nesting within the prepositional structure", *Proceedings of the National Symposium on Machine Translation* (Englewood Cliffs, N.J.), 267–279.
1962   "A fourth level of linguistic analysis", *Proceedings of the First International Conference on Machine Translation of Languages and Applied Language Analysis* (London: Her Majesty's Stationary Office), 160–173.
Zarechnak, M., J. Pyne
1957   *The range of machine search of translation of Russian pronouns*, Georgetown University Research Project in Machine Translation, Seminar Work Paper MT-22 (Washington, D.C.: Georgetown University Institute of Languages and Linguistics).
Žolkovskij, A. *et al.*
1961   "O principial'nom ispol'zovanii smysla pri mašinnom perevode", *Mašinnyj perevod i prikladnaja lingvistika*, vyp. 2.

Machine translation samples

The following pages contain samples of machine translation from Oak Ridge National Laboratory, Tennessee.

ACADEMY OF SCIENCES UKRAINIAN SSR MARITIME HYDRATED
GEOPHYSICAL INSTITUTE .
HYDRODYNAMICS OF SUPERFICIAL AND INTERNAL WAVES .
PUBLISHING-HOUSE OF NAIKOV OF DUMKA .
IN OBTAINED EXPRESSION (1.28) THERE IS CONSIDERED (
WITH ERROR OF ORDER SP5 IN COMPARISON WITH UNITY)
INFLUENCE OF VISCOSITY ON WAVE , WHICH MOVES IN IDEAL
LIQUID WITH RATE S WITHOUT CHANGE OF SHAPE OF HALF-WAVE
OF COSINE CURVE .
EXPRESSION (1.29) PRESENTS TRACE , LEFT ON FREE SURFACE
AFTER PASSAGE OF MAIN WAVE (1.28) .
PRESENCE OF THIS TRACE STIPULATEDLY EXCLUSIVELY BY STU OF
VISCOSITY .
IT COMPLETELY IS LACKING , WHEN UPON SOLUTION OF
ANALOGOUS PROBLEM BY INFLUENCE VISCOSITIES NEGLECT .
IT IS EASY TO SEE , THAT DEPENDENT ON FORCES OF VISCOSITY
WAVE TRACE PRESENTS WAVE OF INCREASE SP10 , AMPLITUDE
WHICH DECREASES WITH INCREASE OF DISTANCE FROM REAR FRONT
OF MAIN WAVE (1.28) .
INTEGRALS IS , ENTERING IN (1.29) , ARE DETERMINED
THROUGH INCOMPLETE GAMMA-FUNCTION BY FOLLOWING WAY (LONG
FORMULA) WHERE $P25
USING ASYMPTOTIC PRESENTATION G AT GREATER VALUES ET Z .
WE OBTAIN FOR 5$ SUCH AN EXPRESSION OF WAVE TRACE (1.29
) : LN4 CORRECT FOR 25$, WHERE 5$ - COORDINATE OF POINT
, WHICH DISTANT FROM REAR FRONT OF MAIN WAVE ON GREAT
DISTANCE IN COMPARISON WITH 30$ MAXIMUM VALUE OF TIME .

AKADEMI4 NAUK UKRAINSKOI SSR MORSKOI GIDROFIZICESKII
INSTITUT *
GIDRODINAMIKA POVERXNOSTNYX I VNUTRENNIX VOLN *
IZDATEL6STVO NAUKOVA DUMKA *
V POLUCENNOM VYRAJENII (1.28) UCITYVAEIS4 (S OWIBKOI
PORQDKA $S SP5 PO SRAVNE4IH S EDINICEI) VLI4NIE V4ZKOSTI
NA VOLNU , DVIJUSUHS4 V IDEAL6NOI JIDKUSTI SU SKUKUSIOH
LS S 8EZ IZMENENI4 FORAY POLUVOLNY KOSINUSOIDY *
VYRAJENIE (1.29) PREDSTAVL4EI SUKOI SLED , OSTAV4IIS4
NA SVOROJNOI POVERXNOSTI POSLE PROXOJDENI4 OSNOVNOI VOLNY
(1.28) *
NALICIE 3IOGO SLEDA OBUSLOVLENO ISKLHCITEL6NO SILAMI
V4ZKOSTI *
ON POLNOSTOH OTSUTSTVUET , KOGDA PRI REWENII ANALOGICNOI
ZADACI VLI4NIEM V4ZKOSTI PRENEBREGAHT *
LEGKO VIDET6 , CTO OBUSLVLENNYI SILAMI V4ZKOSTI VOLNOVOI
SLED PREDSTAVL4EI SOBOI VOLNU POVYMENI4 $$ SP10 .
AMPLITUDA KOTOROI OBYVAEI S UVELICENIEM RASSIOHNI4 UI
ZADNEGO FRONTA OSNOVNOI VOLNY (1.28) *
INTEGRALY IS , VXODQSIE V (1.29) , OPREDEL4HIS4 CEREZ
NEPOLNUH GAMMA - FUNKQIH SLEDUHSIA OBRAZUM (FBHF) , GDE
$$ SP25 *
ISPOL6ZU4 ASIMPTOTICESKOE PREDSTAVLENIE G PRI BOLUWIX
ZNACENI4X $$ EI Z , POLUCAEM DL4 5$ TAKOE VYRAJENIE
VOLNOVOGO SLEDA (1.29) : $$ LN4 SPRAVEDLIVUE DL4 25$.
GDE 5$ --- KOORDINATA TOCKI , OTSTOQSEI OI ZADNEGO FRONTA
USNOVNOI VOLNY NA BOLOWOA RASSIOHNII PO SRAVNENIH S 30$

VIII . OPUXOLI VIII .

OPUXOLI .

CERTAIN GIVEN ACCORDING TO OF SICK RATE AND MORTALITIES .

TO NUMBER OF MOST PUZZLING PHENOMENA IN ANIMAL WORLD

RELATE OPUXOLI (BLASTOMY , OR NEOPLASM) . BEING STUDIED

IN SPECIAL SECTION OF MEDICINE - IN ONKOLOGII . OPUXOL6

PRESENTS BIOLOGICAL PHENOMENON , WIDELY WIDESPREAD AT MAN

. LESS AT OTHER EXISTENCES . BUT HOWEVER VSTRECAHSEES>

ALMOST IN ALL CLASSES , FAMILIES AND FORMS .

IN MASSIVE SCALE OF OPUXOLI ARE OBSERVED . SOMETIMES IN

FORM OF WHOLE EPIDEMICS , AT OSETROVYX FISH . DOMESTIC

HENS . ESPECIALLY ON SPECIAL FACTORIES , I . E . INCUBATOR

PRODUCTION .

FREQUENT (ABOUT 5 X NATURAL RESULTS IS NECESSARY TO

COUNT OPUXOLI AT MICE . DOGS , KOWEK . SLIGHTLY LESS

FREQUENT - AT RATS , HORSES (ABOUT 0.5-2X) . STILL MORE

RARELY THEY ARE ENCOUNTERED AT AMPHIBIOUS , FOR EXAMPLE

AT FROGS , SALAMANDR . .

VERY RARE OPUXOLI AT MONKEYS .

THUS . ON MATERIAL , WHICH EMBRACES 1178 MONKEYS OF

PITOMNIKA OF ACADEMY OF SCIENCES IN USSR IN SUKHUMI ,

ZLOKACESTVENNYE NEOPLASM WERE ENCOUNTERED ONLY TWO TIMES

TAK, MOST FREQUENT AT MAN OF SHAPE OF RAKA

GASTRIC-INTESTINAL . AT MONKEYS WERE NOT OBSERVED TO TIME .

UNIVERSAL LITERATURE DOES NOT CONTAIN NOT ONE INFORMAFION

ON DISCOVERY ZLOKACESTVENNYX OPUXOLEI AT MONKEYS . ONLY

VIII . OPUXOLI VIII .

OPUXOLI *

NEKOTORYE DANNYE PO ZABOLEVAEMOSTI I SMERTNOSTI *

K CISLU NAIBOLEE ZAGADOCNYX 4VLENII V JIVOTNOM MIRE

OTNOS4TS4 OPUXOLI (BLASTOMY , ILI NOVOOBRAZOVANI4) .

IZUCAEMYE V SPECIAL6NOM RAZDELE MEDICINY -- V UNKOLOGII

.* OPUXOL6 PREDSTAVL4ET SOBOI BIOLOGICESKOE 4VLENIE .

WIROKO RASPROSTRANENNOE U CELOVEKA . MENOWE U DRUGIX

SUSESTV , NO VSE JE VSTRECAHSEESS POCTI VO VSEX KLASSAX .

SEMEISTVAX I VIDAX *

V MASSOVOM MASWTABE OPUXOLI NABLHUAHTS4 . INOGDA V VIDE

QELYX 3PIDEMII , U OSETROVYX RYB . DOMAWNIX KUR .

OSOBENNO NA SPECIAL6NYX FABRIKAX , T . E . INKUBATORNOGO

PROIZVODSTVA *

CASTYMI (OKOLO 5 X ESTESTVENNYX ISXODOV SLEDUEI SCITAI6

OPUXOLI U MYWEI . SOBAK . KOWEK . NESKOLOKO MENEE CASTYMI

-- U KRYS , LOWADEI (OKOLO 0.5 - 2X) . ESE REJE UNI

VSTRECAHTS4 U ZEMNOVODNYX . NAPKIMER U L4GUWEK .

SALAMANDR . *

OCENO REDKI OPUXOLI U OBEZ64N *

TAK . NA MATERIALE . OXVATYVAHSEM 1178 OBEZ64N PITOMNIKA

AKADEMII NAUK V SSSR V SUKHUMI . ZLOKACESTVENNYE

NOVOOBRAZOVANI4 VSTRETILIS6 TOL6KO DVA RAZA *

TAK . NAIBOLEE CASTYE U CELOVEKA FORMY RAKA JELUDOCNO -

KINECNOGO U OBEZ64N NE NABLHDALIS6 NI KAZU *

MIROVA4 LITERATURA NE SODERJIT NI ODNOGO UKAZANI4 NA

OBNARUJENIE ZLOKACESTVENNYX OPUXOLEI U OBEZ64N . TOL6KO

Russian (transliterated)	English
CTO VYVEZENNYX IZ MEST IX ESTESIVENNUGO OBITANI4 *	THAT EXPORTED FROM PLACES OF THEIR NATURAL INHABITATION .
ZNACITELSNYE TRUDNOSTI VOZNIKLI I PRI 3KSPERIMENTALSNUM	SIGNIFICANT DIFFICULTIES AROSE AND UPON EXPERIMENTAL
POLUCENII OPUXOLEI U OBEZ64N *	OBTAINING OF OPUXOLEI AT MONKEYS .
REDKIMI 4VL4HTS4 OPUXOLI U TAKIX LABURATORNYX JIVUINYX ,	RARE ARE OPUXOLI AT SUCH LABORATORY ANIMAL , AS KROLIKI,
KAK KROLIKI, MORSKIE SVINKI *	MARITIME PIGLETS .
UPISANY OPUXOLI U KASTENII — TABAKA,TOMATOV I DR. *	DESCRIBED OPUXOLI AT PLANTS — TABAKA,TOMATOV ETC.
UDNAKO PUDLINNO BLASTOMATOZNA4 PRIRODA OPUXOLEI	HOWEVER GENUINELY BLASTOMATOZNA4 NATURE OF OPUXOLEI BY
NEKUTORYMI AVTURAMI USPARIVAETS4 *	CERTAIN AUTHORS IS DISPUTED .
IZ PRIVEDENNYX MATERIALUJ SLEDUET , CTO CASTOTU OPUXOLEI	FROM GIVEN MATERIALS FOLLOWS , THAT FREQUENCY OF OPUXOLEI
U RAZLICNYX JIVUTNYX NELbZ4 OB74SNIT6 S 3VOLHOIONNO -	AT DIFFERENT ANIMAL IT IS NOT POSSIBLE TO EXPLAIN FROM
ISTORICESKIX POZIQII *	EVOLUTIONARY-HISTORICAL POSITIONS .
ONA NE ZAVISIT UI FILOGENETICESKUGU POLOJENI4 V PREDELAX	IT DOES NOT DEPEND ON PHILOGENETIC POSITION WITHIN THE
POOTIPA I SUSTAVL4E1 SKOREE PRIVILEGIH UIDELSNYX	LIMITS OF SURTYPE AND CONSTITUTES SOONER PRIVILEGE OF
SISTEMATICESKIX GRUPP *	SEPARATE SYSTEMATIC GROUPS .
MOJNO LIW6 UTMETIT6 , CTO NI UDNO JIVUTNUE NE IDET V	IT IS POSSIBLE ONLY TO NOTE , THAT NONE ANIMAL GOES IN
SRAVNENIE S CELUVEKUM PU CASTOTE RAZVITI4 OPUXOLEI I PU	COMPARISON WITH MAN ACCORDING TO FREQUENCY OF DEVELOPMENT
IX RAZNOUBRAZIH *	OF OPUXOLEI AND ACCORDING TO THEIR VARIETY .
MUJNO SDELAT6 I DRUGUI VYVID .CTO DOMESTIOIROVANNYE	IT IS POSSIBLE TO MAKE AND OTHER CONCLUSION .CTO
JIVUTNYE ,OBITAHSEE V SREDE DE4TELSNUSTI CELUVEKA (SUBAKI	DOMESTIOIROVANNYE ANIMAL ,OBITAHSEE IN ENVIRONMENT OF
, KOWKI , MYMI , KRYSY , LUWADI ,TAKJE JE KAK I JIVUTNYE	ACTIVITY OF MAN OF (SOBAKI , KOWKI , MICE , RATS , HORSE
V ISKUSSTVENNUI SREDE UBITANI4 (ZUUPARKI, VOLGERY ,	,TAKJE HOWEVER AS ALSO ANIMAL IN ARTIFICIAL ENVIRONMENT
PTIQEFABRIKI I T.P.) , ZNACITELGNO CABE BOLENT OPUXOL4MI	OF INHABITATION (ZOOPARKI, VOLGERY, POULTRY FACTORIES
, CEM VUUB5E MLEKUPIIAHSIE I POZVUNUCNYE *	AND T.P.) , SIGNIFICANTLY MORE FREQUENTLY BOLENT BY
3TO OTNOSITS4 TAKJE K KUKAM , RYBAM *	OPUXOLG4MI , THAN, IN GENERAL, MAMMALS AND VERTEBRAL .
UVELICENIE ILI , VERNEE, RASKAYTIE PUULINNOI	THIS RELATES ALSO TO HENS , FISH .
ZABULEVAEMUSTI V KAKUI - TO MERE SLEDUET UINESTI ZA SCEI	INCREASE OR , VERNEE, OPENING OF GENUINE SICK RATE IN
TUGU , CTO URGANY ZDRAVUOXRANENI4 V NASTU45EE VREM4	SOME MEASURE IS NECESSARY TO RELATE AT THE EXPENSE OF THE
	FACT THAT ORGANY HEALTH PROTECTIONS AT PRESENT PRACTICE

AT PRESENT CONDUCTING OF WIDE PROPHYLACTIC EXAMINATIONS

OF POPULATION , DETECTING MOST INITIAL FORMS BOLEZNI, AND

AND ALSO ** PREDRAKOVYE ** STATES .

ESPECIALLY HIGH FIGURES OF ILLNESS BY OPUXOL4MI GIVE

CARNIVOROUS ANIMAL (DOGS , KOWKI) , AND ALSO HENS .

CONTAINED ON M4SOKOSTNOI FLOUR .

HOWEVER CERTAIN FIGURES , CONCERNED BY OPUXOLEI OF MAN

AND ANIMAL , IN THEMSELVES SPEAK LITTLE .

SPECIAL INTEREST PRESENTS CONTENT OF THESE FIGURES ,

CHARACTER AND LOKALIZA OPUXOLEI .

ON THE OTHER HAND AT DOGS APPARENT PLACE OCCUPIES RAK

SITOVIDNOI JELEZY .

CERTAIN FORMATION OF FIGURES AT CELOVEKA,LOWADI,SOBAKI

AND HORNED CATTLE WE FIND ME FIND IN RELATION TO RAKOV OF

SKIN .

AT ANIMAL THERE IS NOTED RELATIVE MONOTONY IN

LOCALIZATION OF OPUXOLEI SO AT MICE THIS ALMOST

EXCLUSIVELY RAKI GRUDNYX IRON . AS AT DOGS AND KOWEK .

AND AT COWS - RAKI MOCEPOLOVOI SYSTEM .

ON THE ONE HAND , WE SPEAK CONCERNING BIOLOGICAL

VARIABILITY .

ON THE OTHER HAND ,DOMAWNIE ANIMAL ARE SUBJECTED TO

ACTION OF DIFFERENT KANQEROGENOV IN IMMEASURABLY GREATER

DEGREE , BY WHICH ANIMAL ON LIBERTY .

FAKOTORY SUPPLIES (OR OTKARMLIVANI4) ALSO HAVE

CONSIDERABLE VALUE .

EVEN MORE SIGNIFICANTLY TO CONSIDER VOZRASTNYE RELATIONS

PRAKTIKUHT V NASTU4SEE VREM4 PROVEDENIE MIRUKIX

PROFILAKTICESKIX OSMOTRUV NASELENI4 , VY4VL4* SAMYE

NACALONYE FORMY BOLEZNI , A TAKJE [** PREDRAKOVYE **

SOSTO4NI4 *

OSOBENNO VYSOKIE QIFRY ZABOLEVANI4 OPUXOL4MI DAHI

PLOTO4DNYE JIVOTNYE (SUBAKI , KOWKI) , A TAKJE KURY ,

SODERJASIES4 NA M4SUKOSTNOI MUKE *

UDNAKO TE ILI INYE QIFRY , KASAHSIES4 OPUXOLEI CELOVEKA I

JIVOTNYX , SAMI PO SEBE GOVOR4T MALO *

USOBYI INTERES PREDSTAVL4ET SODERJANIE 3TIX QIFR ,

XARAKTER I LOKALIZA OPUXOLEI *

ZATO U SOBAK VIDNOE MESTO ZANIMAEI RAK SITUVIDNOI JELEZY

*

NEKOTOROE SOLIJENIE QIFR U CELOVEKA,LOWADI,SUBAKI I

ROGATOGO SKOTA NAXODIM NAXODIM V OTNOWENII RAKOV KOJI *

U JIVOTNYX OTMECAETS4 OINOSITELONOE ODNOOBRAZIE V

LOKALIZAQII OPUXOLEI TAK U MYWEI 3TO POCTI ISKLHCITELONO

RAKI GRUDNYX JELEZ , KAK U SOBAK I KOWEK , A U KOROV --

RAKI MOCEPOLOVOI SISTEMY *

S ODNOI STORONY , REC6 IDET O BIOLOGICESKOI IZMENCIVOSTI

*

S DRUGOI STORONY ,DOMAWNIE JIVOTNYE PODVERGAHTS4 DEISTVIH

RAZLICNYX KANQEROGENOV V NEIZMERIMO BOLOWEI STEPENI , CEM

JIVOTNYE NA VOLE *

FAKUTORY PITANI4 (ILI OTKARMLIVANI4) TAKJE IMEHT

NEMALOE ZNACENIE *

ESE BOLEE VAJNO UCIITYVATO VOZRASTNYE OTNOWENI4 *

DEVELOPMENT OF OPUXOLEI , AS A RULE , REQUIRES MANY   RAZVITIE OPUXOLEI , KAK PRAVILO , TREBUET MNOGIX MESxOEV
MONTHS , AND MORE FREQUENTLY THAN YEARS .   , A ČASE LEI *
THE SAME PHENOMENON DEVELOPS UPON COMPARISON DIFFERENT   TO JE 4VLENIE OBNARUJIVAEIS4 PRI SRAVNENII RAZNYX
HUMAN POPUL4 & (WITH HIGH AND LOW CONTINUANCE OF LIFE . ČELOVEČESKIX POPUL4 & (S VYSOKOI I NIZKOI
                                                         PRODDLJITEL6NOSTbH JIZNI *
HERE BE ONE OF IMPORTANT CAUSES THIS , WHY AT ANIMAL , IN ZDES6 KROETS4 ODNA IZ VAJNYX PRIČIN TOGO , POČEMU U
MAJORITY ITS/THEIR POSSESSING RELATIVELY BY SMALL   JIVOTNYX , V BOL6WINSTVE SVOEM OBLADAH3IX OTNOSITEL6NU
CONTINUANCE OF LIFE , RAKOVA4 SICK RATE SO LOW IN   MALOI PRODDLJITEL6NOST6H JIZNI , RAKOVA4 ZABOLEVAEMOSI6
COMPARISON WITH SUCH AT MAN .   STOL6 NIZKA PU SRAVNENIH S TAKOVOI U ČELOVEKA *
SOCIAL FACTORS , AND JUST IMPROVEMENT OF CONDITIONS OF   SOUIAL6NYE FAKTORY , A IMENNO ULUČWENIE USLOVII JIZNI .
LIFE , PERMITTED TO EXTEND LIFE OF MAN .   POZVOLILI PRODLIT6 JIZN6 ČELOVEKA *
WE ENTERED IN STREAM .   MY VSTUPILI V POTOK *
NOW TO GO OUT FROM IT CANNOT WE .   TEPER6 VYITI IZ NEGO NE MOJEM *
STONES MANY .   KAMNEI MNOGUH*

Author Index

Bar-Hillel, Yehoshua, 3–4, 34, 34–35, 35–36, 37–38, 39–40, 41, 45–46, 59–60, 76–77, 151, 152, 154, 155, 192
Bloomfield, Leonard, 17–18, 43–44
Booth, A. D., 3–4, 9, 9–10, 11–12, 12–13, 13–14, 35–36, 65–66, 85

Chafe, Wallace, L., 76, 77, 78, 79, 80, 81
Chaloupka, Bedrich, 77, 78
Chomsky, Noam, 58, 59, 60–61
and machine translation, 58–59

Dostert, Léon E., 6, 13–14, 15, 17–18, 20, 22, 30, 31, 32, 61

Fangmeyer, Dr., 150, 167
see also EURATOM

Garvin, Paul, 6, 17–18, 20, 21–22, 24–25, 26, 27–28, 48, 69–70, 152, 153, 180, 181
Gerrard, Martha:
as user of machine translations, 163
Gifford, F. A.:
see NOAA, 163

Harper, Kenneth E., 6, 13–14, 34–35, 64, 65
Hays, David G., 6, 34–35, 43–44, 47–48, 49–50, 59, 76, 83

Josselson, Henry, 6, 37, 38, 38–39, 41, 42, 43, 46, 56

Kertesz, Dr. F., 150, 157, 167
see also Oak Ridge
Klein, W., 6, 60, 61, 62

Knul, C. M. A., 162
see also ETC
Kulagina, Olga S., 6, 65, 66, 67, 69, 70, 71, 73

Lecerf, Y., 69
Lehmann, Winifred P., 6, 36, 37, 48, 57, 58, 59, 60
Ljapunov, A. A., 66, 72, 73
Ljudskanov, A., 62, 63
Locke, W. N., 9, 10, 14, 15, 65, 66

Macdonald, Ross, 6, 20, 27–28, 31–32, 33
Masterman, Margaret, 38
Mathias, Jim, 76, 83, 84
Mel'čuk, Igor' A., 6, 65, 66, 67, 68, 69, 70, 71
Mukhin, I. S., 66, 72–73

Nida, Eugene, 152

Oettinger, Anthony, G., 14, 15, 16, 35, 36, 45–46, 47–48, 61–62

Pankowicz, Zbigniew L., 46
Panov, Yurij, 66, 72–73
Path, W., 45–46
Pendergraft, Eugene, 14, 15, 17, 18, 20, 21
Perschke, Dr. Sergei, 63, 150, 157
see also EUROTOM
Petrick, S. R., 78–87
Pierce, John R., 47–48, 54

Reichenbach, Hans, 10–11
Reifler, Ervin, 9, 13, 15, 17

Rhodes, Ida, 44, 45, 46

Stachowitz, R. A., 57–58, 59

Tesnière, L., 43–44, 58–59, 60–61, 62
Trijssenaar, J. A.:
  see ETC, 162
Trojanskij, P. P., 7, 8, 9, 85

Van Bergeijk, D., 162
  see also ETC

Vauquois, B., 57–58

Weaver, W., 5, 6, 9, 10, 11, 12, 13, 18, 85
Wilks, Yorick, 78

Yngve, Victor, 14, 15, 16, 17, 18, 19

Zarechnak, Michael, 20, 30, 31, 32, 42, 43, 59, 60, 154, 155, 192

Subject Index

AEC Technical Documentation Center, as user of machine translations, 163
ALPAC's views on machine translation results, 46
report, 150
Academy of Sciences of USSR, machine translation at, 28–29
algorithm, 132, 135, 137 ff., 140
aspects of models, 74
and models, re Petrick, 81–82
operations, re Garvin, 26–27
simulating mental process of human translator, 77–78
All-Union Translation Center, creation in USSR, 74–75
ambiguity, 153
American Journal of Computational Linguistics, proceedings from Rosslyn Seminar by, 76
analysis, 7–8, 8–9
analytical approach to machine translation, re Ljapunov, Panov, and Mukhim, 72–73
analyzing language problems, re Booth, 12–13
automatic, experience in USSR, 74–75
automatic syntactic, re Klein, 60–61
automatic text, and synthesis, 71–72
consecutive local method of, re Y. Lecerf, 69–70
contrastive, re Josselson, 42–43
of conversational language, re Reichenbach, 10–11
dictionary entries, coding of word-by-word, 29
discourse, 78
discrete, re Kulagina and Mel'čuk, 70–71
formal, re Panov, 67
of GAT, 32, 115, 134
general, 28–29
»General Analysis Technique« (GAT), 30–31, 134 ff.
and generating structures in natural language, 86–87
group of Dostert, 18–19
immediate constituents, 17–18
of linguistic base of GAT, re Brown, 32
logical, for translation problems, 25
machine translation groups, diagnostic guide (analysis) for comparison to others, 41
machine, aspects in word formation and inflection, 74–75
morphological, 91, 93, 105, 107 ff., 119 ff., 134 ff., 143
operational, in machine translation, 13–14
of by Z. Pankowitz, ALPAC, 46
predictive, re Josselson, 43–44
predictive, for sentence parsing, 45–46
of real data, re Petrick, 81
of Russian language for machine translation, 28–29
of source and target language, 42–43
syntactic, at Georgetown University, 17–18
Arabic, 96
articles, definite and indefinite, 126
artificial intelligence, researchers in, 78, 92, 124
Atomic Energy Commission at Oak Ridge, Tennessee, 59–60

automatic sentence parsing routines, 41
Automatic translation group at Georgetown University, 59–60
available machine-aided translation systems, 76

binary machine translation algorithm in
USSR, 64–65
bipartite system, 130 ff.
blank, importance of, 100
Bloomfieldian concepts as in machine
translation operational influence,
43–44
boldface, 101
Brussels, adaptation of GAT in, 33
brute force system, 78–79

Cambridge group, criticism of Bar-Hillel's arguments, 38
capitalization, 100
Centre National de Documentation
Scientifique et Technique (National
Center for Scientific and Technical Documentation), Brussels, Belgium, as
user of machine translations, 161
Chinese, 32, 96
choice-determining diacritics, 18–19
clerk translators, number working
worldwide and in USA, 51–52
coding, 105 ff., 130, 133 ff., 141, 143
expanded, 105 ff., 145
word under consideration, 19
collocations, see Idioms
comma, 99
computers
  IBM 705 and 709, 31–32
  type to be used, 94
Conference on machine translation in
Texas in 1971, 38
context, 152, 156, 194–195
free, 136, 143
sensitive, 68–69, 131
coordination, 117
core language, 28–29
Cyrillic alphabet, 97

decision-making system, 131
decision-postponing system, 132
dependency grammar, 135
dependency trees in machine translation
work, 58–59

dictionary, 102 ff., 130, 135 ff., 141
codes and syntactic rules, 28
coding, 9
look-up, studying improvement of procedure, re Booth and Richens,
12–13
storage of in computer, 16–17
text based, 29–30
discontinuous structures, 142

ETC (European Translations Centre),
Delft, Holland, 150
activity relative to machine translations, 161–162
EURATOM (European Atomic Energy
Community), 149, 154, 157–163
computers at, 157
in Italy, 33
elektromechanical model, 9
empirical systems, 103, 130 ff., 144
endings, 142
endocentric structure, 116
English-French machine translation system, on EVM BESM, 55, 72–73
entry, 102 ff., 133 ff.
Europe, linguistic theory and linguistic
procedures in, 57–58
exclusion, 113, 115, 134
exocentric structure, 117
experiment, 1954, L. Dostert, 20
experiment before theory, 54–55

First International Conference on Machine Translation of Language and
Applied Language Analysis, September 1961, Teddington, England, 41–42
fixed-length entries, 112
formant, 132, 136 ff.
formulae, 101
French-Russian translation algorithm, 64
French transcription, 98
fulcrum approach, 43–44
fully automatic high quality translation
(FAHQT), 35–36, 36, 37
function-class, 116

gap analysis, 115, 134
GAT, 29–30, 32, 134 ff.
Georgetown University machine transla-
tion project, 133

philosophy and guiding principles, 149
system, use of, 149, 157
German transcription, 98
gloss, 105, 126, 133 ff.
grammar, 132, 135 ff., 141, 144
    rules (sentence structure), 149,
    155, 203
Great Britain, machine translation activity in, 45–46
Grenoble, designing of general analyzer for any language, 57–58, 144

history of machine translation in USSR, 72–73
human translation, 181–182, 183
    comparison with machine translation, 153, 195, 196–197
    cost, 179
    versus post-edited translation, 55–56
    wait time, 184
hyphen, 99

idioms, 43–44, 111, 134, 142, 143
    expressions, 8–9
    treatment of with large capacity computers, 17
inference, notion of, re Wilks, 74–75
inflections, 126, 143
inseparability in machine translation systems, 67–68
intermediary language, 8–9
interpolation, 114, 134, 143
italics, 101

keypunching, 94
keypunch format, 95 ff.

LIMAS group, Bonn, 58–59
language
    experiment with models, re H. Brooks, 56
    intermediary, 8–9
    programming, 32
    traditional description of machine translation system, 44–45
Latin alphabet, 96, 97
lexical choice, 123, 134
linguistic system, ideal, close, re Josselson, 41

linguistic theory
    in Europe, 56–57
    in USSR, re Harper, 64–65
lower case, 100

M.A.N. (Maschinenfabrik [motor vehicle factory]) Augsburg-Nürnberg, Germany as user of machine translations, 161
machine translation and systems
    comparison with human, 195, 196–197
    completeness, 154, 155, 192–193
    conference at Princeton, 30–31
    consistency, 153
    cost, 157, 178–179
    definitions of in ALPAC report, 52
    desirable improvements in, 203–204
    at EURATOM, 157–163
    experiments in USA, USSR, and England, 57–58
    at Foreign Technology Division, USAF, Dayton, Ohio, 46–47
    goals and scope, Bulgaria, Ljudskanov, 62
    groups at Cambridge, Bonn, and Milan, 57–58
    historical background, re Booth, 11–12
    informativeness, 154, 180–181, 193
    monitoring programs in, Kulagina and Mel'čuk, 71
    multilevel operations in third generation, Kulagina and Mel'čuk, 71
    number of, 160
    at Oak Ridge, 157–163
    preference for, 155, 156, 185–186
    in present stage, 81
    procedure in obtaining, 158
    quality, 152–154, 155, 186–187, 200–201
    readability, 154, 192–193
    reasons for using, 174–175, 177–180 passim
    recommendability, 202–203
    records, 150, 159
    report on Georgetown University research project on, Macdonald, 28–29
    research, USA government's attitude toward after ALPAC, 56–57

researchers, re Josselson, 41
scanning, 153, 180, 181
situation, adaptation to any, of SLC, 32–33
speed, 152, 153, 155, 160, 184–185
studies of by E. Reifler, 13
style, getting used to, 201–222
style of, 193–194
symposia in Los Angeles, February 1960, 30–31
test by GAT in 1959, 29–30
three phases of development, 85
time to read, 153, 195–197
in USA, beginning, re Bar-Hillel, 34
in USA, existing after ten years of research, 15
understandability, 187–190
uniformativeness, 153, 197–200
unintelligibility, 193
usefulness, 155, 177–180
use pattern of, 176–177
users comments and evaluation of, 36–37, 162, 164, 220–244
using algorithmic processes, 81
in Western Europe, 57–58
wait time, 155, 184–185
working systems, based on length of single sentence, re Josselson, 42–43
melded system, 143
monitoring, 141
morphological analysis, see Analysis
morphological synthesis, 134
multiple-pass system, 109, 116, 131 ff.
multi-level system, 131

NASA (National Aeronautic and Space Administration) as user of machine translations, 163
NOAA (National Oceanic and Atmospheric Administration) as user of machine translations, 163
nesting, 119
noun, 116 ff., 126, 135, 141

Oak Ridge (National Laboratory at Oak Ridge, Tennessee), 149, 157–163
computer at, 157
Occasional papers, 27–28
optical character recognition, 76
optical scanner, 95

output, 135, 143
outside evaluator, 21–22

Paris, UNESCO Conference, July 1959, 30–31
period, 99
phrase structure, 135
polutornye machine translation systems, 71
polysemantic words, 122 ff.
polysemy in Russian mathematical text, 63
poly-variantness principle, 69, 70
post-editing, 15, 55–56, 122, 128 ff.
predictive analysis, 135
pre-editing, 94
prefixing, 100
preposition, 117, 134
procedure, 130 ff.
proclitics, 101
programming language of Brown, 32
protocol, 102, 144
punctuation, 98 ff.
push-down store in predictive analysis, 38

Questionnaire
1964, 149, 154
1972–1973, 150, 165–215 passim
comparison of 1964 and 1972–1973, 154–155
detailed analysis of results, 170–205
summary of contents, 165–166, full
summary of results, 170–171, 206–208
text of, 210–215

Rand Corporation, machine translation activities of, 43
rearrangement, 118, 127, 134
problems, 16–17
research work on problems of machine translation from Chinese to English, 32
resultant, 132, 136 ff.
Roget, 123
Round Table Conference of Linguistics, 8th annual, 35–36
rule format, 132, 136, 141, 145
Rumania, machine translation activities in, 45–46

running source text, individual words in, 15–16
Russian transcription, 97

SLC, 28, 134
Saussurian »all or nothing«, 68–69
segmentation, 109, 134
semantics, re ALPAC, 53
 analysis, algorithm for, re Ljudskanov, 63
 analysis, 75, 92, 121, 143
 categories, 123 ff., 143
 codes for dictionary, 76
 coding, 37–38
 component in machine translation, research in Europe, 57–58
 computational, 41–42
 contextual meaning, 9–10
 deep meaning structure, 78
 experimental method of analysis, 78
 grammatical multiple meaning solution of, 18–19
 information, re Kulagina and Mel'čuk, 71
 level of machine translation systems, 27–28
 lexical rules and grammar, multiple meaning of, re Klein, 61–62
 machine translation
  groups using information of, 58–59
  roots, development of artificial intelligence, 56
  as tool for rapid dissemination of scientific and technical information, 71–72
 meaning, universal transformations, 73–74
 multiple choice routines, 41
 polysemic nature, words of, re Weaver, 11–12
 prerequisites for machine translation, re Chafe, 76–77
 removing ambiguity, 13
 selecting from available target equivalent, 15–16
 »sense-text« model, problems of using, 73–74, 74
 sentence, minimum carrier of meaning, 9–10

solving problems of meaning, technical dictionaries for, 28–29
statistical, 9–10, 11
syllable as a carrier of semantic unit, 16–17
system of semantic translation for machine translation, 74
units, 78–79
sentences
 in machine translations, 190–193
 as minimum structures, 85–86
 and words, codes assigned to, 19
sentence-by-sentence method, 29
single-level system, 133
single-pass system, 110, 115, 133, 140, 143
single-path system, Harvard University, re Murray Sherry, 45–46
source language, adequate knowledge of, 51
split dictionary entries, 104
stem, 104 ff., 142
stratificational grammar theory, 43–44
subject matter, familiarity with, 152, 153, 155, 156, 188–189
subroutine, 131
surface structure, 86–87
symbolization and verbalization, re Chafe, 86–87
syntactic
 analysis, 91, 93, 105, 115 ff., 134, 143
 rules, re Zarechnak, 59–60
 structures, understanding of, 27–28
 synthesis, 134
syntagmatic
 analysis, 116 ff., 134
 axis, 27–28
 linguistic level, 69
synthesis of target language, 126 ff.
system(s)
 American linguist studying someone else's machine translation system, 14–15
 of American machine translation, compared by E. Pendergraft, 14–15
 of Bunker Ramo, re ALPAC, 55–56
 binarity in machine translation, re Kulagina and Mel'čuk, 67
 computational linguistic, 79–80
 decision-making, 131

editorial intervention in current commercial machine translation, D. Hays, 83
empirical, 103, 130 ff., 144
English-French machine translation, 78
evaluation of Georgetown University machine translation, 14–15, 20
»fulcrum«, at National Physical Laboratory, England and Georgetown University, 56–57
of GAT, producing English output phrases, 81–82, 87
Georgetown University
fulcrum, 70–71
machine translation, in ALPAC, 54–55
machine translation, re Klein, 85
of grammar, 74
Grenoble Russian-to-French machine translation, 71
hardware, selecting, re J. Mathias, 70–71
machine translation
cheaper and faster than human translator, 72–73
components of, re Josselson, 44–45
criteria for good, 31–32
differences existing between, 74–75
elaboration and improvement, 27–28
evaluation of unedited output quality, re Petrick, 87
features of third generation, Kulagina and Mel'čuk, 71
research and development, D. Hays, 83
support for creation of practical, in USSR, 74–75
Xonics, 77–78
multipath, re W. Path, 45–46
practical, embodying theory in, 21–22
of SLC, programming, 28
translation, word-for-word, 73–74

terse coding, 106, 132, 145
Texas, 135, 152, 155
texts, suitability of, 93
theoretical systems, 106, 121, 130 ff., 144

theories, checking of, 54–55
transcription, 95 ff.
transfer, 134
in two senses, re Kulagina and Mel'čuk, 68–69
Translated text, naturalness and fidelity of, 81–82
translation
algorithm, re Garvin, 26–27
correctness, 152, 153
as impossible, re Klein, 60–61
macro- and micro-glossaries for, 13
quality and cost of courses of, 53–54
of random data, 56
sentence-for-sentence, V. Yngve, 18–19
tripartite system, V. Yngve, 69
understandability, 152
treatment of idioms, re Josselson, 43–44
tripartite system, 132
»turning point« in machine translation development, 85

univariantness in machine translation systems, re Kulagina and Mel'čuk, 67
unsplit dictionary entries, 104
upper case, 100
users, 149
analysis of attitudes, 152
attitudes, 151, 167
characteristics of, 170
comments of, 164, 220–244
discussions with, 150, 165, 167–168
evaluations, 149
familiarity with English, 172; with Russian, 173
field of work, 173
as judge, 152
knowledge of subject matter, 155, 156
nationality, 171
native language, 172
need, 152
number of, 169
partial list of, 216–219
reasons for using machine translation, 174–175, 177–180 passim
use patterns of machine translation, 176–177
variable-length entries, 112

variation in translation, 128
verb, 109, 116 ff., 126, 134, 141
vocabulary, 149, 155, 157, 191–193, 203

word
  frequency, analysis of in machine translation, 13–14

minimum carrier of meaning, 9–10
rearrangement in post-editing, 15
word-for-word translation system, 74

Yugoslavia, machine translation activity in, 45–46